CONFUCIUS

THE ANALECTS
(Lun yü)

TRANSLATED WITH
AN INTRODUCTION BY
D.C. LAU

PENGUIN BOOKS

PENGUIN BOOKS

Published by the Penguin Group
27 Wrights Lane, London w8 5tz, England
Viking Penguin Inc., 40 West 23rd Street, New York, New York 10010, USA
Penguin Books Australia Ltd, Ringwood, Victoria, Australia
Penguin Books Canada Ltd, 2801 John Street, Markham, Ontario, Canada l3r 1b4
Penguin Books (NZ) Ltd, 182–190 Wairau Road, Auckland 10, New Zealand

Penguin Books Ltd, Registered Offices: Harmondsworth, Middlesex, England

This translation first published 1979
Reprinted 1982, 1983, 1984, 1986, 1987, 1988

Printed and bound in Great Britain by
Cox & Wyman Ltd, Reading
Set in Monotype Fournier

PENGUIN  CLASSICS

THE ANALECTS

ADVISORY EDITOR: BETTY RADICE

CONFUCIUS (551–479 B.C.), though of noble descent, was born in rather humble circumstances in the state of Lu in modern Shantung, at a time when imperial rule was breaking down. He was a great admirer of the Duke of Chou and looked upon himself as a transmitter of early Chou culture, rather than as an innovator. He taught a moral philosophy with man as the centrepiece. In order to meet his moral responsibility, he believed, a man must think for himself. This belief led Confucius to place as much emphasis on thinking as on learning. The central concept of his philosophy was the *chün tzu*, an ideal man whose character embodies the virtue of benevolence and whose acts are in accordance with the rites and rightness. For Confucius, as for the whole of the Chinese tradition, politics is only an extension of morals: provided that the ruler is benevolent, the government will naturally work towards the good of the people.

After over ten years spent in travelling through the various states, Confucius, realizing that there was no hope of converting any of the feudal rulers to his way of thinking, returned to Lu where he spent the rest of his life teaching a group of gifted and devoted disciples.

In the Western Han, Confucianism became the orthodox philosophy and retained this position up until the present century. Inevitably, his teachings became distorted in the course of time. The *Lun yü*, commonly known as the *Analects*, has been as widely read in China throughout the ages as the Bible has been in the West, and is the only reliable record of his teachings.

•

D. C. LAU read Chinese at the University of Hong Kong, and, in 1946, went to Glasgow, where he read philosophy. In 1950 he began a long career teaching Chinese philosophy at the School of Oriental and African Studies in London. In 1965 he was appointed to the newly-created Readership in Chinese Philosophy and in 1970 became Professor of Chinese in the University of London. He is also the translator of the *Tao Te Ching* and the *Mencius*, both published in Penguin Classics. In 1978 Professor Lau returned to Hong Kong to take up the Chair of Chinese Language and Literature in the Chinese University of Hong Kong.

Contents

CONTENTS

Acknowledgement

I wish to thank the following for having read and criticized, in part or in whole, one of the many drafts this translation went through: Roger Ames, Bill Atwell, Heather Karmay, Diana Larry, Ralph Smith and George Weys. Special thanks are due to Paul Thompson whose searching criticism of one draft resulted in a greatly improved final version, and to my brother, T. C. Lau, who, during my many visits to Hong Kong, was always willing to interrupt his own work in order to discuss with me difficult points of interpretation and translation.

Introduction

DESPITE his immense importance in the Chinese tradition, little that is certain is known about Confucius. The *locus classicus* for his life is his biography in Ssu-ma Ch'ien's *Shih chi* (*Records of the Historian*) finished at the beginning of the first century B.C., but by then so much legend had gathered round the figure of the sage that little credence can be given to any of the events in it not independently confirmed by earlier sources. This being the case, we can consider reliable only what we can glean from the *Lun yü* – commonly known in English as the *Analects of Confucius* – itself and from the *Tso chuan* (*The Tso commentary of the Spring and Autumn Annals*). The *Mencius* can be used as a supplementary source. The facts are few.

Confucius was said to have been descended from a noble family in the state of Sung. In the early years of the eighth century B.C., one of Confucius' ancestors died when the young duke of Sung who was in his charge was assassinated, and his descendants fled to Lu and settled in Tsou. In the *Tso chuan* under the tenth year of Duke Hsiang, it is recorded that one Shu He of Tsou held up the portcullis with his bare hands while his comrades made their getaway. The *Shih chi*, however, gives his name as Shu Liang He and added the information that he was Confucius' father. Of Confucius' mother nothing certain is known.

K'ung Ch'iu or K'ung Chung-ni, commonly known in the West as Confucius, was born in either 552 or 551 B.C., and was orphaned at a very early age. Of his youth little is known except that he was poor and fond of learning. He said, ' I was of humble station when young. That is why I am skilled in so many menial things' (IX.6), and 'At fifteen I set my heart on learning' (II.4).

In 517 B.C. Duke Chao of Lu had to flee the state after an unsuccessful attempt to make war on the Chi Family. It is likely that it was at this time when he was thirty-five that Confucius went to Ch'i. If he did, he soon returned to Lu.

It was in the time of Duke Ting of Lu (r. 509–494 B.C.) that he became the police commissioner of Lu. During his term of office two events took place which are recorded in the *Tso chuan.* First, he accompanied the Duke to a meeting with Duke Ching of Ch'i and scored a diplomatic victory. Second, he was responsible for the abortive plan to demolish the main city of each of the three powerful noble families.

It was probably in 497 B.C. that Confucius left Lu, not to return until thirteen years later. An account is given in the *Analects* of how he came to leave Lu: 'The men of Ch'i made a present of singing and dancing girls. Chi Huan Tzu accepted them and stayed away from court for three days. Confucius departed' (XVIII.4). In the *Mencius,* however, a different account is given. 'Confucius was the police commissioner of Lu, but his advice was not followed. He took part in a sacrifice, but, afterwards, was not given a share of the meat of the sacrificial animal. He left the state without waiting to take off his ceremonial cap.' Mencius' comment was: 'Those who did not understand him thought he acted in this way because of the meat, but those who understood him realized that he left because Lu failed to observe the proper rites.'[1] As Mencius was probably right in thinking that Confucius left on some transparent pretext, we need not be surprised if there is no agreement on the exact nature of the pretext.

Confucius first went to Wei, and during the next few years visited a number of other states, offering advice to the feudal lords, and, meeting with no success, returned to Wei in 489 B.C. It is not possible to determine how long Confucius stayed in each state as what little evidence there is tends to be conflicting. Confucius finally returned to Lu in 484 B.C. when he was sixty-eight. At last realizing that there was no hope of putting his ideas into practice, he devoted the rest of his life to teaching. His last years were saddened by the death first of his son and then of his favourite disciple, Yen Hui, at an early age. He himself died in 479 B.C.

Let us turn to Confucius' teachings. Philosophers who are interested in morals can generally be divided into two kinds, those who are interested in moral character and those who are interested in moral acts. Confucius certainly has far more to say about moral

1. *Mencius,* VI.B.6 (p. 176). For works cited, see p. 235.

character than moral acts, but this does not mean that the rightness of acts, in the last resort, is unimportant in his philosophy. But it does mean that in any account of Confucius' philosophy it is reasonable to start with his views on moral character.

Before we proceed to look at what Confucius has to say about moral character, it is convenient, first of all, to dispose of two concepts which were already current in Confucius' time, viz., the Way (*tao*) and virtue (*te*). The importance Confucius attached to the Way can be seen from his remark, 'He has not lived in vain who dies the day he is told about the Way' (IV.8). Used in this sense, the Way seems to cover the sum total of truths about the universe and man, and not only the individual but also the state is said either to possess or not to possess the Way. As it is something which can be transmitted from teacher to disciple, it must be something that can be put into words. There is another slightly different sense in which the term is used. The way is said also to be someone's way, for instance, 'the ways of the Former Kings' (I.12), 'the way of King Wen and King Wu' (XIX.22), or 'the way of the Master' (IV.15). When thus specified, the way naturally can only be taken to mean the way followed by the person in question. As for the Way, rival schools would each claim to have discovered it even though what each school claimed to have discovered turned out to be very different. The Way, then, is a highly emotive term and comes very close to the term 'Truth' as found in philosophical and religious writings in the West.

There seems to be little doubt that the word *te*, virtue, is cognate with the word *te*, to get.[2] Virtue is an endowment men get from Heaven. The word was used in this sense when Confucius, facing a threat to his life, said, 'Heaven is author of the virtue that is in me' (VII.23), but this usage is rare in the *Analects*. By the time of Confucius, the term must have already become a moral term. It is something one cultivates, and it enables one to govern a state well. One of the things that caused him concern was, according to Confucius, his failure to cultivate his virtue (VII.3). He also said that if one guided the common people by virtue they would not only reform themselves but have a sense of shame (II.3).

2. See XII.21.

Both the Way and virtue were concepts current before Confucius' time and, by then, they must have already acquired a certain aura. They both, in some way, stem from Heaven. It is, perhaps, for this reason that though he said little of a concrete and specific nature about either of these concepts, Confucius, nevertheless, gave them high precedence in his scheme of things. He said, 'I set my heart on the Way, base myself on virtue, lean upon benevolence for support and take my recreation in the arts' (VII.6). Benevolence is something the achievement of which is totally dependent upon our own efforts, but virtue is partly a gift from Heaven.

Behind Confucius' pursuit of the ideal moral character lies the unspoken, and therefore, unquestioned, assumption that the only purpose a man can have and also the only worthwhile thing a man can do is to become as good a man as possible. This is something that has to be pursued for its own sake and with complete indifference to success or failure. Unlike religious teachers, Confucius could hold out no hope of rewards either in this world or in the next. As far as survival after death is concerned, Confucius' attitude can, at best, be described as agnostic. When Tzu-lu asked how gods and spirits of the dead should be served, the Master answered that as he was not able even to serve man how could he serve the spirits, and when Tzu-lu further asked about death, the Master answered that as he did not understand even life how could he understand death (XI.12). This shows, at least, a reluctance on the part of Confucius to commit himself on the subject of survival after death. While giving men no assurance of an after life, Confucius, nevertheless, made great moral demands upon them. He said of the Gentleman[3] of purpose and the benevolent man that 'while it is inconceivable that they should seek to stay alive at the expense of benevolence, it may happen that they have to accept death in order to have benevolence accomplished' (XV.9). When such demands are made on men, little wonder that one of Confucius' disciples should have considered that a Gentleman's 'burden is

3. Throughout this book, 'Gentleman' is used as an equivalent for *shih* while 'gentleman' is used for *chün tzu*. *Shih* was the lowest rank of officials while *chün tzu* denoted either a man of moral excellence or a man in authority. For the connection between the two see p. 229.

heavy and the road is long', for his burden was benevolence and the road came to an end only with death (VIII.7).

If a man cannot be assured of a reward after death, neither can he be guaranteed success in his moral endeavours in this life. The gatekeeper at the Stone Gate asked Tzu-lu, 'Is that the K'ung who keeps working towards a goal the realization of which he knows to be hopeless?' (XIV.38). On another occasion, after an encounter with a recluse, Tzu-lu was moved to remark, 'The gentleman takes office in order to do his duty. As for putting the Way into practice, he knows all along that it is hopeless' (XVIII.7). Since in being moral one can neither be assured of a reward nor guaranteed success, morality must be pursued for its own sake. This is, perhaps, the most fundamental message in Confucius' teachings, a message that marked his teachings from other schools of thought in ancient China.

For Confucius there is not one single ideal character but quite a variety. The highest is the sage (*sheng jen*). This ideal is so high that it is hardly ever realized. Confucius claimed neither to be a sage himself nor even to have seen such a man. He said, 'How dare I claim to be a sage or a benevolent man?' (VII.34) and, on another occasion, 'I have no hopes of meeting a sage' (VII.26). The only time he indicated the kind of man that would deserve the epithet was when Tzu-kung asked him, 'If there were a man who gave extensively to the common people and brought help to the multitude, what would you think of him? Could he be called benevolent?' Confucius' answer was, 'It is no longer a matter of benevolence with such a man. If you must describe him, "sage" is, perhaps, the right word' (VI.30).

Lower down the scale there are the good man (*shan jen*) and the complete man (*ch'eng jen*). Even the good man Confucius said he had not seen, but the term 'good man' seems to apply essentially to men in charge of government, as he said, for instance, 'How true is the saying that after a state has been ruled for a hundred years by good men it is possible to get the better of cruelty and to do away with killing' (XIII.11), and 'After a good man has trained the common people for seven years, they should be ready to take up arms' (XIII.29). On the one occasion when he was asked about the

way of the good man, Confucius' answer was somewhat obscure
(XI.20). As for the complete man, he is described in terms applied
not exclusively to him. He 'remembers what is right at the sight of
profit', and 'is ready to lay down his life in the face of danger'
(XIV.12). Similar terms are used to describe the Gentleman (XIX.
1).

There is no doubt, however, that the ideal moral character for
Confucius is the *chün tzu* (gentleman), as he is discussed in more
than eighty chapters in the *Analects*. *Chün tzu* and *hsiao jen* (small
man) are correlative and contrasted terms. The former is used of
men in authority while the latter of those who are ruled.⁴ In the
Analects, however, *chün tzu* and *hsiao jen* are essentially moral
terms. The *chün tzu* is the man with a cultivated moral character,
while the *hsiao jen* is the opposite. It is worth adding that the two
usages indicating the social and moral status are not exclusive,
and, in individual cases, it is difficult to be sure whether, besides
their moral connotations, these terms may not also carry their
usual social connotations as well.

As the gentleman is the ideal moral character, it is not to be
expected that a man can become a gentleman without a great deal of
hard work or cultivation, as the Chinese called it. There is a considerable number of virtues a gentleman is supposed to have and
the essence of these virtues is often summed up in a precept. In
order to have a full understanding of the complete moral character
of the gentleman, we have to take a detailed look at the various
virtues he is supposed to possess.

Benevolence (*jen*) is the most important moral quality a man can
possess. Although the use of this term was not an innovation on the
part of Confucius, it is almost certain that the complexity of its
content and the pre-eminence it attained amongst moral qualities
were due to Confucius. That it is *the* moral quality a gentleman
must posess is clear from the following saying.

4. There is a theory which will be discussed further on that in the *Analects*
there is a distinction between *jen* and *min*. The former is said to refer to men
who had the right to take office and the latter to the common people who had
no such right. On this theory, although the *hsiao jen* were the ruled, as *jen* they,
nevertheless, had the right to take office and were to be distinguished from the
min in spite of the fact that they both belonged to the category of the ruled.
The term *chün tzu* is, in fact, sometimes contrasted with *min* as well.

If the gentleman forsakes benevolence, in what way can he make a name for himself? The gentleman never deserts benevolence, not even for as long as it takes to eat a meal. If he hurries and stumbles, one may be sure that it is in benevolence that he does so. (IV.5)

In some contexts 'the gentleman' and 'the benevolent man' are almost interchangeable terms. For instance, it is said in one place that 'a gentleman is free from worries and fears' (XII.4), while elsewhere it is the benevolent man who is said not to have worries (IX.29, XIV.28). As benevolence is so central a concept, we naturally expect Confucius to have a great deal to say about it. In this we are not disappointed. There are no less than six occasions on which Confucius answered direct questions about benevolence, and as Confucius had the habit of framing his answers with the specific needs of the inquirer in mind, these answers, taken together, give us a reasonably complete picture.

The essential point about benevolence is to be found in Confucius' answer to Chung-kung:

Do not impose on others what you yourself do not desire. (XII.2)

These words were repeated on another occasion.

Tzu-kung asked, 'Is there a single word which can be a guide to conduct throughout one's life?' The Master said, 'It is perhaps the word "*shu*". Do not impose on others what you yourself do not desire.' (XV.24)

By taking the two sayings together we can see that *shu* forms part of benevolence and, as such, is of great significance in the teachings of Confucius. This is confirmed by a saying of Tseng Tzu's. To the Master's remark that there was a single thread binding his way together, Tseng Tzu added the explanation, 'The way of the Master consists in *chung* and *shu*. That is all' (IV.15). There is another saying which is, in fact, also about *shu*. In answer to a question from Tzu-kung, Confucius said,

A benevolent man helps others to take their stand in so far as he himself wishes to take his stand, and gets others there in so far as he himself wishes to get there. The ability to take as analogy what is near at hand can be called the method of benevolence. (VI.30)

From this we can see that *shu* is the method of discovering what other people wish or do not wish done to them. The method consists in taking oneself – 'what is near at hand' – as an analogy [5] and asking oneself what one would like or dislike were one in the position of the person at the receiving end. *Shu*, however, cannot be the whole of benevolence as it is only its method. Having found out what the other person wants or does not want, whether we go on to do to him what we believe he wants and refrain from doing to him what we believe he does not want must depend on something other than *shu*. As the way of the Master consists of *chung* and *shu*, in *chung* we have the other component of benevolence. *Chung* is the doing of one's best and it is through *chung* that one puts into effect what one had found out by the method of *shu*. Tseng Tzu said on another occasion, 'Every day I examine myself on three counts,' and of these the first is 'In what I have undertaken on another's behalf, have I failed to be *chung*?' (I.4). Again, when asked how a subject should serve his ruler, Confucius' answer was that he 'should serve his ruler with *chung*' (III.19). Finally, it is also said that in dealing with others one should be *chung* (XIII.19). In all these cases there is no doubt at all that *chung* means 'doing one's best'.[6]

Another answer Confucius gave to the question about benevolence was, 'Love your fellow men' (XII.22). As he did not elaborate, his meaning is not very clear. But fortunately he used this phrase again on two other occasions. In I.5 he said, 'In guiding a state of a thousand chariots ... avoid excesses in expenditure and love your fellow men; employ the labour of the common people in the right seasons.' Again, the Master, according to Tzu-yu, once said 'that the gentleman instructed in the Way loves his fellow men and that the small man instructed in the Way is easy to command' (XVII.4). In the first case, the love for one's fellow men (*jen*) is contrasted with the employment of the common people

5. There is a more explicit definition of *shu* in one of the philosophers of the Warring States period. The *Shih tzu* says, 'By "*shu*" is meant using oneself as a measure.' (*Ch'ün shu chih yao*, 36.19b).

6. Translators tend to use 'loyal' as the sole equivalent for *chung* even when translating early texts. This mistake is due to a failure to appreciate that the meaning of the word changed in the course of time. In later usage, it is true, *chung* tended to mean 'loyalty' in the sense of 'blind devotion', but this was not its meaning at the time of Confucius.

(min) in the right seasons, while in the second the gentleman's loving his fellow men is contrasted with the small man's being easy to command. If we remember that the small man was probably different from the common people, we cannot rule out the possibility that when Confucius defined benevolence in terms of loving one's fellow men he did not have the common people in mind as well.[7] Even if this is the case, it is perhaps not as strange as it may seem at first sight, and in order to see it in perspective, we should first take a look at the basis of Confucius' system of morals.

Confucius had a profound admiration for the Duke of Chou[8] who, as regent in the early part of the reign of his young nephew, King Ch'eng, was the architect of the Chou feudal system some five hundred years before Confucius' time. It is beyond the scope of this introduction to discuss in detail the influence of the Duke on Chinese society and the Chinese political system. It is sufficient simply to single out for mention his most important contribution,

7. It is to be emphasized that the theory mentioned above concerning the distinction between *jen* and *min* has not been established beyond doubt. For instance, there are two chapters in the *Analects* (VI.30 and XIV.42) in which Confucius describes the task of taking care of the people as a task difficult even for the sage kings Yao and Shun. The wording is so similar that it is possible that they are versions of the same saying. What is interesting for our present purpose is that in the one (VI.30) *min* (the common people) is contrasted with *chung* (multitude) while in the other (XIV.42) *pai hsing* (the people) is contrasted with *jen*. As *chung* and *jen* are similar in usage, (see, e.g., I.6) it would seem that *min* and *pai hsing* are also used as near synonyms. As *pai hsing* – literally 'the hundred surnames' – must have been people with surnames, if it is a term synonymous with *min*, then *min*, too, must also be people with surnames. In that case, they would hardly be totally without political privileges. This shows how difficult it is to establish the usage of a term even within the narrow compass of a single work. Further, it has to be pointed out that even if we were to concede that *jen*, when used in contradistinction to *min*, most probably had a class connotation, there are other uses of the word which certainly did not have such a connotation. First, *jen* is used to mean others in contradistinction to oneself (*chi*). For instance, 'Do not impose on others (*jen*) what you yourself (*chi*) do not desire' (XII.2). Second, *jen* is certainly the word for human beings in general. For instance, 'A man (*jen*) devoid of constancy will not make a shaman or a doctor' (XIII.22). In the translation, to help the reader who does not read Chinese, *jen* is rendered 'fellow men' whenever it is likely to have a class connotation.

8. See, e.g., VII.5.

the clan inheritance system known as *tsung fa*. Under this system, succession passes to the eldest son by the principal wife. Younger sons or sons by concubines become founders of their own noble houses. Thus the feudal lord stands to the king in a double relationship. In terms of political relationship he is a vassal while in terms of blood ties he is the head of a cadet branch of the royal clan. Political allegiance has as its foundation family allegiance. This social system founded by the Duke of Chou proved its soundness by the durability of the Chou Dynasty.

Following the footsteps of the Duke of Chou, Confucius made the natural love and obligations obtaining between members of the family the basis of a general morality. The two most important relationships within the family are those between father and son and between elder and younger brother. The love one owes to one's parents is *hsiao* while the respect due one's elder brother is *t'i*. If a man is a good son and a good younger brother at home, he can be counted on to behave correctly in society. Tzu-yu said,

> It is rare for a man whose character is such that he is good as a son (*hsiao*) and obedient as a young man (*t'i*) to have the inclination to transgress against his superiors; it is unheard of for one who has no such inclination to be inclined to start a rebellion. (I.2)

He goes on to draw the logical conclusion that 'being good as a son and obedient as a young man is, perhaps, the root of a man's character'.

In later Confucianism an undue emphasis was put on being a good son, but we can see here that even in early Confucian teachings *hsiao* was one of the most basic virtues.

If being a good son makes a good subject, being a good father will also make a good ruler. Love for people outside one's family is looked upon as an extension of the love for members of one's own family. One consequence of this view is that the love, and so the obligation to love, decreases by degrees as it extends outwards. Geographically, one loves members of one's own family more than one's neighbours, one's neighbours more than one's fellow villagers, and so on. Socially, one loves members of one's own social class more than those of another class. Thus it would not be surprising if benevolence was confined to one's fellow men (*jen*), but what is much more important to remember is that this does not mean that one does not love the common people at all. One loves them, but to a lesser degree and, perhaps, in a different manner. In Confucius' terminology, one should be generous (*hui*) to the common people (V.16). This is in keeping with Confucius' general attitude towards obligations. Our obligation towards others should be in proportion to the benefit we have received from them. This seems to be the case even between parents and children. In commenting on Tsai Yü who wanted to cut short the three-year mourning period, Confucius said, 'Was Yü not given three years' love by his parents?' (XVII.21). This may be taken to mean that the observance of the three-year mourning period is, in some sense, a repayment of the love received from one's parents in the first years of one's life. If this is so, it is not difficult to see why the obligations we owe to other people should also be in proportion to the closeness of our relationship to them. As to how a ruler should treat the common people, this is a topic to which we shall return.

Concerning the nature of benevolence, there is another answer given by Confucius which is of great importance because the question was put to him by his most talented disciple.

Yen Yüan asked about benevolence. The Master said, 'To return to the observance of the rites through overcoming the self constitutes benevolence. If for a single day a man could return to the observance of the rites through overcoming himself, then the whole Empire would consider benevolence to be his. However, the practice of benevolence depends on oneself alone, and not on others.' (XII.1)

There are two points in this definition of benevolence which deserve attention. First, benevolence consists in overcoming the self. Second, to be benevolent one has to return to the observance of the rites.

Take the first point first. It is a central tenet in the teachings of Confucius that being moral has nothing to do with self-interest. To be more precise, to say that two things have nothing to do with each other is to say that there is no relationship whatsoever between them, either positive or negative. If being moral has nothing to do with pursuing one's own interest, neither has it anything to do with deliberately going against it. Why, then, it may be asked, is it so important to emphasize this lack of relationship between the two? The answer is this. Of all the things that are likely to distort a man's moral judgement and deflect him from his moral purpose, self-interest is the strongest, the most persistent and the most insidious. Confucius was well aware of this. That is why he said, more than once, that at the sight of profit one should think of what is right (XIV.12, XVI.10 and XIX.1). In another context he warned men in their old age against acquisitiveness (XVI.7). He also asked, 'Is it really possible to work side by side with a mean fellow in the service of a lord? Before he gets what he wants, he worries lest he should not get it. After he has got it, he worries lest he should lose it, and when that happens he will not stop at anything' (XVII.15). Confucius came to the conclusion that he would not remain in undeserved wealth or position in spite of their being desirable objects (IV.5).

The point about returning to the observance of the rites is equally important. The rites (*li*) were a body of rules governing action in every aspect of life and they were the repository of past insights into morality. It is, therefore, important that one should, unless there are strong reasons to the contrary, observe them. Though there is no guarantee that observance of the rites necessarily leads, in every case, to behaviour that is right, the chances are it will, in fact, do so. To this point we shall return. For the moment, it is enough to say that Confucius had great respect for the body of rules which went under the name of *li*. That is why when Yen Yüan pressed for more specific details, he was told not to look or listen, speak or move, unless it was in accordance with the rites (XII.1). This, in Confucius' view, was no easy task, so much so that 'if for a single day a man could return to the observance of the rites through overcoming himself, then the whole Empire would consider benevolence to be his'.

There are two occasions when answers are given which emphasize another aspect of benevolence. When Fan Ch'ih asked about benevolence, the Master said, 'The benevolent man reaps the benefit only after overcoming difficulties' (VI.22). Similarly, when Ssu-ma Niu asked about benevolence, the Master said, 'The mark of the benevolent man is that he is loath to speak,' and then went on to explain, 'When to act is difficult, is it any wonder that one is loath to speak?' (XII.3). That he considered benevolence difficult can be seen from his reluctance to grant that anyone was benevolent. He would not commit himself when asked whether Tzu-lu, Jan Ch'iu and Kung-hsi Ch'ih were benevolent (V.8). Nor would he grant that either Ling Yin Tzu-wen or Ch'en Wen Tzu was benevolent (V.19). He refused to claim benevolence for himself (VII.32). This is no more than one would expect from a man of modesty. However, he did say of Yen Yüan, 'in his heart for three months at a time Hui does not lapse from benevolence,' while 'the others attain benevolence merely by fits and starts' (VI.7). This emphasis on the difficulty of practising benevolence is echoed, as we have seen, by Tseng Tzu who described benevolence as 'a heavy burden' (VIII.7). But although Confucius emphasized the difficulty of practising benevolence, he also made it abundantly clear that whether we succeed or not depends solely on ourselves. As we have already seen, he said in answer to Yen Yüan's question that 'the practice of benevolence depends on oneself alone, and not on others' (XII.1). He was quite clear that failure to practise benevolence was not due to lack of strength to carry it through. He said, 'Is there a man who, for the space of a single day, is able to devote all his strength to benevolence? I have not come across such a man whose strength proves insufficient for the task' (IV.6). Thus when Jan Ch'iu excused himself by saying, 'It is not that I am not pleased with your way, but rather that my strength gives out,' Confucius' comment was, 'A man whose strength gives out collapses along the course. In your case you set the limits beforehand' (VI.12). Confucius stated his conviction unambiguously when he said, 'Is benevolence really far away? No sooner do I desire it than it is here' (VII.30). On the lines of the *Odes*

> The flowers of the cherry tree,
> How they wave about!
> It's not that I do not think of you,
> But your home is so far away,

Confucius commented, 'He did not really think of her. If he did, there is no such thing as being far away' (IX.31). He must have made this comment with its possible application to benevolence in mind.

Besides benevolence there is a host of other virtues which the gentleman is supposed to possess, and we must discuss at least the more important of these. There are two virtues which are often mentioned together with benevolence. They are wisdom or intelligence (*chih*) and courage (*yung*). For instance, Confucius said, 'The man of wisdom is never in two minds; the man of benevolence never worries; the man of courage is never afraid' (IX.29), and 'There are three things constantly on the lips of the gentleman none of which I have succeeded in following: "A man of benevolence never worries; a man of wisdom is never in two minds; a man of courage is never afraid"' (XIV.28).

A man of wisdom is never in two minds in his judgement about right and wrong. A man who lacks wisdom, however, can easily mistake the specious for the genuine. This can happen with borderline cases where the application of a rule or a definition becomes uncertain, particularly in the sphere of morals. Take a concrete example. When a ruler gives his concubine the same privileges as his consort or his younger son the same privileges as the heir, doubt is sown in the minds of the people. To all outward appearance, the concubine is indistinguishable from the consort or the younger son from the heir. It takes a man of wisdom not to be perplexed by such phenomena. Another attribute of the wise man is that he has knowledge of men. In other words, he is a good judge of character. In the Chinese view, the most important factor contributing to the difficulty of predicting the future lies in the unpredictable nature of man. Thus, the study of human character, through which the only hope of gaining some degree of control over future events lies, was considered a matter of vital importance to the ruler, as the present and future stability of his state often depended on his choice of ministers. This kind of study of human character which was to become from the Eastern Han onwards one of the major preoccupations of Chinese thinkers, was already of great importance in Confucius' day. Thus, when Fan Ch'ih asked about wisdom, the Master said, 'Know your fellow men' (XII.22).

But is wisdom acquired? It is true, Confucius said, 'Those who are born with knowledge are the highest. Next come those who attain knowledge through study. Next again come those who turn to study after having been vexed by difficulties. The common people, in so far as they make no effort to study even after having been vexed by difficulties, are the lowest' (XVI.9), but he made no claim to be amongst those born with knowledge. In fact he explicitly rejected this when he said, 'I was not born with knowledge but, being fond of antiquity, I am quick to seek it' (VII.20). He further said this of himself, 'I use my ears widely and follow what is good in what I have heard; I use my eyes widely and retain what I have seen in my mind. This constitutes a lower level of knowledge' (VII.28). He did not seem to have granted that anyone was actually born with knowledge. All he did was to leave open the possibility of there actually being such a category of people. Judging by the tremendous emphasis he placed on learning, what mattered to him was that it was possible to acquire knowledge through learning. Learning, is, to him, a process that can never be completed. As Tzu-hsia said, 'A man can, indeed, be said to be eager to learn who is conscious, in the course of a day, of what he lacks and who never forgets, in the course of a month, what he has mastered' (XIX.5). Indeed, according to Confucius, 'A man is worthy of being a teacher who gets to know what is new by keeping fresh in his mind what he is already familiar with' (II.11).

The most important thing in our attitude towards knowledge is being honest with ourselves. Confucius said to Tzu-lu, 'Yu, shall I tell you what it is to know? To say you know when you know, and to say you do not when you do not, that is knowledge' (II.17). On another occasion when Tzu-lu offered what Confucius considered an ill-judged comment, he admonished him by saying, 'Where a gentleman is ignorant, one would expect him not to offer any opinion' (XIII.3). For his part, Confucius never proposed anything that was not founded on knowledge. 'There are', he said, 'presumably men who innovate without possessing knowledge, but that is not a fault I have' (VII.28). This responsible attitude towards knowledge is most important to the teacher. One of the counts that Tseng Tzu daily examined himself on was, 'Have I passed on to others anything that I have not tried out myself?' (I.4).

Courage was counted one of the major virtues. This is clear from the following saying attributed to Confucius in the *Chung yung* (*The Mean*) 'Wisdom, benevolence and courage, these three are virtues universally acknowledged in the Empire.'[9] In the *Analects* Confucius' attitude towards courage is, in fact, much more critical. True, it is an indispensable virtue in a gentleman if he is to see his moral purpose through, because he has to pursue that purpose fearlessly, and only 'the man of courage is never afraid' (IX.29, XIV.28). 'Faced with what is right, to leave it undone,' according to Confucius, 'shows a lack of courage' (II.24). Hence Confucius said, 'A benevolent man is sure to possess courage,' but he goes on immediately to add, 'A courageous man does not necessarily possess benevolence' (XIV.4). Courage is, indeed, a double-edged sword. In the hands of the good, it is a means to the realization of goodness, but in the hands of the wicked, it is equally a means to the realization of wickedness. To put this in even stronger terms, neither great goodness nor great wickedness can be accomplished by men devoid of courage. Confucius showed that he was well aware of this. He said, 'Unless a man has the spirit of the rites . . . in having courage he will become unruly' (VIII.2). On another occasion he said of the gentleman 'He dislikes those who, while possessing courage, lack the spirit of the rites' (XVII. 24). Equally, 'being fond of courage while detesting poverty will lead men to unruly behaviour' (VIII.10). Courage, to be a virtue, must be in the service of morality. Hence, when asked whether the gentleman considered courage a supreme quality, Confucius answered, 'For the gentleman it is morality that is supreme. Possessed of courage but devoid of morality, a gentleman will make trouble while a small man will be a brigand' (XVII.23).

There remain two major virtues to be dealt with. First, there is *hsin*. This is a concept which has no exact equivalent in English.

9. *Li chi chu shu*, 52.19a.

To be *hsin* is to be reliable in word. An important part of this has, of course, to do with promise-keeping. But when Confucius talks of being *hsin* in word (I.7, XIII.20, XV.6), he means more than that. To be *hsin* in word applies to *all* one's words. It concerns, besides promises, resolutions concerning future conduct, or even plain statements of fact. Not to carry out a resolution is to fail to be *hsin*; to have made a statement not borne out by facts – whether they be present or future facts – is equally to fail to be *hsin*.

In this connection, Confucius often opposes the terms *yen* (word) and *hsing* (deed). For one's deed to fail to match one's word is to fail to be *hsin*. Hence the importance of seeing to it that one lives up to one's word. 'The gentleman is ashamed of his word outstripping his deed' (XIV.27), and 'claims made immodestly are difficult to live up to' (XIV.20). Hence 'in antiquity men were loath to speak' 'because they counted it shameful if their person failed to keep up with their words' (IV.22). The safest course to take is never to make any claims until the deed is done. Thus, the gentleman 'puts his words into action before allowing his words to follow his action' (II.13). Confucius' general advice is that one should be quick to act but slow to speak (I.14, IV.24).

Concerning *hsin* there is one saying which is particularly interesting. Yu Tzu said, 'To be trustworthy in word (*hsin*) is close to being moral in that it enables one's words to be repeated' (I.13). The tragedy of the boy who cried 'Wolf!' is that when he repeated his cry nobody took him seriously because he was not *hsin* on the previous occasions. Being trustworthy in word is close to being moral precisely because of this aspect of trustworthiness, and it is to this aspect that Yu Tzu wanted to draw our attention.[10] But to say that trustworthiness in word is *close to* being moral is to say that the two are not identical. There are bound to be cases where an inflexible adherence to the principle of trustworthiness in word will lead to action that is not moral. Confucius describes 'a man who insists on keeping his word and seeing his actions through to the end' as showing 'a stubborn petty-mindedness' (XIII.20).

10. For a fuller discussion of the interpretation of the quotation from I.13, see D. C. Lau, 'On the expression *fu yen*', *Bulletin of the School of Oriental and African Studies*, XXXVI, 2, (1973), pp. 324-33.

Second, there is *ching* (reverence). This is a rather ancient
concept. In early Chou literature *ching* describes the frame of mind
of a man taking part in a sacrifice. It is different from that shown
in other religions. In other religions, there is fear and abject sub-
mission in face of the power of the deity. *Ching*, on the other hand,
is born of the awareness of the immensity of one's responsibility
to promote the welfare of the common people. It is a combination
of the fear of failing in the responsibility one is charged with and
the solemn single-mindedness directed towards the satisfactory
discharging of that responsibility. In the *Analects*, *ching* still shows
a remnant of this connection with religion. There is one passage in
which it is mentioned in connection with sacrifice. Confucius said,
'To keep one's distance from the gods and spirits while showing
them reverence can be called wisdom' (VI.22). Otherwise, *ching*
is mentioned always in connection with affairs of government and
the service of one's superiors.

Ching, reverence, is to be distinguished from *kung*, respectfulness. The latter is a matter of visible appearance and manner. *Kung*
is mostly mentioned in connection with the observance of the rites.
For instance, the gentleman 'is respectful towards others and observant of the rites' (XII.5), and he is said to turn his thought to
'appearing respectful when it comes to his demeanour' (XVI.10).
A man should be respectful in his intercourse with others because
by so doing he can hope to be spared insults and humiliations.
'If a man is respectful he will not be treated with insolence' (XVII.
6). 'To be respectful is close to being observant of the rites in that
it enables one to stay clear of disgrace and insult' (I.13).

This more or less completes the account of the major moral
virtues which go into the make-up of the gentleman. I have,
however, deliberately left *yi* to the end. *Yi* is a word which
can be used of an act in which case it can be rendered as 'right',
or it can be used of an act an agent ought to perform in which case
it can be rendered as 'duty', or it can be used of an agent in which
case it can be rendered as 'righteous' or 'dutiful'. When used in a
general sense, sometimes the only possible rendering is 'moral'
or 'morality'. In a sense most of the words denoting moral
virtues can be applied to both agents and acts. Nevertheless, in this

respect, *yi* is different from other moral words. Let us contrast it with benevolence, for instance. Of course an act as well as an agent can be described as benevolent, but benevolence is basically a character of agents and its application to acts is only derivative. A benevolent act is the act of a benevolent man. As a character of moral agents, benevolence has more to do with disposition and motive than objective circumstances. The reverse is true of rightness. Rightness is basically a character of acts and its application to agents is derivative. A man is righteous only in so far as he consistently does what is right. The rightness of acts depends on their being morally fitting in the circumstances and has little to do with the disposition or motive of the agent. It is here that the distinction between agent-ethics and act-ethics becomes relevant. Earlier we have said that Confucius was more interested in the moral virtues of men than in the moral qualities of their acts. But no moral system can be solely based on moral virtues, and Confucius' system is no exception. We have seen that in the question of self-interest, the opposition is between profit and rightness. Again, in the test whether courage is a virtue it is *yi* that is the standard. Although Confucius does not state it explicitly, one cannot help getting the impression that he realizes that in the last resort *yi* is the standard by which all acts must be judged while there is no further standard by which *yi* itself can be judged. After all, even benevolence does not carry its own moral guarantee. 'To love benevolence without loving learning is liable to lead to foolishness' (XVII.8). As we shall see, the object to be pursued in learning, in this context, is likely to have been the rites, and the rites, as rules of conduct, can, in the final analysis, only be based on *yi*. We can say, then, that in Confucius' moral system, although benevolence occupies the more central position, *yi* is, nevertheless, more basic.

No account of the gentleman will be complete unless something is said about his attitude towards *t'ien* (Heaven) and *t'ien ming* (Heaven's Decree), but this task turns out to present some difficulty. First, apart from *t'ien ming* – literally Heaven's command – *ming* is also used by itself, and there seems to be a basic difference between the two expressions. Second, the term *t'ien ming* is to be found only twice in the *Analects*, and it is difficult to rest an interpretation on such a scanty basis. However, the attempt has to be made as the distinction between *t'ien ming* and *ming* seems vital to the understanding of Confucius' position.

Although *t'ien ming* occurs only twice in the whole of the *Analects*, it is fortunate for us that it is a term of considerable antiquity. The belief in the Decree of Heaven most probably goes back to a time considerably before the founding of the Chou Dynasty towards the end of the second millenium B.C. The theory concerning the Decree of Heaven was, however, most probably an innovation on the part of the Duke of Chou. According to this theory, Heaven cares profoundly about the welfare of the common people and the Emperor is set up expressly to promote that welfare. He rules in virtue of the Decree of Heaven and remains Emperor only so long as he fulfils that purpose. As soon as he forgets his function and begins to rule for his own sake, Heaven will withdraw the Decree and bestow it on someone more worthy. Thus the Decree of Heaven is a moral imperative and, as such, has nothing to do with the agency of Heaven in bringing about what comes to pass. The only development by Confucius' time was that the Decree of Heaven was no longer confined to the Emperor. Every man was subject to the Decree of Heaven which enjoined him to be moral and it was his duty to live up to the demands of that Decree. Confucius said, 'At fifty, I understood (*chih*) *t'ien ming*' (II.4). This implies that *t'ien ming* is something difficult to understand, but it also shows unmistakeably that it can be understood. The only other mention of *t'ien ming* in the *Analects* is when Confucius said that it was one of the things the gentleman stood in awe of (XVI.8).

Whether *ming* was simply used as an abbreviation for *t'ien ming* in early texts, there is no doubt that by Confucius' time, it had developed into a term with a different and independent meaning. This meaning is best illustrated by the saying quoted by Tzu-hsia in a conversation with Ssu-ma Niu: 'life and death are a matter of *ming*; wealth and honour depend on Heaven' (XII.5). The context shows that *ming* is used in the sense of Destiny and that Heaven is only a synonym for *ming*. There is a remark by Mencius where Heaven and Destiny are also juxtaposed as synonyms which can serve as a gloss on these terms. Mencius said, 'When a thing is done though by no one, then it is the work of Heaven; when a thing comes about though no one brings it about, then it is decreed' (V.A.6).[11] Thus there are certain things which are brought about, not by human agency, but by Destiny. These are things over which human endeavour has no effect. Whether or not a man is going to end up with wealth, honour and long life is due to Destiny. No amount of effort on his part will make any difference to the outcome. Thus, in the context of the fortunes of an individual, *ming* is his lot. For instance, twice Confucius said of Yen Yüan who died young that 'unfortunately his allotted span (*ming*) was a short one' (VI.3, XI.7). Again, he rebuked Tzu-kung for refusing to accept his lot (*ming*) and indulging in speculation (XI.19). The reason why so much importance is attached to *ming* is this. If a man is convinced that all the desirable things in life are due to Destiny, he is more likely to see the futility of pursuing them and instead bend his efforts to the pursuit of morality. Morality is the only object a man ought to pursue because being moral lies in making just such an effort and not in the successful outcome of one's action. This is the meaning of the saying, 'A man has no way of becoming a gentleman unless he understands Destiny (*chih ming*)' (XX.3). The phrase *chih ming* (understanding Destiny) looks very much like the phrase *chich t'ien ming* (understanding Heaven's Decree) which, we have seen, Confucius used of himself at the age of fifty; but the meaning, in fact, is very different in the two cases. To understand Heaven's Decree is to understand *why* Heaven should so decree, but to understand Destiny is to know *that* certain things in life come under the sway of Destiny and *that* it is futile to pursue them.

The difference between *t'ien ming* and *ming* can be summed up in this way. *T'ien ming*, as moral imperative, is concerned with what man ought to do; *ming*, in the sense of Destiny, has to do with the bringing about of what comes to pass. *T'ien ming*, necessarily difficult to understand is, nevertheless, understandable; *ming* is a total mystery. What *t'ien ming* enjoins we ought to obey; what falls within the domain of *ming* we should leave alone.

11. *Mencius*, p. 145.

If *ming* and *t'ien ming* are terms different in meaning, equally there are two different senses of *t'ien* (Heaven), each correlated with one of the two terms. We have already seen that Heaven was used as a synonym of Destiny in Tzu-hsia's remark. This is also the case in lamentations and exclamations of faith. Take these two cases for instance. When Yen Yüan died, Confucius said, 'Alas! Heaven has bereft me! Heaven has bereft me!' (XI.9). However, when Jan Po-niu was stricken with a horrible disease, Confucius said, 'It must be Destiny!' (VI.10). In these two remarks, Heaven and Destiny seem to be interchangeable terms. On the other hand, there are cases where Heaven seems very different from Destiny. For instance, when his life was endangered in Sung, Confucius said, 'Heaven is author of the virtue that is in me. What can Huan T'ui do to me?' (VII.23). On the occasion when Tzu-lu was slandered he, however, said, 'What can Kung-po Liao do in defiance of Destiny?' (XIV.36). The two remarks seem to me to be very different in meaning. In the latter case, Confucius was, in effect, saying, 'What will be will be.' In the former, however, he was saying that Heaven had endowed him with special virtue so that he could shoulder the *t'ien ming* of awakening the Empire to its moral purpose and that if Huan T'ui was allowed to kill him Heaven would be frustrating its own purpose.

Heaven, as a synonym of *ming*, is the agency which brings about what comes to pass, but where moral purpose and moral imperative are concerned, Heaven is the source of the Decree. Whether in the last analysis it is the same Heaven that is responsible both for events that are destined and for the issuing of moral imperatives, and further whether *ming* as Destiny which brings about what comes to pass has also an imperative aspect, we have no way of deciding, but what is important is that, for practical purposes, between them *ming* and *t'ien ming* define for us the legitimate sphere of human endeavour. Earlier we have seen the importance of the distinction between *li* (profit) and *yi* (rightness). The distinction between *ming* and *t'ien ming* is, in effect, the same distinction viewed from a different angle. *Li* pertains to *ming* and is, therefore, not a proper object of pursuit. *Yi* pertains to *t'ien ming* and is, therefore, something we ought to follow.

So far we have only dealt with the moral qualities of the gentle-man. To give these qualities their fullest realization the gentleman must take part in government. This, however, does not mean that the arduous process of self-cultivation is a mere means to the end of personal preferment. Hence, Confucius said, 'It is not easy to find a man who can study for three years without thinking about earning a salary' (VIII.12), and he showed approval when Min Tzu-ch'ien considered himself not yet ready when offered a post (VI.9). But as a man can only be prepared for office through studying, in so far as he studies he is, in fact, preparing himself for an official career at the same time (XV.32). Study and the holding of office are the twin activities inseparable from the concept of the gentleman. 'When a man in office finds that he can more than cope with his duties, then he studies; when a student finds that he can more than cope with his studies, then he takes office' (XIX.13). But that a man should have adequately prepared himself for office is not the only precondition for his actually taking office. The times must be right as well. For a man to be so keen that he is ready to take office whether order prevails in the state or not is condemned by Confucius. 'It is shameful,' he said, 'to make salary your sole object, irrespective of whether the Way prevails in the state or not' (XIV.1). The reason is that when the Way does not prevail in a state one can only stay in office by bending one's principles. If one does not do so one is liable to be putting oneself in danger. In such a situation, one's only choice is to stay clear of trouble, devoting oneself to the pursuit of the highest moral standard in one's life as a private citizen. Shih Yü was straight as an arrow whether the Way prevailed in the state or not. All Confucius was willing to grant him was that he was straight. In contrast, Ch'ü Po-yü who took office when the Way prevailed in the state but allowed himself to be furled and put away when the Way fell into disuse was de-scribed by Confucius as gentlemanly (XV.7). This is an attitude we find Confucius expressing time and time again. 'The Master said of Nan-jung that when the Way prevailed in the state he was not cast aside and when the Way fell into disuse he stayed clear of the humiliation of punishment' (V.2). Ning Wu Tzu was intelli-gent when the Way prevailed in the state, but appeared stupid when it did not. Confucius' comment was, 'Others may equal his intelligence, but they cannot equal his stupidity' (V.21). The way to stay clear of trouble while maintaining one's moral integrity, according to Confucius, is this. 'When the Way prevails in the state, speak and act with perilous high-mindedness; when the Way does not prevail, act with perilous high-mindedness but speak with self-effacing diffidence' (XIV.3). This is in keeping with his general view that one should not concern oneself with matters of government unless they are the responsibility of one's office and Tseng Tzu's view that the gentleman does not allow his thoughts to go beyond his office (XIV.26). That he considered this no easy advice to follow is shown by his saying to Yen Yüan, 'Only you and I have the ability to go forward when employed and to stay out of sight when set aside' (VII.11).

However, when the Way prevails in the state, it is not only one's duty to take office, but the taking of office is the culmination of the years of preparation for just such an eventuality. Thus, according to Confucius, not only is it 'a shameful matter to be rich and noble when the Way falls into disuse in the state', it is equally 'a shameful matter to be poor and humble when the Way prevails in the state' (VIII.13).

The ultimate purpose of government is the welfare of the common people (min). This is the most basic principle in Confucianism and has remained unchanged throughout the ages. The promotion of the welfare of the common people begins with satisfying their material needs. 'Tzu-kung asked about government. The Master said, "Give them enough food"' (XII.7). In order to achieve this aim, the labour of the common people must be employed in the right seasons (I.5), i.e., they must not be taken away from their work on the land during the busy seasons. In broader terms, Tzu-ch'an was said to be generous in caring for the people and just in employing their services (V.16). But besides the necessities of life, the common people must also be provided with sufficient arms. However, before they can be sent to war, they must also be given adequate training. Confucius said, 'To send the common people to war untrained is to throw them away' (XIII.30). As to what this training consists of we are not told. Although the training the ruler gives the common people is likely to be very different from the teaching Confucius gives his disciples, it is inconceivable that this training should be exclusively of a military nature. It must include a strong moral element. Otherwise, it is difficult to see why it should take so long, for, according to Confucius, 'After a good man has trained the common people for seven years, they should be ready to take up arms' (XIII.29).[12] However, food and arms are not the most important things the people should have. Above all, they must have trust in the ruler and must look up to him. In answer to Tzu-kung's question about government, Confucius said, 'Give them enough food, give them enough arms and the common people will have trust in you.' When he was asked which of the three should be given up first, his answer was, 'Give up arms.' This is no surprise given Confucius' attitude towards the use of force in war, but his next answer is surprising. When pressed to say which of the remaining two should be given up first, his answer was, 'Give up food.' He then went on to explain, 'Death has always been with us since the beginning of time, but when there is no trust the common people will have nothing to stand on' (XII.7).

This emphasis on the moral basis of government is fundamental to Confucius' teaching. He said,

> Guide them by edicts, keep them in line with punishments, and the common people will stay out of trouble but will have no sense of shame.

Compulsion and punishment can, at best, ensure outward conform-

12. There is support for this view in the *Tso chuan*. Under the twenty-seventh year of Duke Hsi, an account is given of how Duke Wen of Chin came to be the Leader of the Feudal Lords. On his return to Chin, the Duke began to train the common people. After two years of training, he wanted to go to war, but Tzu-fan advised him that before this could be done the common people should first be made to understand what is right, trustworthiness in word and the rites. The Duke accepted his advice. The *Tso chuan* concluded the account with the remark, 'That Duke Wen succeeded in becoming the Leader of the Feudal Lords was due to the training he gave the common people' (*Tso chuan chu shu*, 16.13a). This shows very clearly that in the training of the common people, the moral side is far more important than the purely military.

ity. The common people will stay clear of trouble not because they are ashamed of doing wrong but because they fear punishment. In contrast to this:

> Guide them by virtue, keep them in line with the rites, and they will, besides having a sense of shame, reform themselves. (II.3)

When the people reform themselves and have a sense of shame, the law and its attendant threat of punishment need never be invoked.

Guidance by virtue, however, cannot be effective unless the ruler sets a moral example for his people. Here, perhaps, we should take note of the fact that the Chinese word *cheng* (to govern) and *cheng* (to correct) are cognate.

> Chi K'ang Tzu asked Confucius about government. Confucius answered, 'To govern (*cheng*) is to correct (*cheng*). If you set an example by being correct, who would dare to remain incorrect?' (XII.17)

There is a positive and a negative point to this. The negative point is that if the ruler fails to be correct himself but insists on punishing his subjects for being incorrect, he will be setting himself above the law and the common people will be conscious of the injustice. The positive point is that the common people always look up to their betters and if those in position of authority set an example this will be imitated even if the people are not ordered to do so. This point comes out clearly in the following passage:

> The Master said, 'If a man is correct in his own person, then there will be obedience without orders being given, but if he is not correct in his own person, there will not be obedience even though orders are given.' (XIII.6)

Moral example is far more effective than edicts, and where edicts contradict the example, it is the example that the common people will heed rather than the edicts. This point is most persuasively put by Confucius on another occasion.

> Chi K'ang Tzu asked Confucius about government, saying, 'What would you think if, in order to move closer to those who possess the Way, I were to kill those who do not follow the Way?'
>
> Confucius answered, 'In administering your government, what

need is there for you to kill? Just desire the good yourself and the
common people will be good. The virtue of the gentleman is like
wind; the virtue of the small man is like grass. Let the wind blow
over the grass and it is sure to bend.' (XII.19)

Here, Confucius was talking about 'the small man' – who presumably enjoyed political power though he belonged to the class of
the ruled – and not about the common people, but what is true of
the small man will *a fortiori* be true of the common people. Moral
example has an influence which, though imperceptible, is, in fact,
irresistible. It is, therefore, of the greatest importance to put the
upright in position of authority. In answer to the question put to
him by Duke Ai, 'What must I do before the common people will
look up to me?' Confucius said, 'Raise the straight and set them
over the crooked and the common people will look up to you.
Raise the crooked and set them over the straight and the common
people will not look up to you' (II.19). On another occasion, in
talking to Fan Ch'ih, Confucius enlarged on the point. The raising
of the straight and setting them over the crooked 'can make the
crooked straight' (XII.22). Tzu-hsia, to whom Fan Ch'ih reported
the remark, illustrated the saying from history. By raising the
straight to positions of authority, Shun and T'ang put those who
were not benevolent at a distance.

Since moral influence works in an imperceptible manner, the
ideal ruler is often characterized not only as doing nothing but
as appearing to the populace as having done nothing for which he
could be praised. 'The rule of virtue can be compared to the Pole
Star which commands the homage of the multitude of stars without leaving its place' (II.1). T'ai Po abdicated his right to rule,
'yet he left behind nothing the common people could acclaim'
(VIII.1). Yao was the king who modelled himself upon Heaven
which alone is great, yet 'he was so boundless that the common
people were not able to put a name to his virtues' (VIII.19).
This description of the ideal ruler is very like that offered by the
Taoists but the two are really very different. The Taoist ruler
genuinely does nothing because the Empire functions best when
left alone. The Confucian ruler only appears to do nothing because
the moral influence he exerts works imperceptibly.

We cannot leave the subject of government without discussing Confucius' attitude towards the common people (*min*). He did not disguise the fact that, in his view, the common people were very limited in their intellectual capacity. He said, 'The common people can be made to follow a path but not to understand it' (VIII.9). They cannot understand why they are led along a particular path because they never take the trouble to study. He said, 'Those who are born with knowledge are the highest. Next come those who attain knowledge through study. Next again come those who turn to study after having been vexed by difficulties. The common people, in so far as they make no effort to study even after having been vexed by difficulties, are the lowest' (XVI.9). It is not surprising that Confucius should have taken such a view. Study, as conceived by Confucius, is an arduous process which is never accomplished. The common people are greatly handicapped. They rarely have the capacity and practically never the opportunity. When on the rare occasion they have both the capacity and the opportunity, they are unlikely to be able to put up with the hardship. Confucius described how his favourite disciple, Yen Hui, was able to pursue unswervingly his studies in these words. 'How admirable Hui is! Living in a mean dwelling on a bowlful of rice and a ladleful of water is a hardship most men would find intolerable, but Hui does not allow this to affect his joy. How admirable Hui is!' (VI.11).

Confucius may not have had too high an opinion of the intellectual and moral capacities of the common people, but it is emphatically not true that he played down their importance in the scheme of things. Perhaps, it is precisely because the people are incapable of securing their own welfare unaided that the ruler's supreme duty is to work on their behalf in bringing about what is good for them. The common people should be treated with the same loving care given to babies who cannot fend for themselves. This is stated in a memorable remark in the *Book of History* quoted by Mencius: the ancient rulers acted 'as if they were tending a new-born babe'.[13] Mencius describes such rulers as father and mother to the people. It is thus undeniable that Confucius advocated a strong paternal-

13. *Mencius*, III.A.5 (p. 105).

ism in government and this remained unchanged as a basic principle throughout the whole history of Confucianism.

The importance of the common people and their welfare is emphasized time and time again in the *Analects*. For instance,

> Tzu-kung said, 'If there were a man who gave extensively to the common people and brought help to the multitude, what would you think of him? Could he be called benevolent?'
>
> The Master said, 'It is no longer a matter of benevolence with such a man. If you must describe him, "sage" is, perhaps, the right word. Even Yao and Shun would have found it difficult to accomplish as much.' (VI.30)

If we remember in what esteem Yao and Shun were held by Confucius and how unwilling he was to grant the epithet "sage" to anyone, we can see the immense significance of the remark. Finally, Confucius said that if he praised anyone, one might be sure that he had been put to the test. The test turns out to be the governing of the common people, for he went on to say, 'These common people are the touchstone by which the Three Dynasties were kept to the straight path' (XV.25). The sole test of a good ruler is whether he succeeds in promoting the welfare of the common people.

So far we have looked only at the moral qualities indispensable to the gentleman, but the ideal of the gentleman is wider than that of the moral man. More is necessary if we are to have the perfect gentleman. In order to understand this, we must first take a look at a pair of terms, *wen* and *chih*. *Chih* is the easier of the two to understand. It is the basic stuff or native substance a thing or a man is made of. *Wen* is more difficult to grasp because of its far-ranging application. In the first place *wen* signifies a beautiful pattern. For instance, the pattern of the stars is the *wen* of heaven, and the pattern on the skin of a tiger is its *wen*. Applied to man, it refers to the beautiful qualities he has acquired through education. Hence the contrast to *chih*. What a man acquires through education covers a wide range of accomplishments. It includes skills like archery and charioteering, writing and mathematics, but the most important fields are literature and music, and conduct befitting the gentleman.

Literature in Confucius' time meant basically the *Odes*, while music for Confucius was the music performed on court occasions and sacrificial ceremonies. Behaviour befitting the gentleman meant observance of the rites which included amongst other things the code of correct conduct. Besides denoting the accomplishments of an individual, *wen* can also be used for the culture of a society as a whole. Thus *wen* is a word with a wide range of meanings covered by a variety of words in English, such as ornament, adornment, refinement, accomplishment, good breeding and culture.

It is not enough for a man to be born with good native substance. A long process of nurture is necessary to give him the breeding that is indispensable to the gentleman. When Chi Tzu-ch'eng said, 'The important thing about the gentleman is the stuff he is made of. What does he need refinement for?' Tzu-kung's comment was that one could not separate refinement from the stuff, for 'the pelt of a tiger or a leopard, shorn of hair, is no different from that of a dog or a sheep' (XII.8). What Tzu-kung is saying is that it is the total qualities of the gentleman – stuff as well as refinement – that distinguish him from the small man, and it is futile to separate the stuff from the refinement in the mistaken attempt to single it out as the basic factor. Elsewhere we find Confucius emphasizing the importance of the balance between the two elements. He said, 'When there is a preponderance of native substance over acquired refinement, the result will be churlishness. When there is a preponderance of acquired refinement over native substance, the result will be pedantry. Only a well-balanced admixture of these two will result in gentlemanliness' (VI.18).

There is one place where a remark of Confucius' throws some light on the nature of this native substance. He said, 'The gentleman has morality as his basic stuff and by observing the rites puts it into practice . . . Such is a gentleman indeed' (XV.18). Here we see that the relation between *chih* and *wen* corresponds to the relation between morality (*yi*) and the rites (*li*). It is not enough for a man to be inclined towards doing what is right by nature, it is essential that he should be versed in the way this inclination can be given refined expression. A man may have a strong urge to show respect towards another man in a given society, but unless he knows the code of behaviour by which this respect is given expression, he will either fail completely to express it or, at most, succeed only in expressing it in a manner not altogether acceptable in that society. This brings out an important point about the rites. Morality does not only consist in action which affects the welfare of other people. It also sometimes requires behaviour which expresses an attitude towards them. This accounts for the fact that the word *li*, though it includes the moral code, is more appropriately rendered in English as 'rites' or 'ritual'.

As we have seen, besides the observance of the rites, the most important part of *wen* is poetry and music. That is why when an equivalent had to be found to the Western term 'literature', the expression used was naturally '*wen hsüeh*'. This may be a convenient point at which to take a look at Confucius' attitude to poetry and music, as the influence he exercised on subsequent ages was immense. The first point that should be made is that in Confucius' time the connection between poetry and music was a close one. Though there was bound to be music which did not involve words, all poetry could probably be sung. For this reason, Confucius had probably the same attitude towards both.

Let us begin with the following passage:

> The Master said of the *shao* that it was both perfectly beautiful and perfectly good, and of the *wu* that it was perfectly beautiful but not perfectly good.' (III.25)

We can see from this passage that Confucius required of music, and, by implication, of literature, not only perfect beauty but perfect goodness as well. The *shao* was the music of Shun who, chosen for his virtue, succeeded to the throne through the abdication of Yao, while the *wu* was the music of King Wu who, in spite of his virtue, won the Empire only after resorting to force – hence the name *wu* 'military force'. For this reason the former was not only perfectly beautiful but also perfectly good while the latter, though perfectly beautiful, left something to be desired in its goodness. That Confucius should consider the *wu* inferior to the *shao* is not surprising if we remember his abhorrence of force which was said to be among the things he never talked about (VII.21).

For Confucius perfect goodness was more important than perfect beauty. Whether a piece of music is acceptable or not depends on its moral quality. Perfect beauty is important because it is the only appropriate vehicle for conveying perfect goodness. It is to perfectly beautiful music that one can listen with joy, but it is only when perfect goodness is fused with perfect beauty that joy can be experienced which goes beyond our expectations.

> The Master heard the *shao* in Ch'i and for three months did not notice the taste of the meat he ate. He said, 'I never dreamt that the joys of music could reach such heights.' (VII.14)

It is no accident that the music that enthralled Confucius should be precisely the *shao* that he praised for its perfect goodness as well as its perfect beauty.

When asked how a state should be governed, Confucius said, 'As for music, adopt the *shao* and the *wu*. Banish the tunes of Cheng and keep plausible men at a distance. The tunes of Cheng are wanton and plausible men are dangerous' (XV.11). He further said, 'I detest purple for displacing vermillion. I detest the tunes of Cheng for corrupting classical music. I detest clever talkers who overturn states and noble families' (XVII.18).

There is no doubt that Confucius detested 'the tunes of Cheng', but he did so not because of their lack of beauty but because of their wantonness. It should be noted that each of the things Confucius detested bore a superficial resemblance to the proper thing, and it is because of this superficial resemblance that the specious can be mistaken for the genuine. Confucius' abhorrence is directed against this spuriousness. The 'tunes of Cheng' are grouped with 'clever talkers' and 'plausible men', since like 'clever talkers' and 'plausible men', the 'tunes of Cheng' are capable of worming their way into our favour if we are not on our guard. They are, then, not unattractive as music. In the end it is not the lack of beauty but the lack of goodness that marks the kind of music typified by the 'tunes of Cheng'.

The 'tunes of Cheng' certainly did not refer to the music alone. What is said about the tunes applies to the words as well, the wantonness being as much in the meaning of the words as in the allure of the music. In contrast to the tunes of Cheng, we find Confucius praising the *Kuan chü* with which the *Odes* open:

> In the *Kuan chü* there is joy without wantonness, and sorrow without self-injury. (III.20)

This shows that it was not the expression of pleasure as such but the expression of immoderate pleasure that was the reason for Confucius' condemnation of the tunes of Cheng. By contrast, the *Kuan chü* is an example of the expression of pleasure and sorrow in exactly the right measure.

Confucius summed up his views on poetry in the following words:

> The *Odes* are three hundred in number. They can be summed up in one phrase:
> Swerving not from the right path. (II.2)

Edification, however, is not the only purpose which poetry serves. Amongst other things, the Odes 'may serve to stimulate the imagination' (XVII.9). When reading poetry, one becomes alive to the underlying similarity between phenomena which, to the unimaginative, appear totally unconnected.

> Tzu-hsia asked,
> > 'Her entrancing smile dimpling,
> > Her beautiful eyes glancing,
> > Patterns of colour upon plain silk.
> What is the meaning of these lines?'
> The Master said, 'The colours are put in after the white.'
> 'Does the practice of the rites likewise come afterwards?'
> The Master said, 'It is you, Shang, who have thrown light on the text for me. Only with a man like you can one discuss the *Odes*.' (III.8)

The Master praised Tzu-hsia for his understanding of the *Odes* because he saw that just as in a painting the colours are put in after the outline is sketched in white so the refinement of observing the rites is inculcated in a man who is already born with the right substance.[14]

14. In I.15, Tzu-kung is similarly praised for his understanding of the *Odes*.

The *Odes* have another use and that is to enable a man to speak well. Confucius' son reported a conversation he once had with his father. 'Have you studied the *Odes*?' 'No.' 'Unless you study the *Odes*, you will be ill-equipped to speak' (XVI.13). The *Odes* was an anthology every educated man was thoroughly acquainted with, so an apt quotation from it could be used to convey one's meaning in polite or delicate situations. An ability to speak through the guise of a quotation was particularly useful in diplomatic exchanges. It is for this reason that Confucius said, 'If a man who knows the three hundred *Odes* by heart . . . proves incapable of exercising his own initiative when sent to foreign states, then what use are the *Odes* to him, however many he may have learned?' (XIII.5).

This way of using the *Odes* is not limited to diplomatic occasions. In criticizing the ruler and his government, one should also resort to quotations from the *Odes*. As the anonymous author of the Preface to the *Kuan chü* put it, 'The one who speaks gives no offence, while the one who hears can take warning'.[15] This is important in political systems where offence given to those in power can easily get a man into serious trouble. There is a further advantage. When one's true meaning is couched in a quotation it is always possible for one to deny, at a subsequent date, that any such meaning was ever intended. For this reason, such practices have continued to the present day.

There is a good example of this manner of veiled speaking in the *Analects*. Prince K'uai K'ui, the son of Duke Ling of Wei, fled to Chin after an unsuccessful attempt on the life of Nan Tzu, the notorious wife of his father. On the death of Duke Ling, K'uai K'ui's son, Che, known in history as the Ousted Duke, succeeded his grandfather. With the backing of the Chin army, Prince K'uai K'ui installed himself in a border city in Wei, waiting for an opportunity to oust his son. Jan Yu wanted to know whether Confucius was on the side of Che, but since both he and Confucius were visitors to the state it was not fitting for them to be seen openly discussing the politics of Wei, and if a straight question was put to him, Confucius would in all likelihood have refused to

15. *Shih ching chu shu*, 1.11b.

answer. Tzu-kung who had the reputation of a skilful speaker (XI.3) volunteered to go and find out. This is how the conversation went.

> He went in and said, 'What sort of men were Po Yi and Shu Ch'i?'
> 'They were excellent men of old.'
> 'Did they have any complaints?'
> 'They sought benevolence and got it. So why should they have any complaints?'

There was not a word about Wei, but Tzu-kung was satisfied that he had got the answer. He came out and said, 'The Master is not on his side' (VII.15). Po Yi and Shu Ch'i were the sons of the lord of Ku Chu. The father intended Shu Ch'i, the younger son, to succeed him, but when he died neither of his sons was willing to deprive the other of the succession and they both fled to the mountains and led the lives of recluses. By approving of Po Yi and Shu Ch'i in their attempt to yield the succession each to the other, Confucius was implicitly disapproving of Che who was engaged in an unseemly struggle with his own father for the throne.

So far we have only looked at the moral teachings of Confucius in connection with his ideal of the gentleman. There is, however, another side to his teaching which has been largely neglected by scholars who write about Confucius. This is his concern with what might be described as matters of method. At the heart of this aspect of his teaching is the opposition between *hsüeh* (learning) and *ssu* (thinking).

Before we can see the significance of this opposition we must, first of all, find out what constituted learning. A brief look at the difficulties one encounters in translating the word *hsüeh* will prove illuminating. The natural choice in English for an equivalent is the verb 'to learn', but very often one is forced by the demands of the English language to use 'to study' instead. The reason is this. The verb 'to learn' needs an expressed object. For instance, we do not say, 'He learns.' We can, of course, say, 'He learns quickly,' or 'He is willing to learn,' but these are special cases where the focal point of the sentence is not in the word 'learn'. We do, on the other hand, say, 'He studies.' There is, however, another difference between 'learning' and 'studying'. We tend to 'learn' some things but 'study' others. For instance, a child learns to walk but an entomologist studies the behaviour of ants. We learn something practical; we study something theoretical. In learning the focus is on the learner; in studying the focus is on the subject. In learning something new, a man improves himself. He either acquires a new skill or becomes more proficient in an old one. In studying, a man acquires new knowledge but this new knowledge need not make any difference to him as a practical man. This difference in usage between 'learn' and 'study' is relevant to the understanding of *hsüeh*. *Hsüeh* is much closer to 'learning' than to 'studying'. Like learning, *hsüeh* makes a difference to a man as a person. It is an activity that enables a man to acquire a new skill or become more proficient in an old one. But in the Confucian context the most important point to remember is that *hsüeh* enables a man to become a better man morally. Thus morals, in the Confucian view, are akin to a skill. They can be transmitted from teacher to pupil. It is because of this possibility that Confucius placed so much emphasis on *hsüeh*. Although 'learn' is much more satisfactory an equivalent for *hsüeh* than 'study', an attempt to keep rigidly to the use of 'learn' can itself give rise to difficulties. When, for instance, Confucius talks about *hsüeh shih*, it is natural to render this as 'to study the *Odes*', but this, as we have seen, changes a practical activity to a theoretical one. Yet to render the phrase as 'to learn the *Odes*' suggests learning the *Odes* by heart. Though this certainly is part of the meaning, it definitely is not the whole or even the most important part of the meaning. As we have seen, the main purpose of *hsüeh shih* is both to improve one's sensibility and to enable one to use lines from the *Odes* to convey one's meaning in veiled terms.[16]

16. There is a further difference between 'learn' and *hsüeh*. 'Learn' in the perfect tense is an achievement word; *hsüeh*, on the other hand, is not. The question '*hsüeh shih hu?*' simply asks whether one has made an attempt to master the *Odes*, but 'Have you learned the *Odes?*' is a question about achievement. In this respect 'study' is a more satisfactory equivalent. For a fuller treatment of the problem of translating the word *hsüeh* see D. C. Lau, 'Translating Philosophical Works in Classical Chinese – Some Difficulties', (*The Art and Profession of Translation*, 1976, Hong Kong, pp. 52–60).

Thus, sometimes the translator is hard put to it to find a suitable equivalent for *hsüeh*.

Learning is concerned with the accumulated wisdom of the past. Although this does not exclude theoretical knowledge, the emphasis, as is to be expected, is on moral insight. Moral insight is mainly epitomized in the form of precepts. The rites were, of course, a code of just such precepts, though there must also have been precepts falling outside this code. That the rites formed a major part of what one has to learn is confirmed by two passages in the *Analects*. In the first one Confucius said, 'Unless a man has the spirit of the rites . . . in having courage he will become unruly, and in being forthright he will become intolerant' (VIII.2). However, in the other he said, 'To love forthrightness without loving learning is liable to lead to intolerance' (XVII.8). The two sayings are practically identical except that in one we have 'the rites' while in the other we have 'learning'.

If it plays such an important part in Confucius' teaching why is it that learning does not figure more frequently in the *Analects* than it actually does? This is because 'learning' is not the only term that is used for the activity. Very often Confucius uses *wen* (to hear) and, very occasionally, *chien* (to see) instead.[17] In particular, 'hearing' is used where the learning of specific precepts is concerned or where learning is contrasted with putting into practice what is learned. Here are examples of having been taught a specific precept.

The Master said, 'I have heard it said, A gentleman gives to help the needy and not to maintain the rich in style.' (VI.4)

Ch'en Ssu-pai said, 'I have heard that the gentleman does not show partiality. Does he show it nevertheless?' (VII.31)

Tzu-hsia said, 'I have heard it said: life and death are a matter of Destiny; wealth and honour depend on Heaven.' (XII.5)

17. That *wen* and *chien* are equivalent to *hsüeh* can be seen from the two following passages. In VII.28, we find 'I use my ears (*wen*) widely and follow what is good in what I have heard; I use my eyes (*chien*) widely and retain what I have seen in my mind,' while in XV.3 we have 'a man who learns (*hsüeh*) widely and retains what he has learned in his mind'.

Confucius said, 'What I have heard is that the head of a state or a noble family worries not about underpopulation but about uneven distribution, not about poverty but about instability.' (XVI.1)

Tzu-yu answered, 'Some time ago I heard it from you, Master, that the gentleman instructed in the Way loves his fellow men and that the small man instructed in the Way is easy to command.' (XVII.4)

Tzu-lu said, 'Some time ago I heard it from you, Master, that the gentleman does not enter the domain of one who in his own person does what is not good.' (XVII.7)

Tzu-chang said, 'That is different from what I have heard. I have heard that the gentleman honours his betters and is tolerant towards the multitude and that he is full of praise for the good while taking pity on the backward.' (XIX.3)

The connection between hearing and putting into practice what one has heard is clearly brought out in the following passages.

The Master said, 'Use your ears (*wen*) widely but leave out what is doubtful; repeat the rest with caution and you will make few mistakes. Use your eyes (*chien*) widely and leave out what is hazardous; put the rest into practice with caution and you will have few regrets.' (II.18)

Before he could put into practice something he had heard, the only thing Tzu-lu feared was that he should be told something further. (V.14)

The Master said, 'It is these things that cause me concern . . . inability, when I am told (*wen*) what is right, to move to where it is.' (VII.3)

The Master said, ' . . . I use my ears widely and follow what is good in what I have heard; I use my eyes widely and retain what I have seen in my mind.' (VII.28)

Tzu-lu asked, 'Should one immediately put into practice what one has heard?' (XI.22)

The connection between learning and putting into practice what one has learned is a close one, because amongst the things one learns are precepts and what would be the point of learning a precept if one made no attempt to put it into practice? Hence

Confucius' concern over his inability to move to a new position as soon as he has learned that it is morally right, and Tzu-lu's fear of a backlog building up if precepts come at a brisker pace than he can cope with. But this does not mean that one should put a precept into practice simply because it is a precept. One should, first of all, think deeply about its rightness. That is why Confucius is constantly giving the advice that one should choose from what one has learned only what is good and leave out what is doubtful. The only way to do so is through thinking. This brings us back to the subject of learning and thinking. There is a well-known saying in the *Analects*, 'If one learns from others but does not think, one will be bewildered. If, on the other hand, one thinks but does not learn from others, one will be in peril' (II.15). One must learn from wise men of the past and the present, but, at the same time, one must try to improve on what one has learned. Although both learning and thinking are indispensable, Confucius seems to consider learning to be, in some sense, more basic. He said, 'I once spent all day thinking without taking food and all night thinking without going to bed, but I found that I gained nothing from it. It would have been better for me to have spent the time in learning' (XV.31). Here Confucius is saying that if we were to indulge in a one-sided pursuit, then learning would be more rewarding than thinking. A moment's reflection will show that this is not an unreasonable view. If one's aim is to make advances in knowledge, both thinking and learning are equally necessary, but in cases where one has no such aim, through learning one can at least gain something by acquainting oneself with what is already known, but one is unlikely to make any gains at all if one thinks *in vacuo*.

Let us take an example which illustrates the way Confucius thought about the existing rites.

The Master said, 'A ceremonial cap of linen is what is prescribed by the rites. Today black silk is used instead. This is more frugal and I follow the majority. To prostrate oneself before ascending the steps is what is prescribed by the rites. Today one does so after having ascended them. This is casual and, though going against the majority, I follow the practice of doing so before ascending.' (IX.3)

Here we have a clear case of Confucius taking a critical look at the rites. He concluded that in the one case he was prepared to follow the majority, but not in the other. He came to this conclusion by going back to the principles underlying the rites concerned. In the second case, the underlying principle is respect, while in the first case there is frugality as well. That respect should be the under- lying principle of a rite is only to be expected, but that frugality should be such a principle may seem surprising until we remember Confucius' answer to a question about the basis of the rites. Part of this answer was, 'With the rites, it is better to err on the side of frugality than on the side of extravagance' (III.4). All things being equal, it is better to be frugal. The black silk cap is more frugal but loses nothing in respect. Hence Confucius' approval. Prostration after ascending the steps, on the other hand, is casual, in other words, less respectful, and has no compensating gains. Hence Confucius' disapproval.

As we have seen, precepts are often introduced by the formula, 'I have heard it said.' Very often, however, this formula is dis- pensed with, particularly in cases where the precept is to be ex- amined. In such cases, the question, 'What do you think of this saying?' is simply posed. For instance,

> Tzu-kung said, ' "Poor without being obsequious, wealthy without being arrogant." What do you think of this saying?'
> The Master said, 'That will do, but better still "Poor yet delight- ing in the Way, wealthy yet observant of the rites." ' (I.15)

Here the precept cited by Tzu-kung concerns the overcoming of poverty and wealth as obstacles to a moral character. Confucius examines the precept in this spirit and proposes an improved version.

> Someone said,
> 'Repay an injury with a good turn.
> What do you think of this saying?'
> The Master said, 'What, then, do you repay a good turn with? You repay an injury with straightness, but you repay a good turn with a good turn.' (XIV.34)

Here Confucius is criticizing the existing precept 'Repay an injury with a good turn' for being over-generous, leaving nothing with which to repay a good turn. It is enough, in Confucius' view, that we should not be motivated by vindictiveness. What Confucius is advocating is the middle way between vindictiveness and excessive generosity.

From these examples where Confucius examined existing precepts critically we can glean something of his general approach to the problem of the rule and the principle. In Confucius' day if one were to state the problem it would be natural to state it in terms of *li* (the rites) and *yi* (rightness). We have already touched on the relationship between the two in the context of the morality of acts and agents. Now we shall take a closer look at this relationship. The rites are a code of rules of behaviour. Although as something handed down from antiquity, the rites carried great authority, nevertheless, this authority cannot guarantee their rightness. Whether they are right or not depends on whether they measure up to the demands of rightness. Rightness, on the other hand, is the standard by which all acts have, in the last resort, to be measured. Thus there is an intimate relationship between *li* and *yi*. Confucius' critical examination of existing precepts is precisely the subjection of rules to the yardstick of rightness. But why should a rule which had been found right in the past be subjected to fresh scrutiny? The answer is this. First, a rule once formulated in precise terms cannot adapt itself to changing circumstances. What was right in a previous age need not continue to be right in a subsequent age. This awareness that rules have to keep pace with changing times is clearly felt by Confucius. He said, 'The Yin built on the rites of the Hsia. What was added and what was omitted can be known. The Chou built on the rites of the Yin. What was added and what was omitted can be known' (II.23). Here we can see that although the rites of a subsequent age were based on those of the previous one, because of the lapse of time new rules had to be added and obsolete ones omitted. This awareness that what is appropriate changes with the times was one of the outstanding features of Confucius' thought, so much so that Mencius describes him as 'the sage whose actions were timely' (*Mencius*, V.B.1). Second, circumstances may arise where one rule comes into conflict with another. Such a conflict can only be resolved by appealing to basic moral principle. Third, even with a rule which may be satisfactory in itself, there are occasions when the observance of it conflicts with the spirit behind the rule. For all these reasons, one has to be constantly on the alert to the possibility that a rule may need rethinking at any moment and on any occasion. So far we have only looked at the problem from the point of view of the subordination of rule to principle. Equally, principle cannot do without rules which give it effect. Moral principles need to be put into effect, and any act that puts a moral principle into effect will, in fact, be an exemplification of some rule or other. This is, as we have seen, particularly so where the purpose of an act is to show a certain attitude, e.g., respect. No action is inherently a sign of respect. An action can only serve to show respect given a certain convention and a convention can only be stated in a rule. Thus while a rule can remain right only if it is constantly measured against the demands of principles, a principle cannot do without rules if it is to be put into effect. This dialogue between rule and principle constitutes the essence of Confucius' moral thinking.

In this connection, Confucius' approach may have something to offer in the debate whether morals are objective or conventional. The argument runs something like this. If morality is conventional it has no objectivity. One can only judge moral rules within the conventions of a given social system of which they form part. There is no way of adjudicating between different systems. On the other hand, if morality is objective, how we come to know these objective realities poses epistemological problems. Confucius' approach seems to offer a way out. All moral rules have implicit in them some principle or principles. A rule can thus always be judged by its success in realizing these principles. In other words, moral rules have built-in standards by which they can be judged. If they are found wanting, this points to the way of their improvement. On the other hand, the implicit principles are ideals which become clearer to us as they are used as standards to criticize the rules. We gain greater insight into a moral principle by discovering the inadequacies of the rules which give it effect.

Apart from reflecting on moral insights of the past, thinking also is important if we are to be able to see connections between phenomena that may seem unconnected at first sight. We have seen that this is important both in the sphere of literature and in the sphere of morals. In literature, we have seen that the *Odes* can stimulate the imagination so that we can see underlying similarities between disparate phenomena. In morals, it is by means of the method of *shu* that we can hope to be able to practise benevolence, and *shu* consists in using ourselves as analogy to find out about the likes and dislikes of other human beings. Confucius would not tolerate any student who, because he failed to think, was unable to discover new applications for known principles. He said, 'When I have pointed out one corner of a square to anyone and he does not come back with the other three, I will not point it out to him a second time.' Indeed, Confucius believed so much in the value of the student making the utmost effort to think things out for himself that he said on the same occasion, 'I never enlighten anyone who has not been driven to distraction by trying to understand a difficulty or has not got into a frenzy trying to put his ideas into words' (VII.8). We have seen that Confucius praised Tzu-hsia as someone worth discussing the *Odes* with (III.8). In praising Tzu-kung in similar vein he added this remark, 'Tell such a man something and he can see its relevance to what he has not been told' (I.15). This is also the quality essential to a teacher. 'A man is worthy of being a teacher who gets to know what is new by keeping fresh in his mind what he is already familiar with' (II.11).

Intelligence is something Confucius valued greatly. His highest praise was reserved for Yen Hui who was not only superior to his fellow disciples in moral attainment but also in intelligence. When Tzu-kung who was himself a man of no mean intelligence remarked, 'How dare I compare myself with Hui? When he is told one thing he understands ten. When I am told one thing I understand only two,' Confucius consoled him by saying, 'You are not as good as he is. Neither of us is as good as he is' (V.9).

Confucius was both a great thinker and a great human being. As a thinker he held up an ideal for all men. This consisted of perfecting one's own moral character. Realizing this ideal involves not

only being benevolent to other individuals but also working
unstintingly for the welfare of the common people. For this Confucius could hold out no hope of a reward either in this life or in
the next. The reward lies in the doing of what is good, and this
constitutes the joy of following the Way. He had great respect for
the wisdom of the past but he did not accept it uncritically. For him
the only way of making progress is to reflect on what has been
handed down to us from the past. He was anything but dogmatic:
he 'refused to entertain conjectures or insist on certainty; he refused
to be inflexible or to be egotistical' (IX.4). In characterizing himself he said, 'I have no preconceptions about the permissible and
the impermissible' (XVIII.8). It cannot be denied that, over the
centuries, Confucianism acquired a lot of dogmas and developed
authoritarian tendencies, but it would be as grossly unfair to lay
these at Confucius' door as to blame Jesus for the excesses of the
Church in later ages.

Confucius was modest about his own achievement. He said,
'How dare I claim to be a sage or a benevolent man?' (VII.34).
In spite of this modesty, he must have realized his own ideal to a
great extent. Otherwise, it would be impossible to account for the
reverence and affection shown him by his disciples who were
widely different in talent and temperament.

Yen Hui, who was outstanding in morals and intelligence said,
when Confucius thought he had died in an armed siege, 'While
you, Master, are alive, how would I dare to die?' (XI.23). He
described the ideal of the Master and his method of teaching as
follows:

> The more I look up at it the higher it appears. The more I bore into
> it the harder it becomes. I see it before me. Suddenly it is behind me.
> The Master is good at leading one on step by step. He broadens
> me with culture and brings me back to essentials by means of the
> rites. I cannot give up even if I wanted to, but, having done all I
> can, it seems to rise sheer above me and I have no way of going
> after it, however much I may want to. (IX.11)

Tzu-kung, the man of the world who had a successful career
both as a diplomat and as a merchant, made this comment when
someone disparaged Confucius,

Chung-ni cannot be defamed. In other cases, men of excellence are like hills which one can climb over. Chung-ni is like the sun and the moon which one has no way of climbing over. Even if someone wanted to cut himself off from them, how could this detract from the sun and the moon? It would merely serve the more to show that he did not know his own measure. (XIX.24)

He further said,

The Master cannot be equalled just as the sky cannot be scaled . . . In life he is honoured and in death he will be mourned. How can he be equalled? (XIX.25)

Tseng Tzu, the disciple who took his moral responsibility so seriously (VIII.7), said, according to the *Mencius*, this of Confucius:

Washed by the River and the Han, bleached by the autumn sun, so immaculate was he that his whiteness could not be surpassed. (III.A.4)

Mencius echoed this sentiment when he said,

Ever since man came into this world, there has never been one greater than Confucius. (II.A.2)

For his part, Confucius never claimed to be either superior in intelligence or in moral qualities. He said, 'I was not born with knowledge but, being fond of antiquity, I am quick to seek it' (VII.20), and 'In a hamlet of ten households, there are bound to be those who are my equal in doing their best for others and in being trustworthy in what they say, but they are unlikely to be as eager to learn as I am' (V.28). In both sayings, all he would claim was his eagerness to learn. This was matched only by his eagerness to teach. He said, 'Quietly to store up knowledge in my mind, to learn without flagging, to teach without growing weary, these present me with no difficulties' (VII.2). Again, in denying he was a sage, he said, 'Perhaps it might be said of me that I learn without flagging and teach without growing weary' (VII.34). As a teacher he was capable of both criticizing his disciples with firmness as well as speaking to them in jest. When Tsai Yü took a nap in the daytime Confucius said, 'A piece of rotten wood cannot be carved, nor can a wall of dried dung be trowelled' (V.10). Again, when the same disciple doubted the wisdom of the three-year mourning period, Confucius said, 'How unfeeling Yü is! . . . Was Yü not given three years' love by his parents?' (XVII.21). On the occasion Confucius went to Wu Ch'eng and found Tzu-yu teaching the people music, he poked fun at him by saying, 'Surely you don't need to use an ox-knife to kill a chicken.' When Tzu-yu took this seriously and started defending his action, Confucius admitted that he was only joking (XVII.4).

The predominant impression one gets of Confucius from the *Analects* is a man whose life was full of joy. When the governor of She asked Tzu-lu what kind of man Confucius was, Tzu-lu made no answer. Confucius' comment was,

> Why did you not simply say something to this effect: he is the sort of man who forgets to eat when he tries to solve a problem that has been driving him to distraction, who is so full of joy that he forgets his worries and who does not notice the onset of old age? (VII.19)

He describes this joy in more concrete terms when he said,

> In the eating of coarse rice and the drinking of water, the using of one's elbow for a pillow, joy is to be found. Wealth and rank attained through immoral means have as much to do with me as passing clouds. (VII.16)

There is no doubt that part of this joy came from the pursuit of the Way. Confucius said, 'At seventy I followed my heart's desire without overstepping the line' (II.4). When after a lifetime of moral cultivation he found that what he desired naturally coincided with what was moral, that he should have experienced joy is understandable. But the joy was not confined to the moral side of his life. On the occasion when he was with a group of disciples, Confucius asked them to state what they would like to do. When they had finished, Confucius showed that his sympathies were with Tseng Hsi who said,

> In late spring, after the spring clothes have been newly made, I should like, together with five or six adults and six or seven boys, to go bathing in the River Yi and enjoy the breeze on the Rain Altar and then to go home chanting poetry. (XI.26)

Here is a man who, indeed, appreciated the joys of living.

Anyone who has read the sayings of Confucius carefully and without prejudice will surely find it difficult to recognize the die-hard conservative and arch-villain that he has sometimes been made out to be. Confucius is, perhaps, yet another instance of the proverbial prophet.

D.C.L.

THE ANALECTS

BOOK I

1. The Master said, 'Is it not a pleasure, having learned something, to try it out at due intervals? Is it not a joy to have friends come from afar? Is it not gentlemanly not to take offence when others fail to appreciate your abilities?'

2. Yu Tzu[1] said, 'It is rare for a man whose character is such that he is good as a son and obedient as a young man to have the inclination to transgress against his superiors; it is unheard of for one who has no such inclination to be inclined to start a rebellion. The gentleman devotes his efforts to the roots, for once the roots are established, the Way will grow therefrom. Being good as a son and obedient as a young man is, perhaps, the root of a man's character.' [1][2]

3. The Master said, 'It is rare, indeed, for a man with cunning words and an ingratiating face to be benevolent.'

4. Tseng Tzu said, 'Every day I examine myself on three counts. In what I have undertaken on another's behalf, have I failed to do my best? In my dealings with my friends have I failed to be trustworthy in what I say? Have I passed on to others anything that I have not tried out myself?'

5. The Master said, 'In guiding a state of a thousand chariots, approach your duties with reverence and be trustworthy in what you say; avoid excesses in expenditure and love your fellow men; employ the labour of the common people only in the right seasons.'

6. The Master said, 'A young man should be a good son at home and an obedient young man abroad, sparing of speech but trustworthy in what he says, and should love the multitude at large but

1. For names of persons and places see Glossary.
2. Numbers in square brackets refer to Textual Notes on p. 234.

cultivate the friendship of his fellow men.³[2] If he has any energy
to spare from such action, let him devote it to making himself
cultivated.'

7. Tzu-hsia said, 'I would grant that a man has received instruction
who appreciates men of excellence where other men appreciate
beautiful women, who exerts himself to the utmost in the service
of his parents and offers his person to the service of his lord,
and who, in his dealings with his friends, is trustworthy in what
he says, even though he may say that he has never been taught.'

8. The Master said, 'A gentleman who lacks gravity does not in-
spire awe. A gentleman who studies is unlikely to be inflexible.
  'Make⁴ it your guiding principle to do your best for others and
to be trustworthy in what you say. Do not accept as friend anyone
who is not as good as you.
  'When you make a mistake, do not be afraid of mending your
ways.'

9. Tseng Tzu said, 'Conduct the funeral of your parents with
meticulous care and let not sacrifices to your remote ancestors be
forgotten, and the virtue of the common people will incline towards fullness.'

10. Tzu-ch'in asked Tzu-kung, 'When the Master arrives in a
state, he invariably gets to know about its government. Does he
seek this information? or is it given him?'
  Tzu-kung said, 'The Master gets it through being cordial,
good, respectful, frugal and deferential. The way the Master seeks
it is, perhaps, different from the way other men seek it.'

11. The Master said, 'Observe what a man has in mind to do when
his father is living, and then observe what he does when his father

  3. For the contrast of *jen* (fellow men) with *chung* (multitude) see XVII.6
and for a discussion of the word *jen* see Introduction pp. 14 and 17.
  4. The whole of what follows is found also in IX.25 while the opening
sentence is found also in XII.10.

is dead. If, for three years, he makes no changes to his father's ways, he can be said to be a good son.'[5]

12. Yu Tzu said, 'Of the things brought about by the rites, harmony is the most valuable. Of the ways of the Former Kings, this is the most beautiful, and is followed alike in matters great and small, yet this will not always work: to aim always at harmony without regulating it by the rites simply because one knows only about harmony will not, in fact, work.'

13. Yu Tzu said, 'To be trustworthy in word is close to being moral in that it enables one's words to be repeated.[6] To be respectful is close to being observant of the rites in that it enables one to stay clear of disgrace and insult. If, in promoting good relationship with relatives by marriage, a man manages not to lose the good will of his own kinsmen, he is worthy of being looked up to as the head of the clan.'[7]

14. The Master said, 'The gentleman seeks neither a full belly nor a comfortable home. He is quick in action but cautious in speech.[8] He goes to men possessed of the Way to be put right. Such a man can be described as eager to learn.'

15. Tzu-kung said, ' "Poor without being obsequious, wealthy without being arrogant." What do you think of this saying?'
    The Master said, 'That will do, but better still "Poor yet delighting in the Way,[2] wealthy yet observant of the rites." '
    Tzu-kung said, 'The *Odes* say,

> Like bone cut, like horn polished,
> Like jade carved, like stone ground.

Is not what you have said a case in point?'

5. This sentence is found again in IV.20. Cf. also XIX.18.
6. For a discussion of the interpretation of this sentence see D. C. Lau, 'On the expression *fu yen*', *Bulletin of the School of Oriental and African Studies*, XXXVI, 2, (1973), pp. 424–33.
7. The sense of this last sentence is rather obscure. The present translation, though tentative, is based on a comment of Cheng Hsüan's on the word *yin* in the *Chou li* (*Chou li chu shu*, 10.24b).
8. cf. IV.24.

16. The Master said, 'Ssu, only with a man like you can one discuss the *Odes*. Tell such a man something and he can see its relevance to what he has not been told.'

The Master said, 'It is not the failure of others to appreciate your abilities that should trouble you, but rather your failure to appreciate theirs.'

BOOK II

1. The Master said, 'The rule of virtue can be compared to the Pole Star which commands the homage of the multitude of stars without leaving its place.'

2. The Master said, 'The *Odes* are three hundred in number. They can be summed up in one phrase,

Swerving not from the right path.'[1]

3. The Master said, 'Guide them by edicts, keep them in line with punishments, and the common people will stay out of trouble but will have no sense of shame. Guide them by virtue, keep them in line with the rites, and they will, besides having a sense of shame, reform themselves.'

4. The Master said, 'At fifteen I set my heart on learning; at thirty I took my stand; at forty I came to be free from doubts; at fifty I understood the Decree of Heaven; at sixty my ear was atuned;[2] at seventy I followed my heart's desire without overstepping the line.'

5. Meng Yi Tzu asked about being filial. The Master answered, 'Never fail to comply.'

Fan Ch'ih was driving. The Master told him about the interview, saying, 'Meng-sun asked me about being filial. I answered, "Never fail to comply."'

Fan Ch'ih asked, 'What does that mean?'

The Master said, 'When your parents are alive, comply with the rites in serving them; when they die, comply with the rites in burying them; comply with the rites in sacrificing to them.'

1. This line is from Ode 297 where it describes a team of horses going straight ahead without swerving to left or right.

2. The expression *erh shun* is very obscure and the translation is tentative.

6. Meng Wu Po asked about being filial. The Master said, 'Give your father and mother no other cause for anxiety than illness.'

7. Tzu-yu asked about being filial. The Master said, 'Nowadays for a man to be filial means no more than that he is able to provide his parents with food. Even hounds and horses are, in some way, provided with food. If a man shows no reverence, where is the difference?'

8. Tzu-hsia asked about being filial. The Master said, 'What is difficult to manage is the expression on one's face. As for the young taking on the burden when there is work to be done or letting the old enjoy the wine and the food when these are available, that hardly deserves to be called filial.'

9. The Master asked, 'I can speak to Hui all day without his disagreeing with me in any way. Thus he would seem to be stupid. However, when I take a closer look at what he does in private after he has withdrawn from my presence, I discover that it does, in fact, throw light on what I said. Hui is not stupid after all.'

10. The Master said, 'Look at the means a man employs, observe the path he takes and examine where he feels at home.[3] In what way is a man's true character hidden from view? In what way is a man's true character hidden from view?'

11. The Master said, 'A man is worthy of being a teacher who gets to know what is new by keeping fresh in his mind what he is already familiar with.'

12. The Master said, 'The gentleman is no vessel.'[4]

13. Tzu-kung asked about the gentleman. The Master said, 'He puts his words into action before allowing his words to follow his action.'

3. cf. 'The benevolent man feels at home in benevolence.' (IV.2)
4. i.e., he is no specialist, as every vessel is designed for a specific purpose only.

14. The Master said, 'The gentleman enters into associations but not cliques; the small man enters into cliques but not associations.'

15. The Master said, 'If one learns from others but does not think, one will be bewildered. If, on the other hand, one thinks but does not learn from others, one will be in peril.'

16. The Master said, 'To attack a task from the wrong end can do nothing but harm.'

17. The Master said, 'Yu, shall I tell you what it is to know. To say you know when you know, and to say you do not when you do not, that is knowledge.'

18. Tzu-chang was studying with an eye to an official career. The Master said, 'Use your ears widely but leave out what is doubtful; repeat the rest with caution and you will make few mistakes. Use your eyes widely and leave out what is hazardous; put the rest into practice with caution and you will have few regrets. When in your speech you make few mistakes and in your action you have few regrets, an official career will follow as a matter of course.'

19. Duke Ai asked, 'What must I do before the common people will look up to me?'

Confucius answered, 'Raise the straight and set them over the crooked[5] and the common people will look up to you. Raise the crooked and set them over the straight and the common people will not look up to you.'

20. Chi K'ang Tzu asked, 'How can one inculcate in the common people the virtue of reverence, of doing their best and of enthusiasm?'

The Master said, 'Rule over them with dignity and they will be reverent; treat them with kindness and they will do their best; raise the good and instruct those who are backward and they will be imbued with enthusiasm.'

5. cf. XII.22.

21. Someone said to Confucius, 'Why do you not take part in government?'

The Master said, 'The *Book of History* says, "Oh! Simply by being a good son and friendly to his brothers a man can exert an influence upon government."[6] In so doing a man is, in fact, taking part in government. How can there be any question of his having actively to "take part in government"?'

22. The Master said, 'I do not see how a man can be acceptable who is untrustworthy in word? When a pin is missing in the yoke-bar of a large cart or in the collar-bar of a small cart, how can the cart be expected to go?'

23. Tzu-chang asked, 'Can ten generations hence be known?'

The Master said, 'The Yin built on the rites of the Hsia. What was added and what was omitted can be known. The Chou built on the rites of the Yin. What was added and what was omitted can be known. Should there be a successor to the Chou, even a hundred generations hence can be known.'

24. The Master said, 'To offer sacrifice to the spirit of an ancestor not one's own is obsequious.

'Faced with what is right, to leave it undone shows a lack of courage.'

6. This is from a lost chapter of the *Shu ching* but has been incorporated in a modified form into the spurious *Chün shih* chapter. See *Shu ching chu shu,* 18.10a.

BOOK III

1. Confucious said of the Chi Family, 'They use eight rows of eight dancers each[1] to perform in their courtyard. If this can be tolerated, what cannot be tolerated?'

2. The Three Families[2] performed the *yung*[3] when the sacrificial offerings were being cleared away. The Master said,

> 'In attendance were the great lords,
> In solemn dignity was the Emperor.

What application has this to the halls of the Three Families?'

3. The Master said, 'What can a man do with the rites who is not benevolent? What can a man do with music who is not benevolent?'

4. Lin Fang asked about the basis of the rites. The Master said, 'A noble question indeed! With the rites, it is better to err on the side of frugality than on the side of extravagance; in mourning, it is better to err on the side of grief than on the side of formality.'

5. The Master said, 'Barbarian tribes with their rulers are inferior to Chinese states without them.'

6. The Chi Family were going to perform the sacrifice to Mount T'ai.[4] The Master said to Jan Ch'iu,[5] 'Can you not save the situation?'
'No. I cannot.'

1. A prerogative of the Emperor.
2. The three noble families of the state of Lu: Meng-sun, Shu-sun and Chi-sun.
3. Ode 282, from which the couplet quoted comes.
4. Not being the lord of the state of Lu, the head of the Chi Family was not entitled to perform the sacrifice to Mount T'ai and it would be a violation of the rites for Mount T'ai to accept the sacrifice.
5. who was in the service of the Chi Family.

The Master said, 'Alas! Who would have thought that Mount T'ai would suffer in comparison with Lin Fang?'[6]

7. The Master said, 'There is no contention between gentlemen. The nearest to it is, perhaps, archery. In archery they bow and make way for one another as they go up and on coming down they drink together. Even the way they contend is gentlemanly.'

8. Tzu-hsia asked,

> 'Her entrancing smile dimpling,
> Her beautiful eyes glancing,
> Patterns of colour upon plain silk.[7]

What is the meaning of these lines?'
   The Master said, 'The colours are put in after the white.'
   'Does the practice of the rites likewise come afterwards?'
   The Master said, 'It is you, Shang, who have thrown light on the text for me. Only with a man like you can one discuss the *Odes*.'

9. The Master said, 'I am able to discourse on the rites of the Hsia, but the state of Ch'i[8] does not furnish sufficient supporting evidence; I am able to discourse on the rites of the Yin, but the state of Sung does not furnish sufficient supporting evidence. This is because there are not enough records and men of erudition. Otherwise I would be able to support what I say with evidence.'

10. The Master said, 'I do not wish to witness that part of the *ti* sacrifice[9] which follows the opening libation to the impersonator.'[10]

6. See III.4 above where Lin Fang showed a concern for the basis of the rites.

7. The first two lines of this quotation are to be found in Ode 57 but not the third.

8. After the overthrow of the two dynasties, the descendants of the Hsia were enfeoffed in the state of Ch'i while those of the Yin were enfeoffed in the state of Sung.

9. An important sacrifice performed by the Emperor, but the privilege of performing it was granted to the Duke of Chou, the founder of the state of Lu.

10. The young boy or girl who impersonates the dead ancestor to whom the offerings are made.

11. Someone asked about the theory of the *ti* sacrifice. The Master said, 'It is not something I understand, for whoever understands it will be able to manage the Empire as easily as if he had[3] it here,' pointing to his palm.

12. 'Sacrifice as if present' is taken to mean 'sacrifice to the gods as if the gods were present.'

The Master, however, said, 'Unless I take part in a sacrifice, it is as if I did not sacrifice.'

13. Wang-sun Chia said,

> 'Better to be obsequious to the kitchen stove
> Than to the south-west corner of the house.[11]

What does that mean?'

The Master said, 'The saying has got it wrong. When you have offended against Heaven, there is nowhere you can turn to in your prayers.'

14. The Master said, 'The Chou is resplendent in culture, having before it the example of the two previous dynasties.[12] I am for the Chou.'

15. When the Master went inside the Grand Temple,[13] he asked questions about everything. Someone remarked, 'Who said that the son of the man from Tsou[14] understood the rites? When he went inside the Grand Temple, he asked questions about everything.'

The Master, on hearing of this, said, 'The asking of questions is in itself the correct rite.'

11. By 'the south-west corner of the house' which is the place of honour Wang-sun Chia, being a minister of Wei, presumably meant to refer to the lord of Wei and by 'the kitchen stove' to himself.

12. The Hsia and the Yin.

13. The temple of the Duke of Chou, the founder of the state of Lu.

14. The man from Tsou refers to Confucius' father.

16. The Master said,

> 'In archery the point lies not in piercing the hide,[15]
> For the reason that strength varies from man to man.

This was the way of antiquity.'

17. Tzu-kung wanted to do away with the sacrificial sheep at the announcement of the new moon. The Master said, 'Ssu, you are loath to part with the price of the sheep, but I am loath to see the disappearance of the rite.'

18. The Master said, 'You will be looked upon as obsequious by others if you observe every detail of the rites in serving your lord.'

19. Duke Ting asked, 'What is the way the ruler should employ the services of his subjects? What is the way a subject should serve his ruler?'

Confucius answered, 'The ruler should employ the services of his subjects in accordance with the rites. A subject should serve his ruler by doing his best.'

20. The Master said, 'In the *kuan chü*[16] there is joy without wantonness, and sorrow without self-injury.'

21. Duke Ai asked Tsai Wo about the altar to the god of earth. Tsai Wo replied, 'The Hsia used the pine, the Yin used the cedar, and the men of Chou used the chestnut (*li*), saying that it made the common people tremble (*li*).'

The Master, on hearing of this reply, commented, 'One does not explain away what is already done, one does not argue against what is already accomplished, and one does not condemn what has already gone by.'

22. The Master said, 'Kuan Chung was, indeed, a vessel of small capacity.'

15. i.e., the bull's eye fixed in the centre of a cloth target.
16. The first ode in the *Odes*.

Someone remarked, 'Was Kuan Chung frugal, then?'

'Kuan Chung kept three separate establishments, each complete with its own staff. How can he be called frugal?'

'In that case, did Kuan Chung understand the rites?'

'Rulers of states erect gate-screens; Kuan Chung erected such a screen as well. The ruler of a state, when entertaining the ruler of another state, has a stand for inverted cups; Kuan Chung had such a stand as well. If even Kuan Chung understood the rites, who does not understand them?'

23. The Master talked of music to the Grand Musician of Lu, saying, 'This much can be known about music. It begins with playing in unison. When it gets into full swing, it is harmonious, clear and unbroken. In this way it reaches the conclusion.'

24. The border official of Yi requested an audience, saying, 'I have never been denied an audience by any gentleman who has come to this place.' The followers presented him. When he came out, he said, 'What worry have you, gentlemen, about the loss of office? The Empire has long been without the Way. Heaven is about to use your Master as the wooden tongue for a bell.'[17]

25. The Master said of the *shao*[18] that it was both perfectly beautiful and perfectly good, and of the *wu*[19] that it was perfectly beautiful but not perfectly good.

26. The Master said, 'What can I find worthy of note in a man who is lacking in tolerance when in high position, in reverence when performing the rites and in sorrow when in mourning?'

17. to rouse the Empire.

18. The music of Shun who came to the throne through the abdication of Yao.

19. The music of King Wu who came to the throne through overthrowing the Yin by military force.

BOOK IV

1. The Master said, 'Of neighbourhoods benevolence is the most beautiful. How can the man be considered wise who, when he has the choice, does not settle in benevolence?'

2. The Master said, 'One who is not benevolent cannot remain long in straitened circumstances, nor can he remain long in easy circumstances.

'The benevolent man is attracted to benevolence because he feels at home in it. The wise man is attracted to benevolence because he finds it to his advantage.'

3. The Master said, 'It is only the benevolent man who is capable of liking or disliking other men.'

4. The Master said, 'If a man sets his heart on benevolence, he will be free from evil.'

5. The Master said, 'Wealth and high station are what men desire but unless I got them in the right way I would not remain in them. Poverty and low station are what men dislike, but even if I did not get them in the right way I would not try to escape from them.[1]

'If the gentleman forsakes benevolence, in what way can he make a name for himself? The gentleman never deserts benevolence, not even for as long as it takes to eat a meal. If he hurries and stumbles one may be sure that it is in benevolence that he does so.'

6. The Master said, 'I have never met a man who finds benevolence attractive or a man who finds unbenevolence[2] repulsive. A man

1. This sentence is most likely to be corrupt. The negative is probably an interpolation and the sentence should read: 'Poverty and low station are what men dislike, but if I got them in the right way I would not try to escape from them.'

2. The word 'unbenevolence' has been coined because the original word has a positive meaning lacking in 'non-benevolence'.

who finds benevolence attractive cannot be surpassed. A man who finds unbenevolence repulsive can, perhaps, be counted as benevolent, for he would not allow what is not benevolent to contaminate his person.

'Is there a man who, for the space of a single day, is able to devote all his strength to benevolence? I have not come across such a man whose strength proves insufficient for the task. There must be such cases of insufficient strength, only I have not come across them.'[3]

7. The Master said, 'In his errors a man is true to type. Observe the errors and you will know the man.'[1]

8. The Master said, 'He has not lived in vain who dies the day he is told about the Way.'

9. The Master said, 'There is no point in seeking the views of a Gentleman[4] who, though he sets his heart on the Way, is ashamed of poor food and poor clothes.'

10. The Master said, 'In his dealings with the world the gentleman is not invariably for or against anything. He is on the side of what is moral.'

11. The Master said, 'While the gentleman cherishes benign rule, the small man cherishes his native land. While the gentleman cherishes a respect for the law, the small man cherishes generous treatment.'[5]

12. The Master said, 'If one is guided by profit in one's actions, one will incur much ill will.'

3. Cf. VI. 12.
4. For the use of 'Gentleman' and 'gentleman' in the present translation see n. 3 on p. 12.
5. The distinction here between 'the gentleman' and 'the small man' is not, as is often the case, drawn between the ruler and the ruled but within the class of the ruled.

13. The Master said, 'If a man is able to govern a state by observing the rites and showing deference, what difficulties will he have in public life?[4] If he is unable to govern a state by observing the rites and showing deference, what good are the rites to him?'

14. The Master said, 'Do not worry because you have no official position. Worry about your qualifications. Do not worry because no one appreciates your abilities. Seek to be worthy of appreciation.'

15. The Master said, 'Ts'an! There is one single thread binding my way together.'

Tseng Tzu assented.

After the Master had gone out, the disciples asked, 'What did he mean?'

Tseng Tzu said, 'The way of the Master consists in doing one's best and in using oneself as a measure to gauge others. That is all.'

16. The Master said, 'The gentleman understands what is moral. The small man understands what is profitable.'

17. The Master said, 'When you meet someone better than yourself, turn your thoughts to becoming his equal. When you meet someone not as good as you are, look within and examine your own self.'

18. The Master said, 'In serving your father and mother you ought to dissuade them from doing wrong in the gentlest way. If you see your advice being ignored, you should not become disobedient but remain reverent. You should not complain even if in so doing you wear yourself out.'

19. The Master said, 'While your parents are alive, you should not go too far afield in your travels. If you do, your whereabouts should always be known.'

20. The Master said, 'If, for three years, a man makes no changes to his father's ways, he can be said to be a good son.'[6]

21. The Master said, 'A man should not be ignorant of the age of his father and mother. It is a matter, on the one hand, for rejoicing and, on the other, for anxiety.'

22. The Master said, 'In antiquity men were loath to speak. This was because they counted it shameful if their person failed to keep up with their words.'

23. The Master said, 'It is rare for a man to miss the mark through holding on to essentials.'

24. The Master said, 'The gentleman desires to be halting in speech but quick in action.'

25. The Master said, 'Virtue never stands alone. It is bound to have neighbours.'

26. Tzu-yu said, 'To be importunate with one's lord will mean humiliation. To be importunate with one's friends will mean estrangement.'

6. This saying also forms part of I.11.

BOOK V

1. The Master said of Kung-yeh Ch'ang that he was a suitable choice for a husband, for though he was in gaol it was not as though he had done anything wrong. He gave him his daughter in marriage.

2. The Master said of Nan-jung that when the Way prevailed in the state he was not cast aside and when the Way fell into disuse he stayed clear of the humiliation of punishment. He gave him his elder brother's daughter in marriage.[1]

3. The Master's comment on Tzu-chien was 'What a gentleman this man is! If there were no gentlemen in Lu where could he have acquired his qualities?'

4. Tzu-kung asked, 'What do you think of me?'
   The Master said, 'You are a vessel.'[2]
   'What kind of vessel?'
   'A sacrificial vessel.'[3]

5. Someone said, 'Yung is benevolent but does not have a facile tongue.'
   The Master said, 'What need is there for him to have a facile tongue? For a man quick with a retort there are frequent occasions on which he will incur the hatred of others. I cannot say whether Yung is benevolent or not, but what need is there for him to have a facile tongue?'

6. The Master told Ch'i-tiao K'ai to take office. Ch't-tiao K'ai said, 'I cannot trust myself to do so yet.' The Master was pleased.

7. The Master said, 'If the Way should fail to prevail and I were to put to sea on a raft, the one who would follow me would no doubt be Yu.' Tzu-lu, on hearing this, was overjoyed. The Master

1. cf. XI.6.   2. cf. II.13.   3. made of jade.

said, 'Yu has a greater love for courage than I, but is lacking in judgement.'

8. Meng Wu Po asked whether Tzu-lu was benevolent. The Master said, 'I cannot say.' Meng Wu Po repeated the question. The Master said, 'Yu can be given the responsibility of managing the military levies in a state of a thousand chariots, but whether he is benevolent or not I cannot say.'

'What about Ch'iu?'

The Master said, 'Ch'iu can be given the responsibility as a steward in a town with a thousand households or in a noble family with a hundred chariots, but whether he is benevolent or not I cannot say.'

'What about Ch'ih?'

The Master said, 'When Ch'ih, putting on his sash, takes his place at court, he can be given the responsibility of conversing with the guests, but whether he is benevolent or not I cannot say.'

9. The Master said to Tzu-kung, 'Who is the better man, you or Hui?'

'How dare I compare myself with Hui? When he is told one thing he understands ten. When I am told one thing I understand only two.'

The Master said, 'You are not as good as he is. Neither of us is as good as he is.'

10. Tsai Yü was in bed in the daytime. The Master said, 'A piece of rotten wood cannot be carved, nor can a wall of dried dung be trowelled. As far as Yü is concerned what is the use of condemning him?' The Master added, 'I used to take on trust a man's deeds after having listened to his words. Now having listened to a man's words I go on to observe his deeds. It was on account of Yü that I have changed in this respect.'

11. The Master said, 'I have never met anyone who is truly unbending.'

Someone said, 'What about Shen Ch'eng?'

The Master said, 'Ch'eng is full of desires. How can he be un-bending?'

12. Tzu-kung said, 'While I do not wish others to impose on me, I also wish not to impose on others.'

The Master said, 'Ssu, that is quite beyond you.'

13. Tzu-kung said, 'One can get to hear about the Master's accomplishments, but one cannot get to hear his views on human nature and the Way of Heaven.'

14. Before he could put into practice something he had heard, the only thing Tzu-lu feared was that he should be told something further.

15. Tzu-kung asked, 'Why was K'ung Wen Tzu called "wen"?'

The Master said, 'He was quick and eager to learn: he was not ashamed to seek the advice of those who were beneath him in station. That is why he was called "wen".'⁴

16. The Master said of Tzu-ch'an that he had the way of the gentleman on four counts: he was respectful in the manner he conducted himself; he was reverent in the service of his lord; in caring for the common people, he was generous and, in employing their services, he was just.

17. The Master said, 'Yen P'ing-chung excelled in friendship: even after long acquaintance he treated his friends with reverence.'

18. The Master said, 'When housing his great tortoise, Tsang Wen-chung had the capitals of the pillars carved in the shape of hills and the rafterposts painted in a duckweed design. What is one to think of his intelligence?'

4. In the chapter dealing with posthumous titles in the *Yi Chou shu* it is said that 'diligence in learning and seeking advice is called "wen"' (p. 196). It is likely that the *Yi Chou shu*, though traditionally taken to be earlier, in fact, took the *Analects* as one of its sources.

19. Tzu-chang asked, 'Ling Yin[5] Tzu-wen gave no appearance of pleasure when he was made prime minister three times. Neither did he give any appearance of displeasure when he was removed from office three times. He always told his successor what he had done during his term of office. What do you think of this?'

The Master said, 'He can, indeed, be said to be a man who does his best.'

'Can he be said to be benevolent?'

'He cannot even be said to be wise. How can he be said to be benevolent?'

'When Ts'ui Tzu assassinated the Lord of Ch'i, Ch'en Wen Tzu who owned ten teams of four horses each abandoned them and left the state. On arriving in another state, he said, "The officials here are no better than our Counsellor Ts'ui Tzu." He left and went to yet another state. Once more, he said, "The officials here are no better than our Counsellor Ts'ui Tzu," and he again left. What do you think of this?'

The Master said, 'He can, indeed, be said to be pure.'

'Can he be said to be benevolent?'

'He cannot even be said to be wise. How can he be said to be benevolent?'

20. Chi Wen Tzu always thought three times before taking action. When the Master was told of this, he commented, 'Twice is quite enough.'

21. The Master said, 'Ning Wu Tzu was intelligent when the Way prevailed in the state, but stupid when it did not. Others may equal his intelligence but they cannot equal his stupidity.'

22. When he was in Ch'en, the Master said, 'Let us go home. Let us go home. Our young men at home are wildly ambitious, and have great accomplishments for all to see, but they do not know how to prune themselves.'

5. This was the title in the state of Ch'u for the prime minister.

23. The Master said, 'Po Yi and Shu Ch'i never remembered old scores. For this reason they incurred little ill will.'

24. The Master said, 'Who said Wei-sheng Kao was straight? Once when someone begged him for vinegar, he went and begged it off a neighbour to give it to him.'

25. The Master said, 'Cunning words, an ingratiating face and utter servility, these things Tso-ch'iu Ming found shameful. I, too, find them shameful. To be friendly towards someone while concealing one's hostility, this Tso-ch'iu Ming found shameful. I, too, find it shameful.'

26. Yen Yüan and Chi-lu were in attendance. The Master said, 'I suggest you each tell me what it is you have set your hearts on.'

Tzu-lu said, 'I should like to share my carriage and horses, clothes[5] and furs with my friends, and to have no regrets even if they become worn.'

Yen Yüan said, 'I should like never to boast of my own goodness and never to impose onerous tasks upon others.'

Tzu-lu said, 'I should like to hear what you have set your heart on.'

The Master said, 'To bring peace to the old, to have trust in my friends, and to cherish the young.'

27. The Master said, 'I suppose I should give up hope. I have yet to meet the man who, on seeing his own errors, is able to take himself to task inwardly.'

28. The Master said, 'In a hamlet of ten households, there are bound to be those who are my equal in doing their best for others and in being trustworthy in what they say, but they are unlikely to be as eager to learn as I am.'

BOOK VI

1. The Master said, 'Yung could be given the seat facing south.'[1]

2. Chung-kung asked about Tzu-sang Po-tzu. The Master said, 'It is his simplicity of style that makes him acceptable.'

Chung-kung said, 'In ruling over the common people, is it not acceptable to hold oneself in reverence and merely to be simple in the measures one takes? On the other hand, is it not carrying simplicity too far to be simple in the way one holds oneself as well as in the measures one takes?'

The Master said, 'Yung is right in what he says.'

3. When Duke Ai asked which of his disciples was eager to learn, Confucius answered, 'There was one Yen Hui who was eager to learn. He did not vent his anger upon an innocent person, nor did he make the same mistake twice. Unfortunately his allotted span was a short one and he died. Now there is no one. No one eager to learn has come to my notice.'

4. Jan Tzu asked for grain for the mother of Tzu-hua who was away on a mission to Ch'i. The Master said, 'Give her one *fu*.'[2] Jan Tzu asked for more. 'Give her one *yü*.' Jan Tzu gave her five *ping* of grain.

The Master said, 'Ch'ih went off to Ch'i drawn by well-fed horses and wearing light furs. I have heard it said, A gentleman gives to help the needy and not to maintain the rich in style.'

5. On becoming his[3] steward, Yüan Ssu was given nine hundred measures of grain which he declined. The Master said, 'Can you not find a use for it in helping the people in your neighbourhood?'

1. the seat of the ruler.
2. *Fu, yü* and *ping* are dry measures in ascending order of capacity.
3. i.e., Confucius'.

6. The Master said of Chung-kung, 'Should a bull born of plough cattle have a sorrel coat and well-formed horns, would the spirits of the mountains and rivers allow it to be passed over even if we felt it was not good enough to be used?'

7. The Master said, 'In his heart for three months at a time Hui does not lapse from benevolence. The others attain benevolence merely by fits and starts.'

8. Chi K'ang Tzu asked, 'Is Chung Yu good enough to be given office?'

The Master said, 'Yu is resolute. What difficulties could there be for him in taking office?'

'Is Ssu good enough to be given office?'

'Ssu is a man of understanding. What difficulties could there be for him in taking office?'

'Is Ch'iu good enough to be given office?'

'Ch'iu is accomplished. What difficulties could there be for him in taking office?'

9. The Chi Family wanted to make Min Tzu-ch'ien the steward of Pi. Min Tzu-ch'ien said, 'Decline the offer for me tactfully. If anyone comes back for me, I shall be on the other side of the Riven Wen.'[4]

10. Po-niu was ill. The Master visited him and, holding his hand through the window, said, 'We are going to lose him. It must be Destiny. Why else should such a man be stricken with such a disease? Why else should such a man be stricken with such a disease?'

11. The Master said, 'How admirable Hui is! Living in a mean dwelling on a bowlful of rice and a ladleful of water is a hardship most men would find intolerable, but Hui does not allow this to affect his joy. How admirable Hui is!'

12. Jan Ch'iu said, 'It is not that I am not pleased with your way,

4. i.e., over the border into the state of Ch'i.

but rather that my strength gives out.' The Master said, 'A man whose strength gives out collapses along the course. In your case you set the limits beforehand.'

13. The Master said to Tzu-hsia, 'Be a gentleman *ju*,[5] not a petty *ju*.'

14. Tzu-yu was the steward of Wu Ch'eng. The Master said, 'Have you made any discoveries there?'

'There is one T'an-t'ai Mieh-ming who never takes short-cuts and who has never been to my room except on official business.'

15. The Master said, 'Meng chih Fan was not given to boasting. When the army was routed, he stayed in the rear. But on entering the gate, he goaded[6] his horse on, saying, 'I did not lag behind out of presumption. It was simply that my horse refused to go forward.'

16. The Master said, 'You may have the good looks of Sung Chao, but you will find it difficult to escape unscathed in this world if you do not, at the same time, have the eloquence of the Priest T'uo.'

17. The Master said, 'Who can go out without using the door? Why, then, does no one follow this Way?'

18. The Master said, 'When there is a preponderance of native substance over acquired refinement, the result will be churlishness. When there is a preponderance of acquired refinement over native substance, the result will be pedantry. Only a well-balanced admixture of these two will result in gentlemanliness.'

5. The original meaning of the word is uncertain, but it probably referred to men for whom the qualities of the scholar were more important than those of the warrior. In subsequent ages, *ju* came to be the name given to the Confucianists.

6. According to the account in the *Tso chuan* under Duke Ai 11, with his arrow (*Tso chuan chu shu*, 58.22a).

19. The Master said, 'That a man lives is because he is straight. That a man who dupes others survives is because he has been fortunate enough to be spared.'

20. The Master said, 'To be fond of something is better than merely to know it, and to find joy in it is better than merely to be fond of it.'

21. The Master said, 'You can tell those who are above average about the best, but not those who are below average.'

22. Fan Ch'ih asked about wisdom. The Master said, 'To work for the things the common people have a right to and to keep one's distance from the gods and spirits while showing them reverence can be called wisdom.'

Fan Ch'ih asked about benevolence. The Master said, 'The benevolent man reaps the benefit only after overcoming difficulties. That can be called benevolence.'[7]

23. The Master said, 'The wise find joy in water; the benevolent find joy in mountains. The wise are active; the benevolent are still. The wise are joyful; the benevolent are long-lived.'

24. The Master said, 'At one stroke Ch'i can be made into a Lu, and Lu, at one stroke, can be made to attain the Way.'

25. The Master said, 'A ku[8] that is not truly a ku. A ku indeed! A ku indeed!'

26. Tsai Wo asked, 'If a benevolent man was told that there was another benevolent man in the well, would he, nevertheless, go and join him?'

The Master said, 'Why should that be the case? A gentleman can be sent there, but cannot be lured into a trap. He can be deceived, but cannot be duped.'

7. cf. XII.22 where Confucius gives different answers to the same questions from Fan Ch'ih.
8. A drinking vessel with a regulation capacity.

27. The Master said, 'The gentleman widely versed in culture but brought back to essentials by the rites can, I suppose, be relied upon not to turn against what he stood for.'

28. The Master went to see Nan Tzu.[9] Tzu-lu was displeased. The Master swore, 'If I have done anything improper, may Heaven's curse be on me, may Heaven's curse be on me!'

29. The Master said, 'Supreme indeed is the Mean as a moral virtue. It has been rare among the common people for quite a long time.'

30. Tzu-kung said, 'If there were a man who gave extensively to the common people and brought help to the multitude, what would you think of him? Could he be called benevolent?'

The Master said, 'It is no longer a matter of benevolence with such a man. If you must describe him, "sage" is, perhaps, the right word. Even Yao and Shun would have found it difficult to accomplish as much. Now, on the other hand, a benevolent man helps others to take their stand in so far as he himself wishes to take his stand,[10] and gets others there in so far as he himself wishes to get there. The ability to take as analogy what is near at hand[11] can be called the method of benevolence.'

9. the notorious wife of Duke Ling of Wei.

10. It is on the rites that one takes one's stand. Cf. 'Take your stand on the rites' (VIII.8) and 'unless you study the rites you will not be able to take your stand' (XVI.13).

11. viz., oneself.

BOOK VII

1. The Master said, 'I transmit but do not innovate; I am truthful in what I say and devoted to antiquity. I venture to compare myself to our Old P'eng.'[1]

2. The Master said, 'Quietly to store up knowledge in my mind, to learn without flagging, to teach without growing weary, these present me with no difficulties.'

3. The Master said, 'It is these things that cause me concern: failure to cultivate virtue, failure to go more deeply into what I have learned, inability, when I am told what is right, to move to where it is, and inability to reform myself when I have defects.'

4. During his leisure moments, the Master remained correct though relaxed.

5. The Master said, 'How I have gone downhill! It has been such a long time since I dreamt of the Duke of Chou.'

6. The Master said, 'I set my heart on the Way, base myself on virtue, lean upon benevolence for support and take my recreation in the arts.'

7. The Master said, 'I have never denied instruction to anyone who, of his own accord, has given me so much as a bundle of dried meat as a present.'

8. The Master said, 'I never enlighten anyone who has not been driven to distraction by trying to understand a difficulty or who has not got into a frenzy trying to put his ideas into words.

'When I have pointed out one corner of a square to anyone and he does not come back with the other three, I will not point it out to him a second time.'

1. It is not clear who Old P'eng was.

9. When eating in the presence of one who had been bereaved, the Master never ate his fill.

10. On a day he had wept, the Master did not sing.

11. The Master said to Yen Yüan, 'Only you and I have the ability to go forward when employed and to stay out of sight when set aside.'

Tzu-lu said, 'If you were leading the Three Armies whom would you take with you?'

The Master said, 'I would not take with me anyone who would try to fight a tiger with his bare hands or to walk across the River[2] and die in the process without regrets. If I took anyone it would have to be a man who, when faced with a task, was fearful of failure and who, while fond of making plans, was capable of successful execution.'

12. The Master said, 'If wealth were a permissible pursuit, I would be willing even to act as a guard holding a whip outside the market place. If it is not, I shall follow my own preferences.'

13. Fasting, war and sickness were the things over which the Master exercised care.

14. The Master heard the *shao*[3] in Ch'i and for three months did not notice the taste of the meat he ate. He said, 'I never dreamt that the joys of music could reach such heights.'

15. Jan Yu said, 'Is the Master on the side of the Lord of Wei?'[4] Tzu-kung said, 'Well, I shall put the question to him.'

2. In ancient Chinese literature, 'the River' meant the Yellow River.
3. The music of Shun. Cf. III.25.
4. i.e., Che, known in history as the Ousted Duke, son of Prince K'uai K'ui who was son of Duke Ling. After failing in an attempt to kill Nan Tzu, the notorious wife of his father, Prince K'uai K'ui fled to Chin. On the death of Duke Ling, Che came to the throne. With the backing of the Chin army, Prince K'uai K'ui managed to install himself in the city of Ch'i in Wei, waiting for an opportunity to oust his son. At that time Confucius was in Wei, and what Jan Yu wanted to know was whether he was for Che.

He went in and said, 'What sort of men were Po Yi and Shu Ch'i?'

'They were excellent men of old.'

'Did they have any complaints?'

'They sought benevolence and got it. So why should they have any complaints?'

When Tzu-kung came out, he said, 'The Master is not on his side.'

16. The Master said, 'In the eating of coarse rice and the drinking of water, the using of one's elbow for a pillow, joy is to be found. Wealth and rank attained through immoral means have as much to do with me as passing clouds.'

17. The Master said, 'Grant me a few more years so that I may study at the age of fifty and[6] I shall be free from major errors.'

18. What the Master used the correct pronunciation for: the *Odes*, the *Book of History* and the performance of the rites. In all these cases he used the correct pronunciation.

19. The Governor of She asked Tzu-lu about Confucius. Tzu-lu did not answer. The Master said, 'Why did you not simply say something to this effect: he is the sort of man who forgets to eat when he tries to solve a problem that has been driving him to distraction, who is so full of joy that he forgets his worries and who does not notice the onset of old age?'

20. The Master said, 'I was not born with knowledge but, being fond of antiquity, I am quick to seek it.'

21. The topics the Master did not speak of were prodigies, force, disorder and gods.

22. The Master said, 'Even when walking in the company of two other men, I am bound to be able to learn from them. The good points of the one I copy; the bad points of the other I correct in myself.'

23. The Master said, 'Heaven is author of the virtue that is in me. What can Huan T'ui do to me?'[5]

24. The Master said, 'My friends, do you think I am secretive? There is nothing which I hide from you. There is nothing I do which I do not share with you, my friends. There is Ch'iu for you.'

25. The Master instructs under four heads: culture, moral conduct, doing one's best and being trustworthy in what one says.

26. The Master said, 'I have no hopes of meeting a sage. I would be content if I met someone who is a gentleman.'

The Master said, 'I have no hopes of meeting a good man. I would be content if I met someone who has constancy.[6] It is hard for a man to have constancy who claims to have when he is wanting, to be full when he is empty and to be comfortable when he is in straitened circumstances.'

27. The Master used a fishing line but not a cable;[7] he used a corded arrow but not to shoot at roosting birds.

28. The Master said, 'There are presumably men who innovate without possessing knowledge, but that is not a fault I have. I use my ears widely and follow what is good in what I have heard; I use my eyes widely and retain what I have seen in my mind.[8] This constitutes a lower level of knowledge.'[9]

29. People of Hu Hsiang were difficult to talk to. A boy was received and the disciples were perplexed. The Master said, 'Approval of his coming does not mean approval of him when he is not here.

5. According to tradition, this was said on the occasion when Huan T'ui, the Minister of War in Sung, attempted to kill him.

6. cf. XIII.22.

7. attached to a net.

8. cf. XV.3.

9. cf. 'The best are those born with knowledge. Next come those who get to know through learning' (XVI.9).

Why should we be so exacting? When a man comes after having purified himself, we approve of his purification but we cannot vouch for his past.'[10]

30. The Master said, 'Is benevolence really far away? No sooner do I desire it than it is here.'

31. Ch'en Ssu-pai asked whether Duke Chao was versed in the rites. Confucius said, 'Yes.'

After Confucius had gone, Ch'en Ssu-pai, bowing to Wu-ma Ch'i, invited him forward and said, 'I have heard that the gentleman does not show partiality. Does he show it nevertheless? The Lord took as wife a daughter of Wu, who thus is of the same clan as himself,[11] but he allows her to be called Wu Meng Tzu.[12] If the Lord is versed in the rites, who isn't?'

When Wu-ma Ch'i recounted this to him, the Master said, 'I am a fortunate man. Whenever I make a mistake, other people are sure to notice it.'[13]

32. When the Master was singing in the company of others and liked someone else's song, he always asked to hear it again before joining in.

33. The Master said, 'In unstinted effort I can compare with others, but in being a practising gentleman I have had, as yet, no success.'

34. The Master said, 'How dare I claim to be a sage or a benevolent man? Perhaps it might be said of me that I learn without flagging and teach without growing weary.'[14] Kung-hsi Hua said, 'This is

10. It has been suggested that this sentence should stand at the beginning of Confucius' remark.

11. bearing the name Chi.

12. when she should be called Wu Chi. Calling her Wu Meng Tzu was an attempt to gloss over the fact that she shared the same clan name of Chi.

13. Being a native of Lu, Confucius would rather be criticized for partiality than appear to be openly critical of the Duke.

14. *Mencius*, II.A.2 (p. 79) contains what seems to be a fuller version of this passage.

precisely where we disciples are unable to learn from your example.'

35. The Master was seriously ill. Tzu-lu asked permission to offer a prayer. The Master said, 'Was such a thing ever done?' Tzu-lu said, 'Yes, it was. The prayer offered was as follows: pray thus to the gods above and below.' The Master said, 'In that case, I have long been offering my prayers.'

36. The Master said, 'Extravagance means ostentation, frugality means shabbiness. I would rather be shabby than ostentatious.'

37. The Master said, 'The gentleman is easy of mind, while the small man is always full of anxiety.'

38. The Master is cordial yet stern, awe-inspiring yet not fierce, and respectful yet at ease.

BOOK VIII

1. The Master said, 'Surely T'ai Po can be said to be of the highest virtue. Three times he abdicated his right to rule over the Empire, and yet he left behind nothing the common people could acclaim.'

2. The Master said, 'Unless a man has the spirit of the rites, in being respectful he will wear himself out, in being careful he will become timid, in having courage he will become unruly, and in being forthright he will become intolerant.[1]

'When the gentleman feels profound affection for his parents, the common people will be stirred to benevolence. When he does not forget friends of long standing, the common people will not shirk their obligations to other people.'

3. When he was seriously ill Tseng Tzu summoned his disciples and said, 'Take a look at my hands. Take a look at my feet. The *Odes* say,

> In fear and trembling,
> As if approaching a deep abyss,
> As if walking on thin ice.[2]

Only now am I sure of being spared,[3] my young friends.'

4. Tseng Tzu was seriously ill. When Meng Ching Tzu visited him, this was what Tseng Tzu said,

> 'Sad is the cry of a dying bird;
> Good are the words of a dying man.

There are three things which the gentleman values most in the Way: to stay clear of violence by putting on a serious countenance,

1. cf. XVII.8.
2. Ode 195.
3. i.e., to have avoided, now that he was on the point of death, the risk of the mutilation of his body – a duty which he owed to his parents.

to come close to being trusted by setting a proper expression on his face, and to avoid being boorish and unreasonable by speaking in proper tones. As for the business of sacrificial vessels, there are officials responsible for that.'

5. Tseng Tzu said, 'To be able yet to ask the advice of those who are not able. To have many talents yet to ask the advice of those who have few. To have yet to appear to want. To be full yet to appear empty.[4] To be transgressed against yet not to mind. It was towards this end that my friend[5] used to direct his efforts.'

6. Tseng Tzu said, 'If a man can be entrusted with an orphan six ch'ih[6] tall, and the fate of a state one hundred li square, without his being deflected from his purpose even in moments of crisis, is he not a gentleman? He is, indeed, a gentleman.'

7. Tseng Tzu said, 'A Gentleman must be strong and resolute, for his burden is heavy and the road is long. He takes benevolence as his burden. Is that not heavy? Only with death does the road come to an end. Is that not long?'

8. The Master said, 'Be stimulated by the *Odes*, take your stand on the rites and be perfected by music.'

9. The Master said, 'The common people can be made to follow a path but not to understand it.'

10. The Master said, 'Being fond of courage while detesting poverty will lead men to unruly behaviour. Excessive detestation of men who are not benevolent will provoke them to unruly behaviour.'

11. The Master said, 'Even with a man as gifted as the Duke of

4. This is in contrast to the man 'who claims to have when he is wanting, to be full when he is empty' (VII.26).
5. According to tradition, this refers to Yen Hui.
6. The ch'ih in Tseng Tzu's time was much shorter than the modern foot.

Chou, if he was arrogant and miserly, then the rest of his qualities would not be worthy of admiration.'

12. The Master said, 'It is not easy to find a man who can study for three years without thinking about earning a salary.'

13. The Master said, 'Have the firm faith to devote yourself to learning, and abide to the death in the good way. Enter not a state that is in peril; stay not in a state that is in danger. Show yourself when the Way prevails in the Empire, but hide yourself when it does not. It is a shameful matter to be poor and humble when the Way prevails in the state. Equally, it is a shameful matter to be rich and noble when the Way falls into disuse in the state.'

14. The Master said, 'Do not concern yourself with matters of government unless they are the responsibility of your office.'[7]

15. The Master said, 'When Chih, the Master Musician, begins to play and when the *Kuan chü*[8] comes to its end, how the sound fills the ear!'

16. The Master said, 'Men who reject discipline and yet are not straight, men who are ignorant and yet not cautious, men who are devoid of ability and yet not trustworthy are quite beyond my understanding.'

17. The Master said, 'Even with a man who urges himself on in his studies as though he was losing ground, my fear is still that he may not make it in time.'

18. The Master said, 'How lofty Shun and Yü were in holding aloof from the Empire when they were in possession of it.'

19. The Master said, 'Great indeed was Yao as a ruler! How lofty! It is Heaven that is great and it was Yao who modelled himself

7. This remark forms part of the saying in XIV.26.
8. The first ode in the *Odes*.

upon it. He was so boundless that the common people were not able to put a name to his virtues. Lofty was he in his successes and brilliant was he in his accomplishments!'

20. Shun had five officials and the Empire was well governed. King Wu said, 'I have ten capable officials.'

Confucius commented, 'How true it is that talent is difficult to find! The period of T'ang and Yü[9] was rich in talent.[10] With a woman amongst them, there were, in fact, only nine.[11] The Chou continued to serve the Yin when it was in possession of two-thirds of the Empire. Its virtue can be said to have been the highest.'

21. The Master said, 'With Yü I can find no fault. He ate and drank the meanest fare while making offerings to ancestral spirits and gods with the utmost devotion proper to a descendant. He wore coarse clothes while sparing no splendour in his robes and caps on sacrificial occasions. He lived in lowly dwellings while devoting all his energy to the building of irrigation canals. With Yü I can find no fault.'

9. T'ang here is the name of Yao's dynasty and Yü the name of Shun's dynasty, not to be confused with T'ang the founder of the Yin or Shang dynasty and Yü the founder of the Hsia dynasty.

10. yet Shun had only five officials.

11. in the case of King Wu.

BOOK IX

1. The occasions on which the Master talked about profit, Destiny and benevolence were rare.

2. A man from a village in Ta Hsiang said, 'Great indeed is Confucius! He has wide learning but has not made a name for himself in any field.' The Master, on hearing of this, said, to his disciples, 'What should I make myself proficient in? In driving? or in archery? I think I would prefer driving.'

3. The Master said, 'A ceremonial cap of linen is what is prescribed by the rites. Today black silk is used instead. This is more frugal and I follow the majority. To prostrate oneself before ascending the steps is what is prescribed by the rites. Today one does so after having ascended them. This is casual and, though going against the majority, I follow the practice of doing so before ascending.'

4. There were four things the Master refused to have anything to do with: he refused to entertain conjectures[1] or insist on certainty; he refused to be inflexible or to be egotistical.

5. When under siege in K'uang, the Master said, 'With King Wen dead, is not culture (*wen*) invested here in me? If Heaven intends culture to be destroyed, those who come after me will not be able to have any part of it. If Heaven does not intend this culture to be destroyed, then what can the men of K'uang do to me?'

6. The *t'ai tsai*[2] asked Tzu-kung, 'Surely the Master is a sage, is he not? Otherwise why should he be skilled in so many things?'

---

1. cf. 'If a man, without anticipating deception . . . is able to be the first to see it, he must be an able man' (XIV.31).
2. This is the title of a high office. It is not clear who the person referred to was or even from which state he came.

Tzu-kung said, 'It is true, Heaven set him on the path to sagehood. However, he is skilled in many things besides.'

The Master, on hearing of this, said, 'How well the *t'ai tsai* knows me! I was of humble station when young. That is why I am skilled in many menial things. Should a gentleman be skilled in many things? No, not at all.'

7. Lao[3] said, 'The Master said, "I have never been proved in office. That is why I am a Jack of all trades."'

8. The Master said, 'Do I possess knowledge? No, I do not. A rustic put a question to me and my mind was a complete blank. I kept hammering at the two sides of the question until I got everything out of it.'[4]

9. The Master said, 'The Phoenix does not appear nor does the River offer up its Chart.[5] I am done for.'

10. When the Master encountered men who were in mourning or in ceremonial cap and robes or were blind, he would, on seeing them, rise to his feet, even though they were younger than he was, and, on passing them, would quicken his step.[6]

11. Yen Yüan, heaving a sigh, said, 'The more I look up at it the higher it appears. The more I bore into it the harder it becomes. I see it before me. Suddenly it is behind me.

'The Master is good at leading one on step by step. He broadens me with culture and brings me back to essentials by means of the rites. I cannot give up even if I wanted to, but, having done all I can, it[7] seems to rise sheer above me and I have no way of going after it, however much I may want to.'

3. The identity of the person referred to here is uncertain.
4. The whole section is exceedingly obscure and the translation is tentative.
5. Both the Phoenix and the Chart were auspicious omens. Confucius is here lamenting the hopelessness of putting the Way into practice in the Empire of his day.
6. as a sign of respect.
7. Throughout this chapter the 'it' refers to the way of Confucius.

12. The Master was seriously ill. Tzu-lu told his disciples to act as retainers.[8] During a period when his condition had improved, the Master said, 'Yu has long been practising deception. In pretending that I had retainers when I had none, who would we be deceiving? Would we be deceiving Heaven? Moreover, would I not rather die in your hands, my friends, than in the hands of retainers? And even if I were not given an elaborate funeral, it is not as if I was dying by the wayside.'

13. Tzu-kung said, 'If you had a piece of beautiful jade here, would you put it away safely in a box or would you try to sell it for a good price?' The Master said, 'Of course I would sell it. Of course I would sell it. All I am waiting for is the right offer.'

14. The Master wanted to settle amongst the Nine Barbarian Tribes of the east. Someone said, 'But could you put up with their uncouth ways?' The Master said, 'Once a gentleman settles amongst them, what uncouthness will there be?'

15. The Master said, 'It was after my return from Wei to Lu that the music was put right, with the ya and the sung[9] being assigned their proper places.'

16. The Master said, 'To serve high officials when abroad, and my elders when at home, in arranging funerals not to dare to spare myself, and to be able to hold my drink – these are trifles that give me no trouble.'

17. While standing by a river, the Master said, 'What passes away is, perhaps, like this. Day and night it never lets up.'

18. The Master said, 'I have yet to meet the man who is as fond of virtue as he is of beauty in women.'[10]

19. The Master said, 'As in the case of making a mound, if, before

8. when Confucius, no longer in office, was not in a position to have them.
9. The ya and the sung are sections in the Odes.
10. This saying is repeated in XV.13.

the very last basketful, I stop, then I shall have stopped. As in the case of levelling the ground, if, though tipping only one basketful, I am going forward, then I shall be making progress.'

20. The Master said, 'If anyone can listen to me with unflagging attention, it is Hui, I suppose.'

21. The Master said of Yen Yüan, 'I watched him making progress, but I did not see him realize his capacity to the full. What a pity!'

22. The Master said, 'There are, are there not, young plants that fail to produce blossoms, and blossoms that fail to produce fruit?'

23. The Master said, 'It is fitting that we should hold the young in awe. How do we know that the generations to come will not be the equal of the present? Only when a man reaches the age of forty or fifty without distinguishing himself in any way can one say, I suppose, that he does not deserve to be held in awe.'

24. The Master said, 'One cannot but give assent to exemplary words, but what is important is that one should rectify oneself. One cannot but be pleased with tactful words, but what is important is that one should reform oneself. I can do nothing with the man who gives assent but does not rectify himself or the man who is pleased but does not reform himself.'

25. The Master said, 'Make it your guiding principle to do your best for others and to be trustworthy in what you say. Do not accept as friend anyone who is not as good as you. When you make a mistake do not be afraid of mending your ways.'[11]

26. The Master said, 'The Three Armies can be deprived of their commanding officer, but even a common man cannot be deprived of his purpose.'

11. This saying has already appeared as part of I.8.

27. The Master said, 'If anyone can, while dressed in a worn-out gown padded with old silk floss, stand beside a man wearing fox or badger fur without feeling ashamed, it is, I suppose, Yu.

> Neither envious nor covetous,
> How can he be anything but good?'[12]

Thereafter, Tzu-lu constantly recited these verses. The Master commented, 'The way summed up in these verses will hardly enable one to be good.'

28. The Master said, 'Only when the cold season comes is the point brought home that the pine and the cypress are the last to lose their leaves.'

29. The Master said, 'The man of wisdom is never in two minds;[13] the man of benevolence never worries;[14] the man of courage is never afraid.'[15]

30. The Master said, 'A man good enough as a partner in one's studies need not be good enough as a partner in the pursuit of the Way; a man good enough as a partner in the pursuit of the Way need not be good enough as a partner in a common stand; a man good enough as a partner in a common stand need not be good enough as a partner in the exercise of moral discretion.'

31.

> The flowers of the cherry tree,
> How they wave about!
> It's not that I do not think of you,
> But your home is so far away.[16]

The Master commented, 'He did not really think of her. If he did, there is no such thing as being far away.'

12. Ode 33.
13. about right and wrong.
14. about the future.
15. This chapter forms part of XIV.28 where the saying about the man of benevolence comes before the one about the man of wisdom.
16. These lines are not to be found in the present *Odes*.

BOOK X

1. In the local community, Confucius was submissive and seemed to be inarticulate. In the ancestral temple and at court, though fluent, he did not speak lightly.

2. At court, when speaking with Counsellors of lower rank he was affable; when speaking with Counsellors of upper rank, he was frank though respectful. In the presence of his lord, his bearing, though respectful, was composed.

3. When he was summoned by his lord to act as usher, his face took on a serious expression and his step became brisk. When he bowed to his colleagues, stretching out his hands to the left or to the right, his robes followed his movements without being disarranged. He went forward with quickened steps, as though he was gliding on wings. After the withdrawal of the guest, he invariably reported, 'The guest has stopped looking back.'

4. On going through the outer gates to his lord's court, he drew himself in, as though the entrance was too small to admit him.

When he stood, he did not occupy the centre of the gateway;[1] when he walked, he did not step on the threshold.

When he went past the station of his lord, his face took on a serious expression, his step became brisk, and his words seemed more laconic.

When he lifted the hem of his robe to ascend the hall, he drew himself in, stopped inhaling as if he had no need to breathe.

When he had come out and descended the first step, relaxing his expression, he seemed no longer to be tense.

When he had reached the bottom of the steps he went forward with quickened steps as though he was gliding on wings.

When he resumed his station, his bearing was respectful.

1. A position which would have been presumptuous.

5. When he held the jade tablet, he drew himself in as though its weight was too much for him. He held the upper part of the tablet as though he was bowing; he held the lower part of the tablet as though he was ready to hand over a gift. His expression was solemn as though in fear and trembling, and his feet were constrained as though following a marked line.

When making a presentation, his expression was genial.

At a private audience, he was relaxed.

6. The gentleman avoided using dark purple and maroon coloured silk for lapels and cuffs. Red and violet coloured silks were not used for informal dress.

When, in the heat of summer, he wore an unlined robe made of either fine or coarse material, he invariably wore it over an under-robe to set it off.

Under a black jacket, he wore lambskin; under an undyed jacket, he wore fawnskin; under a yellow jacket, he wore fox fur.

His informal fur coat was long but with a short right sleeve.

He invariably had a night robe which was half as long again as he was tall.[2]

Their fur being thick, pelts of the fox and the badger were used as rugs.

Once the period of mourning was over, he placed no restrictions on the kind of ornament that he wore.

Other than skirts for ceremonial occasions, everything else was made up from cut pieces.

Lambskin coats and black caps were not used on visits of condolence.

On New Year's Day, he invariably went to court in court dress.

7. In periods of purification, he invariably wore a house robe made of the cheaper sort of material.

In periods of purification, he invariably changed to a more austere diet and, when at home, did not sit in his usual place.

2. It has been suggested that this sentence has got out of place and should follow the first sentence in the next section.

8. He did not eat his fill of polished rice, nor did he eat his fill of finely minced meat.

He did not eat rice that had gone sour or fish and meat that had spoiled. He did not eat food that had gone off colour or food that had a bad smell. He did not eat food that was not properly prepared nor did he eat except at the proper times. He did not eat food that had not been properly cut up, nor did he eat unless the proper sauce was available.

Even when there was plenty of meat, he avoided eating more meat than rice.

Only in the case of wine did he not set himself a rigid limit. He simply never drank to the point of becoming confused.

He did not consume wine or dried meat bought from a shop.

Even when he did not have the side dish of ginger cleared from the table, he did not eat more than was proper.

9. After assisting at a sacrifice at his lord's place, he did not keep his portion of the sacrificial meat overnight. In other cases, he did not keep the sacrificial meat for more than three days. Once it was kept beyond three days he no longer ate it.

10. He did not converse at meals; nor did he talk in bed.

11. Even when a meal consisted only of coarse rice and vegetable broth, he invariably[7] made an offering from them and invariably did so solemnly.

12. He did not sit, unless his mat was straight.

13. When drinking at a village gathering, he left as soon as those carrying walking sticks had left.

14. When the villagers were exorcizing evil spirits, he stood in his court robes on the eastern steps.[3]

15. When making inquiries after someone in another state, he bowed to the ground twice before sending off the messenger.

3. The place for a host to stand.

16. When K'ang Tzu sent a gift of medicine, [Confucius] bowed his head to the ground before accepting it. However, he said, 'Not knowing its properties, I dare not taste it.'

17. The stables caught fire. The Master, on returning from court, asked, 'Was anyone hurt?' He did not ask about the horses.

18. When his lord gave a gift of cooked food, the first thing he invariably did was to taste it after having adjusted his mat. When his lord gave him a gift of uncooked food, he invariably cooked it and offered it to the ancestors. When his lord gave him a gift of a live animal, he invariably reared it. At the table of his lord, when his lord had made an offering before the meal he invariably started with the rice first.

19. During an illness, when his lord paid him a visit, he would lie with his head to the east, with his court robes draped over him and his grand sash trailing over the side of the bed.

20. When summoned by his lord, he would set off without waiting for horses to be yoked to his carriage.

21. When he went inside the Grand Temple, he asked questions about everything.[4]

22. Whenever a friend died who had no kin to whom his body could be taken, he said, 'Let him be given a funeral from my house.'

23. Even when a gift from a friend was a carriage and horses – since it lacked the solemnity of sacrificial meat – he did not bow to the ground.

24. When in bed, he did not lie like a corpse, nor did he sit in the formal manner of a guest[8] when by himself.

25. When he met a bereaved person in mourning dress, even though

4. This forms part of III.15.

it was someone he was on familiar terms with, he invariably assumed a solemn expression. When he met someone wearing a ceremonial cap or someone blind, even though they were well-known to him, he invariably showed them respect.[5]

On passing a person dressed as a mourner he would lean forward with his hands on the cross-bar of his carriage to show respect; he would act in a similar manner towards a person carrying official documents.

When a sumptuous feast was brought on, he invariably assumed a solemn expression and rose to his feet.

When there was a sudden clap of thunder or a violent wind, he invariably assumed a solemn attitude.

26. When climbing into a carriage, he invariably stood squarely and grasped the mounting-cord.

When in the carriage, he did not turn towards the inside, nor did he shout or point.

27. Startled, the bird rose up and circled round before alighting. He said, 'The female pheasant on the mountain bridge, how timely her action is, how timely her action is!' Tzu-lu cupped one hand in the other in a gesture of respect towards the bird which, flapping its wings three times, flew away.

5. cf. IX.10.

BOOK XI

1. The Master said, 'As far as the rites and music are concerned, the disciples who were the first to come to me were rustics while those who came to me afterwards were gentlemen. When it comes to putting the rites and music to use, I follow the former.'

2. The Master said, 'None of those who were with me in Ch'en and Ts'ai ever got as far as my door.'[1]

3. Virtuous conduct: Yen Yüan, Min Tzu-ch'ien, Jan Po-niu and Chung-kung; speech: Tsai Wo and Tzu-kung; government: Jan Yu and Chi-lu; culture and learning: Tzu-yu and Tzu-hsia.

4. The Master said, 'Hui is no help to me at all. He is pleased with everything I say.'

5. The Master said, 'What a good son Min Tzu-ch'ien is! No one can find fault with what his parents and brothers have to say about him.'

6. Nan Jung repeated over and over again the lines about the white jade sceptre.[2] Confucius gave him his elder brother's daughter in marriage.[3]

7. Chi K'ang Tzu asked which of his disciples was eager to learn. Confucius answered, 'There was one Yen Hui who was eager to

---

1. This is a most puzzling saying however it is interpreted.
2. i.e., the lines from Ode 256 which run as follows:

> A blemish on the white jade
>   Can still be polished away;
> A blemish on these words
>   Cannot be removed at all.

3. cf. V.2.

learn, but unfortunately his allotted span was a short one and he died. Now there is no one.'[4]

8. When Yen Yüan died, Yen Lu[5] asked the Master to give him his carriage to pay for an outer coffin for his son. The Master said, 'Everyone speaks up for his own son whether he is talented or not. When Li[6] died, he had a coffin but no outer coffin, I did not go on foot in order to provide him with an outer coffin, because it would not have been proper for me to go on foot, seeing that I took my place after the Counsellors.'

9. When Yen Yüan died, the Master said, 'Alas! Heaven has bereft me! Heaven has bereft me!'

10. When Yen Yüan died, in weeping for him, the Master showed undue sorrow. His followers said, 'You are showing undue sorrow.' 'Am I? Yet if not for him, for whom should I show undue sorrow?'

11. When Yen Yüan died, the disciples wanted to give him a lavish burial. The Master said, 'It would not be proper.' All the same, they gave him a lavish burial. The Master said, 'Hui treated me as a father, yet I have been prevented from treating him as a son. This was none of my choice. It was the doing of these others.'

12. Chi-lu asked how the spirits of the dead and the gods should be served. The Master said, 'You are not able even to serve man. How can you serve the spirits?'

'May I ask about death?'

'You do not understand even life. How can you understand death?'

13. When in attendance on the Master, Min Tzu looked respectful and upright; Tzu-lu looked unbending; Jan Yu and Tzu-kung looked affable. The Master was happy.

4. cf. VI.3 where a similar conversation between Duke Ai of Lu and Confucius is to be found.
5. Yen Yüan's father.
6. Confucius' son.

'A man like Yu will not die a natural death.'[7]

14. The people of Lu were rebuilding the treasury. Min Tzu-ch'ien said, 'Why not simply restore it? Why must it be totally rebuilt?'

The Master said, 'Either this man does not speak or he says something to the point.'

15. The Master said, 'What is Yu's lute doing inside my door?' The disciples ceased to treat Tzu-lu with respect. The Master said, 'Yu may not have entered the inner room, but he has ascended the hall.'

16. Tzu-kung asked, 'Who is superior, Shih or Shang?' The Master said, 'Shih overshoots the mark; Shang falls short.'

'Does that mean that Shih is in fact better?'

The Master said, 'There is little to choose between overshooting the mark and falling short.'

17. The wealth of the Chi Family was greater than that of the Duke of Chou, and still Ch'iu helped them add further to that wealth by raking in the taxes. The Master said, 'He is no disciple of mine. You, my young friends, may attack him openly to the beating of drums.'[8]

18. [The Master said,] 'Ch'ai is stupid; Ts'an is slow; Shih is onesided; Yu is forthright.'

19. The Master said, 'Hui is perhaps difficult to improve upon; he allows himself constantly to be in dire poverty. Ssu refuses to accept his lot and indulges in money making, and is frequently right in his conjectures.'

20. Tzu-chang asked about the way of the good man. The Master

7. This remark seems out of place here. It probably belongs to another context.
8. cf. *Mencius*, IV.A.14.

said, 'Such a man does not follow in other people's footsteps; neither does he gain entrance into the inner room.'⁹

21. The Master said, 'Is one who simply sides with tenacious opinions a gentleman? or is he merely putting on a dignified appearance?'

22. Tzu-lu asked, 'Should one immediately put into practice what one has heard?' The Master said, 'As your father and elder brothers are still alive, you are hardly in a position immediately to put into practice what you have heard.'

Jan Yu asked, 'Should one immediately put into practice what one has heard?' The Master said, 'Yes. One should.'

Kung-hsi Hua said, 'When Yu asked whether one should immediately put into practice what one had heard, you pointed out that his father and elder brothers were alive. Yet when Ch'iu asked whether one should immediately put into practice what one had heard, you answered that one should. I am puzzled. May I be enlightened?'

The Master said, 'Ch'iu holds himself back. It is for this reason that I tried to urge him on. Yu has the energy of two men. It is for this reason that I tried to hold him back.'

23. When the Master was under siege in K'uang, Yen Yüan fell behind. The Master said, 'I thought you had met your death.' 'While you, Master, are alive, how would I dare die?'

24. Chi Tzu-jan asked, 'Can Chung Yu and Jan Ch'iu be called great ministers?'

The Master said, 'I had expected a somewhat different question. It never occurred to me that you were going to ask about Yu and Ch'iu. The term "great minister" refers to those who serve their lord according to the Way and who, when this is no longer possible, relinquish office. Now men like Yu and Ch'iu can be described as ministers appointed to make up the full quota.'

9. For the expression 'inner room' see chapter 15 above.

'In that case, are they the kind that will always do as they are told?'

'No. They will not do so when it comes to patricide or regicide.'

25. On the occasion Tzu-lu made Tzu-kao the prefect of Pi, the Master said, 'He is ruining another man's son.'

Tzu-lu said, 'There are the common people and one's fellow men, and there are the altars to the gods of earth and grain. Why must one have to read books before one is said to learn?'

The Master said, 'It is for this reason that I dislike men who are plausible.'

26. When Tzu-lu, Tseng Hsi, Jan Yu and Kung-hsi Hua were seated in attendance, the Master said, 'Do not feel constrained simply because I am a little older than you are. Now you are in the habit of saying, "My abilities are not appreciated," but if someone did appreciate your abilities, do tell me how you would go about things.'

Tzu-lu promptly answered, 'If I were to administer a state of a thousand chariots, situated between powerful neighbours, troubled by armed invasions and by repeated famines, I could, within three years, give the people courage and a sense of direction.'

The Master smiled at him.

'Ch'iu, what about you?'

'If I were to administer an area measuring sixty or seventy *li* square, or even fifty or sixty *li* square, I could, within three years, bring the size of the population up to an adequate level. As to the rites and music, I would leave that to abler gentlemen.'

'Ch'ih, how about you?'

'I do not say that I already have the ability, but I am ready to learn. On ceremonial occasions in the ancestral temple or in diplomatic gatherings, I should like to assist as a minor official in charge of protocol, properly dressed in my ceremonial cap and robes.'

'Tien, how about you?'

After a few dying notes came the final chord, and then he stood up from his lute. 'I differ from the other three in my choice.'

The Master said, 'What harm is there in that? After all each man is stating what he has set his heart upon.'

'In late spring, after the spring clothes have been newly made, I should like, together with five or six adults and six or seven boys, to go bathing in the River Yi and enjoy the breeze on the Rain Altar, and then to go home chanting poetry.'

The Master sighed and said, 'I am all in favour of Tien.'

When the three left, Tseng Hsi stayed behind. He said, 'What do you think of what the other three said?'

'They were only stating what they had set their hearts upon.'

'Why did you smile at Yu?'

'It is by the rites that a state is administered, but in the way he spoke Yu showed a lack of modesty. That is why I smiled at him.'

'In the case of Ch'iu, was he not concerned with a state?'

'What can justify one in saying that sixty or seventy *li* square or indeed fifty or sixty *li* square do not deserve the name of "state"?'

'In the case of Ch'ih, was he not concerned with a state?'

'What are ceremonial occasions in the ancestral temple and diplomatic gatherings if not matters which concern rulers of feudal states? If Ch'iu plays only a minor part, who would be able to play a major role?'

BOOK XII

1. Yen Yüan asked about benevolence. The Master said, 'To return to the observance of the rites through overcoming the self constitutes benevolence. If for a single day a man could return to the observance of the rites through overcoming himself, then the whole Empire would consider benevolence to be his. However, the practice of benevolence depends on oneself alone, and not on others.'

Yen Yüan said, 'I should like you to list the items.' The Master said, 'Do not look unless it is in accordance with the rites; do not listen unless it is in accordance with the rites; do not speak unless it is in accordance with the rites; do not move unless it is in accordance with the rites.'

Yen Yüan said, 'Though I am not quick, I shall direct my efforts towards what you have said.'

2. Chung-kung asked about benevolence. The Master said, 'When abroad behave as though you were receiving an important guest. When employing the services of the common people behave as though you were officiating at an important sacrifice. Do not impose on others what you yourself do not desire.[1] In this way you will be free from ill will whether in a state or in a noble family.'

Chung-kung said, 'Though I am not quick, I shall direct my efforts towards what you have said.'

3. Ssu-ma Niu asked about benevolence. The Master said, 'The mark of the benevolent man is that he is loath to speak.'

'In that case, can a man be said to be benevolent simply because he is loath to speak?'

The Master said, 'When to act is difficult, is it any wonder that one is loath to speak?'[2]

---

1. This sentence is to be found in XV.24.
2. for fear that one may be unable to live up to one's words. Cf. IV.22, IV.24.

4. Ssu-ma Niu asked about the gentleman. The Master said, 'The gentleman is free from worries and fears.'

'In that case, can a man be said to be a gentleman simply because he is free from worries and fears?'

The Master said, 'If, on examining himself, a man finds nothing to reproach himself for, what worries and fears can he have?'

5. Ssu-ma Niu appeared worried, saying, 'All men have brothers. I alone have none.' Tzu-hsia said, 'I have heard it said: life and death are a matter of Destiny; wealth and honour depend on Heaven. The gentleman is reverent and does nothing amiss, is respectful towards others and observant of the rites, and all within the Four Seas are his brothers. What need is there for the gentleman to worry about not having any brothers?'

6. Tzu-chang asked about perspicacity. The Master said, 'When a man is not influenced by slanders which are assiduously repeated or by complaints for which he feels a direct sympathy, he can be said to be perspicacious. He can at the same time be said to be far-sighted.'

7. Tzu-kung asked about government. The Master said, 'Give them enough food, give them enough arms, and the common people will have trust in you.'

Tzu-kung said, 'If one had to give up one of these three, which should one give up first?'

'Give up arms.'

Tzu-kung said, 'If one had to give up one of the remaining two, which should one give up first?'

'Give up food. Death has always been with us since the beginning of time, but when there is no trust, the common people will have nothing to stand on.'

8. Chi Tzu-ch'eng said, 'The important thing about the gentleman is the stuff he is made of. What does he need refinement for?' Tzu-kung commented, 'It is a pity that the gentleman should have spoken so about the gentleman. "A team of horses cannot catch

up with one's tongue." The stuff is no different from refinement; refinement is no different from the stuff. The pelt of a tiger or a leopard, shorn of hair, is no different from that of a dog or a sheep.'

9. Duke Ai asked Yu Juo, 'The harvest is bad, and I have not sufficient to cover expenditure. What should I do?'

Yu Juo answered, 'What about taxing the people one part in ten?'

'I do not have sufficient as it is when I tax them two parts in ten. How could I possibly tax them one part in ten?'

'When the people have sufficient, who is there to share your insufficiency? When the people have insufficient, who is there to share your sufficiency?'

10. Tzu-chang asked about the exaltation of virtue and the recognition of misguided judgement. The Master said, 'Make it your guiding principle to do your best for others and to be trustworthy in what you say, and move yourself to where rightness is, then you will be exalting virtue. When you love a man you want him to live and when you hate him you want him to die. If, having wanted him to live, you then want him to die, this is misguided judgement.

> If you did not do so for the sake of riches,
> You must have done so for the sake of novelty.'[3]

11. Duke Ching of Ch'i asked Confucius about government. Confucius answered, 'Let the ruler be a ruler, the subject a subject, the father a father, the son a son.' The Duke said, 'Splendid! Truly, if the ruler be not a ruler, the subject not a subject, the father not a father, the son not a son, then even if there be grain, would I get to eat it?'

12. The Master said, 'If anyone can arrive at the truth in a legal dispute on the evidence of only one party, it is, perhaps, Yu.'

Tzu-lu never put off the fulfilment of a promise to the next day.

3. The quotation which is from Ode 188 seems to have no bearing on the subject under discussion. It has been suggested that it does not belong here.

13. The Master said, 'In hearing litigation, I am no different from any other man. But if you insist on a difference, it is, perhaps, that I try to get the parties not to resort to litigation in the first place.'

14. Tzu-chang asked about government. The Master said, 'Over daily routine do not show weariness, and when there is action to be taken, give of your best.'

15. The Master said, 'The gentleman widely versed in culture but brought back to essentials by the rites can, I suppose, be relied upon not to turn against what he stood for.'[4]

16. The Master said, 'The gentleman helps others to realize what is good in them; he does not help them to realize what is bad in them. The small man does the opposite.'

17. Chi K'ang Tzu asked Confucius about government. Confucius answered, 'To govern (*cheng*) is to correct (*cheng*).[5] If you set an example by being correct, who would dare to remain incorrect?'

18. The prevalence of thieves was a source of trouble to Chi K'ang Tzu who asked the advice of Confucius. Confucius answered, 'If you yourself were not a man of desires,[6] no one would steal even if stealing carried a reward.'

19. Chi K'ang Tzu asked Confucius about government, saying, 'What would you think if, in order to move closer to those who possess the Way, I were to kill those who do not follow the Way?'

Confucius answered, 'In administering your government, what need is there for you to kill? Just desire the good yourself and the common people will be good. The virtue of the gentleman is like

4. This is a repetition of VI.27.

5. Besides being homophones, the two words in Chinese are cognate, thus showing that the concept of 'governing' was felt to be related to that of 'correcting'.

6. in other words, if you did not set an example by stealing from the people.

wind; the virtue of the small man is like grass. Let the wind blow over the grass and it is sure to bend.'[7]

20. Tzu-chang asked, 'What must a Gentleman be like before he can be said to have got through?' The Master said, 'What on earth do you mean by getting through?' Tzu-chang answered, 'What I have in mind is a man who is sure to be known whether he serves in a state or in a noble family.' The Master said, 'That is being known, not getting through. Now the term "getting through" describes a man who is straight by nature and fond of what is right, sensitive to other people's words and observant of the expression on their faces, and always mindful of being modest. Such a man is bound to get through whether he serves in a state or in a noble family. On the other hand, the term "being known" describes a man who has no misgivings about his own claim to benevolence when all he is doing is putting up a façade of benevolence which is belied by his deeds. Such a man is sure to be known, whether he serves in a state or in a noble family.'

21. Fan Ch'ih was in attendance during an outing to the Rain Altar. He said, 'May I ask about the exaltation of virtue, the reformation of the depraved and the recognition of misguided judgement?' The Master said, 'What a splendid question! To put service before the reward you get for it, is that not exaltation of virtue?[8] To attack evil as evil and not as evil of a particular man, is that not the way to reform the depraved? To let a sudden fit of anger make you forget the safety of your own person or even that of your parents, is that not misguided judgement?'

22. Fan Ch'ih asked about benevolence. The Master said, 'Love your fellow men.'

He asked about wisdom. The Master said, 'Know your fellow men.' Fan Ch'ih failed to grasp his meaning. The Master said,

7. This saying is quoted in *Mencius*, III.A.2.
8. The two words *te* (to get) and *te* (virtue) seem to be cognate. Virtue is what one makes one's own by the pursuit of the *tao* (Way). (For a discussion of this point in a Taoist context, see the *Tao te ching*, p. 42).

'Raise the straight and set them over the crooked.[9] This can make the crooked straight.'

Fan Ch'ih withdrew and went to see Tzu-hsia, saying, 'Just now, I went to see the Master and asked about wisdom. The Master said, "Raise the straight and set them over the crooked. This can make the crooked straight." What did he mean?'

Tzu-hsia said, 'Rich, indeed, is the meaning of these words. When Shun possessed the Empire, he raised Kao Yao from the multitude and by so doing put those who were not benevolent at a great distance. When T'ang possessed the Empire, he raised Yi Yin from the multitude and by so doing put those who were not benevolent at a great distance.'

23. Tzu-kung asked about how friends should be treated. The Master said, 'Advise them to the best of your ability and guide them properly, but stop when there is no hope of success. Do not ask to be snubbed.'[10]

24. Tseng Tzu said, 'A gentleman makes friends through being cultivated, but looks to friends for support in benevolence.'

9. For this saying, see II.19.
10. cf. IV.26.

BOOK XIII

1. Tzu-lu asked about government. The Master said, 'Encourage the people to work hard by setting an example yourself.' Tzu-lu asked for more. The Master said, 'Do not allow your efforts to slacken.'

2. While he was steward to the Chi Family, Chung-kung asked about government. The Master said, 'Set an example for your officials to follow; show leniency towards minor offenders; and promote men of talent.'

'How does one recognize men of talent to promote?'

The Master said, 'Promote those you do recognize. Do you suppose others will allow those you fail to recognize to be passed over?'

3. Tzu-lu said, 'If the Lord of Wei left the administration (*cheng*) of his state to you, what would you put first?'

The Master said, 'If something has to be put first, it is, perhaps, the rectification (*cheng*)[1] of names.'

Tzu-lu said, 'Is that so? What a roundabout way you take! Why bring rectification in at all?'

The Master said, 'Yu, how boorish you are. Where a gentleman is ignorant, one would expect him not to offer any opinion. When names are not correct, what is said will not sound reasonable; when what is said does not sound reasonable, affairs will not culminate in success; when affairs do not culminate in success, rites and music will not flourish; when rites and music do not flourish, punishments will not fit the crimes; when punishments do not fit the crimes, the common people will not know where to put hand and foot. Thus when the gentleman names something, the name is sure to be usable in speech, and when he says something this is sure to be practicable. The thing about the gentleman is that he is anything but casual where speech is concerned.'

1. For a discussion about the two words pronounced *cheng* see note to XII.17.

4. Fan Ch'ih asked to be taught how to grow crops. The Master said, 'I am not as good as an old farmer.' He asked to be taught how to grow vegetables. 'I am not as good as an old gardener.'

When Fan Ch'ih left, the Master said, 'How petty Fan Hsü is! When those above love the rites, none of the common people will dare be irreverent; when they love what is right, none of the common people will dare be insubordinate; when they love trustworthiness, none of the common people will dare be insincere. In this way, the common people from the four quarters will come with their children strapped on their backs. What need is there to talk about growing crops?'

5. The Master said, 'If a man who knows the three hundred *Odes* by heart fails when given administrative responsibilities and proves incapable of exercising his own initiative when sent to foreign states, then what use are the *Odes* to him, however many he may have learned?'

6. The Master said, 'If a man is correct in his own person, then there will be obedience without orders being given; but if he is not correct in his own person, there will not be obedience even though orders are given.'

7. The Master said, 'In their government the states of Lu and Wei are as alike as brothers.'

8. The Master said about Prince Ching of Wei that he showed a laudable attitude towards a house as a place to live in. When he first had a house, he said, 'It is more or less adequate.' When he had extended it somewhat, he said, 'It has more or less everything.' When it had become sumptuous, he said, 'It is more or less grand enough.'

9. When the Master went to Wei, Jan Yu drove for him. The Master said, 'What a flourishing population!'

Jan Yu said, 'When the population is flourishing, what further benefit can one add?'

'Make the people rich.'

'When the people have become rich, what further benefit can one add?'

'Train them.'[2]

10. The Master said, 'If anyone were to employ me, in a year's time I would have brought things to a satisfactory state, and after three years I should have results to show for it.'

11. The Master said, 'How true is the saying that after a state has been ruled for a hundred years by good men it is possible to get the better of cruelty and to do away with killing.'

12. The Master said, 'Even with a true king it is bound to take a generation for benevolence to become a reality.'

13. The Master said, 'If a man manages to make himself correct, what difficulty will there be for him to take part in government? If he cannot make himself correct, what business has he with making others correct?'[3]

14. Jan Tzu returned from court. The Master said, 'Why so late?' 'There were affairs of state.' The Master said, 'They could only have been routine matters. Were there affairs of state, I would get to hear of them, even though I am no longer given any office.'

15. Duke Ting asked, 'Is there such a thing as a single saying that can lead a state to prosperity?'

Confucius answered, 'A saying cannot quite do that. There is a saying amongst men: "It is difficult to be a ruler, and it is not easy to be a subject either." If the ruler understands the difficulty of being a ruler, then is this not almost a case of a saying leading the state to prosperity?'

'Is there such a thing as a saying that can lead the state to ruin?'

Confucius answered, 'A saying cannot quite do that. There is

2. For the training of the people see chapters 29 and 30 below.
3. For the connection between government and correction see XII.17.

a saying amongst men: "I do not at all enjoy being a ruler, except for the fact that no one goes against what I say." If what he says is good and no one goes against him, good. But if what he says is not good and no one goes against him, then is this not almost a case of a saying leading the state to ruin?'

16. The Governor of She asked about government. The Master said, 'Ensure that those who are near are pleased and those who are far away are attracted.'

17. On becoming prefect of Chü Fu, Tzu-hsia asked about government. The Master said, 'Do not be impatient. Do not see only petty gains. If you are impatient, you will not reach your goal. If you see only petty gains, the great tasks will not be accompished.'

18. The Governor of She said to Confucius, 'In our village there is a man nicknamed "Straight Body". When his father stole a sheep, he gave evidence against him.' Confucius answered, 'In our village those who are straight are quite different. Fathers cover up for their sons, and sons cover up for their fathers. Straightness is to be found in such behaviour.'

19. Fan Ch'ih asked about benevolence. The Master said, 'While at home hold yourself in a respectful attitude; when serving in an official capacity be reverent; when dealing with others do your best. These are qualities that cannot be put aside, even if you go and live among the barbarians.'

20. Tzu-kung asked, 'What must a man be like before he can be said truly to be a Gentleman?' The Master said, 'A man who has a sense of shame in the way he conducts himself and, when sent abroad, does not disgrace the commission of his lord can be said to be a Gentleman.'
  'May I ask about the grade below?'
  'Someone praised for being a good son in his clan and for being a respectful young man in the village.'
  'And the next?'

'A man who insists on keeping his word and seeing his actions through to the end can, perhaps, qualify to come next, even though he shows a stubborn petty-mindedness.'

'What about men who are in public life in the present day?'

The Master said, 'Oh, they are of such limited capacity that they hardly count.'

21. The Master said, 'Having failed to find moderate men for associates, one would, if there were no alternative, have to turn to the undisciplined and the over-scrupulous. The former are enterprising, while the latter will draw the line at certain kinds of action.'

22. The Master said, 'The southerners have a saying: A man devoid of constancy[4] will not make a shaman or a doctor. How well said! "If one does not show constancy in one's virtue, one will, perhaps, suffer shame." '[5] The Master went on to comment, 'The import of the saying is simply that in such a case there is no point in consulting the oracle.'

23. The Master said, 'The gentleman agrees with others without being an echo. The small man echoes without being in agreement.'

24. Tzu-kung asked, ' "All in the village like him." What do you think of that?'

The Master said, 'That is not enough.'

' "All in the village dislike him." What do you think of that?'

The Master said, 'That is not enough either. "Those in his village who are good like him and those who are bad dislike him." That would be better.'

25. The Master said, 'The gentleman is easy to serve but difficult to please. He will not be pleased unless you try to please him by following the Way, but when it comes to employing the services of others, he does so within the limits of their capacity. The small man is difficult to serve but easy to please. He will be pleased

4. cf. VII.26.
5. The text to the third line of hexagram 32 *heng* (constancy).

even though you try to please him by not following the Way, but when it comes to employing the services of others, he demands all-round perfection.'

26. The Master said, 'The gentleman is at ease without being arrogant; the small man is arrogant without being at ease.'

27. The Master said, 'Unbending strength, resoluteness, simplicity and reticence [6] are close to benevolence.'

28. Tzu-lu asked, 'What must a man be like before he deserves to be called a Gentleman?' The Master said, 'One who is, on the one hand, earnest and keen and, on the other, genial deserves to be called a Gentleman – earnest and keen amongst friends and genial amongst brothers.'

29. The Master said, 'After a good man has trained the common people for seven years, they should be ready to take up arms.'

30. The Master said, 'To send the common people to war untrained is to throw them away.'

6. cf. XII.3.

BOOK XIV

1. Hsien asked about the shameful. The Master said, 'It is shameful to make salary your sole object, irrespective of whether the Way prevails in the state or not.'

'Standing firm against the temptation to press one's advantage, to brag about oneself, to harbour grudges or to be covetous may be called "benevolent"?'

The Master said, 'It may be called "difficult", but I don't know about its being benevolent.'

2. The Master said, 'A Gentleman who is attached to a settled home is not worthy of being a Gentleman.'

3. The Master said, 'When the Way prevails in the state, speak and act with perilous high-mindedness; when the Way does not prevail, act with perilous high-mindedness but speak with self-effacing diffidence.'

4. The Master said, 'A man of virtue is sure to be the author of memorable sayings, but the author of memorable sayings is not necessarily virtuous. A benevolent man is sure to possess courage, but a courageous man does not necessarily possess benevolence.'

5. Nan-kung K'uo asked Confucius, 'Both Yi who was good at archery and Ao who could push a boat over dry land met violent deaths, while Yü and Chi who took part in planting the crops gained the Empire.' The Master made no reply.

After Nan-kung K'uo had left, the Master commented, 'How gentlemanly that man is! How he reveres virtue!'

6. The Master said, 'We may take it that there are cases of gentlemen who are unbenevolent, but there is no such thing as a small man who is, at the same time, benevolent.'

7. The Master said, 'Can you love anyone without making him work hard? Can you do your best for anyone without educating him?'

8. The Master said, 'In composing the text of a treaty, P'i Ch'en would write the draft, Shih Shu would make comments, Tzu-yü, the master of protocol, would touch it up and Tzu-ch'an of Tung Li would make embellishments.'

9. Someone asked about Tzu-ch'an. The Master said, 'He was a generous man.' He asked about Tzu-hsi. The Master said, 'That man! That man!' He then asked about Kuan Chung. The Master said, 'He was a man.[1] He took three hundred households from the fief of the Po Family in the city of P'ien, and Po, reduced to living on coarse rice, did not utter a single word of complaint to the end of his days.'

10. The Master said, 'It is more difficult not to complain of injustice when poor than not to behave with arrogance when rich.'

11. The Master said, 'Meng Kung-ch'uo would be more than adequate as steward to great noble families like Chao or Wei, but he would not be suitable as Counsellor even in a small state like T'eng or Hsüeh.'

12. Tzu-lu asked about the complete man.
The Master said, 'A man as wise as Tsang Wu-chung, as free from desires as Meng Kung-ch'uo, as courageous as Chuang-tzu of Pien and as accomplished as Jan Ch'iu, who is further refined by the rites and music, may be considered a complete man.' Then he added, 'But to be a complete man nowadays one need not be all these things. If a man remembers what is right at the sight of profit, is ready to lay down his life in the face of danger, and does not forget sentiments he has repeated all his life even when he has been

1. The text is probably corrupt. In the light of the first answer, an adjective, probably 'benevolent', should precede the word 'man'. See chapters 16 and 17 below where Kuan Chung is said to be 'benevolent'.

in straitened circumstances for a long time, he may be said to be a
complete man.'

13. The Master asked Kung-ming Chia about Kung-shu Wen-tzu,
'Is it true that your Master never spoke, never laughed and never
took anything?'

Kung-ming Chia answered, 'Whoever told you that exaggerated.
My Master spoke only when it was time for him to speak. So people
never grew tired of his speaking. He laughed only when he was
feeling happy. So people never grew tired of his laughing. He
took only when it was right for him to take. So people never grew
tired of his taking.'

The Master said, 'Can that really be the right explanation for
the way he was, I wonder?'

14. The Master said, 'Tsang Wu-chung used his fief to bargain for
a successor to his line. Should it be said that he was not coercing
his lord, I would not believe it.'

15. The Master said, 'Duke Wen of Chin was crafty and lacked
integrity. Duke Huan of Ch'i, on the other hand, had integrity
and was not crafty.'

16. Tzu-lu said, 'When Duke Huan had Prince Chiu killed, Shao
Hu died for the Prince but Kuan Chung failed to do so.' He added,
'In that case, did he fall short of benevolence?' The Master said,
'It was due to Kuan Chung that Duke Huan was able, without a
show of force, to assemble the feudal lords nine times. Such was his
benevolence. Such was his benevolence.'

17. Tzu-kung said, 'I don't suppose Kuan Chung was a benevolent
man. Not only did he not die for Prince Chiu, but he lived to help
Duke Huan who had the Prince killed.'

The Master said, 'Kuan Chung helped Duke Huan to become the
leader of the feudal lords and to save the Empire from collapse. To
this day, the common people still enjoy the benefit of his acts.
Had it not been for Kuan Chung, we might well be wearing our

hair down and folding our robes to the left.² Surely he was not like the common man or woman who, in their petty faithfulness, commit suicide in a ditch without anyone taking any notice.'

18. Counsellor Chuan who had been an official in the household of Kung-shu Wen-tzu was promoted to high office in the state, serving side by side with Kung-shu Wen-tzu. On hearing of this, the Master commented, 'Kung-shu Wen-tzu deserved the epithet "*wen*".'³

19. When the Master spoke of the total lack of moral principle on the part of Duke Ling of Wei, K'ang Tzu commented, 'That being the case, how is it he did not lose his state?'

Confucius said, 'Chung-shu Yü was responsible for foreign visitors, Priest T'uo for the ancestral temple and Wang-sun Chia for military affairs. That being the case, what question could there have been of his losing his state?'

20. The Master said, 'Claims made immodestly are difficult to live up to.'

21. Ch'en Ch'eng Tzu killed Duke Chien. After washing himself ceremonially, Confucius went to court and reported to Duke Ai, saying, 'Ch'en Heng has killed his lord. May I request that an army be sent to punish him?' The Duke answered, 'Tell the three noble lords.'⁴ Confucius said, 'I have reported this to you simply because I have a duty to do so, seeing that I take my place after the Counsellors, and yet you say "Tell the three noble lords."'

He went and reported to the three noble lords, and they refused his request. Confucius said, 'I have reported this to you simply

---

2. i.e., in the fashion of the barbarians.

3. An account of the conferment of the posthumous title "*wen*" on Kung-shu Wen-tzu is to be found in the *T'an kung* chapter of the *Li chi* (*Li chi chu shu*, 10.1a–1b). In the *Yi chou shu*, it is said, among other things, that 'bestowing rank on the common people is called "*wen*"' (p. 196). Cf. note to V.15.

4. i.e., the heads of the three powerful families in Lu.

because I have a duty to do so, seeing that I take my place after the Counsellors.'[5]

22. Tzu-lu asked about the way to serve a lord. The Master said, 'Make sure that you are not being dishonest with him when you stand up to him.'

23. The Master said, 'The gentleman gets through to what is up above; the small man gets through to what is down below.'[6]

24. The Master said, 'Men of antiquity studied to improve themselves; men today study to impress others.'

25. Ch'ü Po-yü sent a messenger to Confucius. Confucius sat with him and asked him, 'What does your master do?' He answered, 'My master seeks to reduce his errors but has not been able to do so.'

When the messenger had left, the Master commented, 'What a messenger! What a messenger!'

26. The Master said, 'Do not concern yourself with matters of government unless they are the responsibility of your office.'[7]

Tseng Tzu commented, 'The gentleman does not allow his thoughts to go beyond his office.'

27. The Master said, 'The gentleman is ashamed of his word outstripping[9] his deed.'

28. The Master said, 'There are three things constantly on the lips of the gentleman none of which I have succeeded in following: "A man of benevolence never worries;[8] a man of wisdom is never in two minds;[9] a man of courage is never afraid." '[10] Tzu-kung said, 'What the Master has just quoted is a description of himself.'

5. The incident is recorded in the *Tso chuan* (*Tso chuan chu shu*, 59.19a–19b).
6. cf. chapter 35 below.
7. This saying is also found in VIII.14.
8. about the future.
9. about right and wrong.
10. cf. IX.29.

29. Tzu-kung was given to grading people. The Master said, 'How superior Ssu is! For my part I have no time for such things.'

30. The Master said, 'It is not the failure of others to appreciate your abilities that should trouble you,[11] but rather your own lack of them.'

31. The Master said, 'Is a man not superior who, without anticipating attempts at deception or presuming acts of bad faith, is, nevertheless, the first to be aware of such behaviour?'

32. Wei-sheng Mu said to Confucius, 'Ch'iu, why are you so restless? Are you, perhaps, trying to practise flattery?'

Confucius answered, 'I am not so impertinent as to practise flattery. It is just that I so detest inflexibility.'

33. The Master said, 'A good horse is praised for its virtue, not for its strength.'

34. Someone said,

'Repay an injury with a good turn.[12]

What do you think of this saying?'

The Master said, 'What, then, do you repay a good turn with? You repay an injury with straightness, but you repay a good turn with a good turn.'

35. The Master said, 'There is no one who understands me.' Tzu-kung said, 'How is it that there is no one who understands you?' The Master said, 'I do not complain against Heaven, nor do I blame Man. In my studies, I start from below and get through to what is up above. If I am understood at all, it is, perhaps, by Heaven.'

36. Kung-po Liao spoke ill of Tzu-lu to Chi-Sun. Tzu-fu Ching-po

11. This sentence is to be found in I.16.

12. cf. 'Do good to him who has done you an injury.' (*Tao te ching*, ch. 63, p. 124)

reported this, saying, 'My master shows definite signs of being swayed by Kung-po Liao, but I still have enough influence to have his carcass exposed in the market place.'

The Master said, 'It is Destiny if the Way prevails; it is equally Destiny if the Way falls into disuse. What can Kung-po Liao do in defiance of Destiny?'

37. The Master said, 'Men who shun the world come first; those who shun a particular place come next; those who shun a hostile look come next; those who shun hostile words come last.'

The Master said, 'There were seven who arose.'[13]

38. Tzu-lu put up for the night at the Stone Gate. The gatekeeper said, 'Where have you come from?' Tzu-lu said, 'From the K'ung family.' 'Is that the K'ung who keeps working towards a goal the realization of which he knows to be hopeless?'

39. While the Master was playing the stone chimes in Wei, a man who passed in front of the door, carrying a basket, said, 'The way he plays the stone chimes is fraught with frustrated purpose.' Presently he added, 'How squalid this stubborn sound is. If no one understands him,[14] then he should give up, that is all.

> When the water is deep, go across by wading;
> When it is shallow, lift your hem and cross.'[15]

The Master said, 'That would be resolute indeed. Against such resoluteness there can be no argument.'

40. Tzu-chang said, 'The *Book of History* says,

Kao Tsung confined himself to his mourning hut, and for three years remained silent.[16]

What does this mean?'

13. This saying must have become detached from its proper context, as it makes little sense here.
14. cf. chapter 35 above.
15. Ode 54.
16. *Shu ching chu shu*, 16.10b.

The Master said, 'There is no need to go to Kao Tsung for an example. This was always so amongst men of antiquity. When the ruler died, all the officials joined together and placed themselves under the prime minister and, for three years, accepted his command.'

41. The Master said, 'When those above are given to the observance of the rites, the common people will be easy to command.'[17]

42. Tzu-lu asked about the gentleman. The Master said, 'He cultivates himself and thereby achieves reverence.'

'Is that all?'

'He cultivates himself and thereby brings peace and security to his fellow men.'

'Is that all?'

'He cultivates himself and thereby brings peace and security to the people. Even Yao and Shun would have found the task of bringing peace and security to the people taxing.'

43. Yüan Jang sat waiting with his legs spread wide. The Master said, 'To be neither modest nor deferential when young, to have passed on nothing worthwhile when grown up, and to refuse to die when old, that is what I call a pest.' So saying, the Master tapped him on the shin with his stick.

44. After a boy of Ch'üeh Tang had announced a visitor, someone asked about him, saying, 'Is he one who is likely to make progress?' The Master said, 'I have seen him presume to take a seat and to walk abreast his seniors. He does not want to make progress. He is after quick results.'

17. cf. XIII.4.

BOOK XV

1. Duke Ling of Wei asked Confucius about military formations. Confucius answered, 'I have, indeed, heard something about the use of sacrificial vessels, but I have never studied the matter of commanding troops.' The next day he departed.

2. In Ch'en when provisions ran out the followers[1] had become so weak that none of them could rise to their feet. Tzu-lu, with resentment written all over his face, said, 'Are there times when even gentlemen are brought to such extreme straits?' The Master said, 'It comes as no surprise to the gentleman to find himself in extreme straits. The small man finding himself in extreme straits would throw over all restraint.'

3. The Master said, 'Ssu, do you think that I am the kind of man who learns widely and retains what he has learned in his mind?'
   'Yes, I do. Is it not so?'
   'No. I have a single thread binding it all together.'[2]

4. The Master said, 'Yu, rare are those who understand virtue.'

5. The Master said, 'If there was a ruler who achieved order without taking any action, it was, perhaps, Shun. There was nothing for him to do but to hold himself in a respectful posture and to face due south.'[3]

6. Tzu-chang asked about going forward without obstruction. The Master said, 'If in word you are conscientious and trustworthy and in deed singleminded and reverent, then even in the lands of the barbarians you will go forward without obstruction. But if you fail

1. of Confucius.
2. cf. IV.15.
3. The seat of the emperor faces south.

to be conscientious and trustworthy in word or to be singleminded and reverent in deed, then can you be sure of going forward without obstruction even in your own neighbourhood? When you stand you should have this ideal there in front of you, and when you are in your carriage you should see it leaning against the handle-bar. Only then are you sure to go forward without obstruction.'

Tzu-chang wrote this down on his sash.

7. The Master said, 'How straight Shih Yü is! When the Way prevails in the state he is as straight as an arrow, yet when the Way falls into disuse in the state he is still as straight as an arrow.

'How gentlemanly Ch'ü Po-yü is! When the Way prevails in the state he takes office, but when the Way falls into disuse in the state he allows himself to be furled and put away safely.'

8. The Master said, 'To fail to speak to a man who is capable of benefiting is to let a man go to waste. To speak to a man who is incapable of benefiting is to let one's words go to waste. A wise man lets neither men nor words go to waste.'

9. The Master said, 'For Gentlemen of purpose and men of benevolence while it is inconceivable that they should seek to stay alive at the expense of benevolence, it may happen that they have to accept death in order to have benevolence accomplished.'

10. Tzu-kung asked about the practice of benevolence. The Master said, 'A craftsman who wishes to practise his craft well must first sharpen his tools. You should, therefore, seek the patronage of the most distinguished Counsellors and make friends with the most benevolent Gentlemen in the state where you happen to be staying.'

11. Yen Yüan asked about the government of a state. The Master said, 'Follow the calendar of the Hsia, ride in the carriage of the Yin, and wear the ceremonial cap of the Chou, but, as for music, adopt the *shao* and the *wu*.[4][10] Banish the tunes of Cheng and

4. For *shao* and *wu* see III.25.

keep plausible men at a distance. The tunes of Cheng are wanton and plausible men are dangerous.'

12. The Master said, 'He who gives no thought to difficulties in the future is sure to be beset by worries much closer at hand.'

13. The Master said, 'I suppose I should give up hope. I have yet to meet the man who is as fond of virtue as he is of beauty in women.'

14. The Master said, 'Has Tsang Wen-chung not occupied a position he is not entitled to? He knew the excellence of Liu Hsia Hui and yet would not yield to him his position.' 5

15. The Master said, 'If one sets strict standards for oneself and makes allowances for others when making demands on them, one will stay clear of ill will.'

16. The Master said, 'There is nothing I can do with a man who is not constantly saying, "What am I to do? What am I to do?"'

17. The Master said, 'It is quite a remarkable feat for a group of men who are together all day long merely to indulge themselves in acts of petty cleverness without ever touching on the subject of morality in their conversation!'

18. The Master said, 'The gentleman has morality as his basic stuff and by observing the rites puts it into practice, by being modest gives it expression, and by being trustworthy in word brings it to completion. Such is a gentleman indeed!'

19. The Master said, 'The gentleman is troubled by his own lack of ability, not by the failure of others to appreciate him.' 6

5. This remark by Confucius, in a slightly different form, is also found in the *Tso chuan* (*Tso chuan chu shu*, 18.14a–b).
6. cf. XIV.30.

20. The Master said, 'The gentleman hates not leaving behind a name when he is gone.'

21. The Master said, 'What the gentleman seeks, he seeks within himself; what the small man seeks, he seeks in others.'

22. The Master said, 'The gentleman is conscious of his own superiority without being contentious, and comes together with other gentlemen without forming cliques.'

23. The Master said, 'The gentleman does not recommend a man on account of what he says, neither does he dismiss what is said on account of the speaker.'

24. Tzu-kung asked, 'Is there a single word which can be a guide to conduct throughout one's life?' The Master said, 'It is perhaps the word "*shu*".[7] Do not impose on others what you yourself do not desire.'

25. The Master said, 'Whom have I ever praised or condemned? If there is anyone I praised, you may be sure that he had been put to the test. These common people are the touchstone by which the Three Dynasties were kept to the straight path.'

26. The Master said, 'I am old enough to have seen scribes who lacked refinement. Those who had horses would permit others to drive them.[8] Nowadays, there are, I suppose, no longer such cases.'

27. The Master said, 'Artful words will ruin one's virtue; the lack of self-restraint in small matters will bring ruin to great plans.'

7. i.e., using oneself as a measure in gauging the wishes of others. Cf. VI.30 and IV.15. It is interesting to note that in V.12 when Tzu-kung remarked that if he did not wish others to impose on him neither did he wish to impose on others, Confucius' comment was that this was beyond his ability.

8. One's carriages and horses are not things one should lightly permit others to use. To do so shows, therefore, a lack of refinement. This, as far as I can understand it, is the interpretation proposed by Professor Chow Tse-tsung. (See his '*Shuo "shih chih ch'üeh wen"*', *Ta lu tsa chih*, XXXVII.4, 1968, pp. 1–16).

28. The Master said, 'Be sure to go carefully into the case of the man who is disliked by the multitude. Be sure to go carefully into the case of the man who is liked by the multitude.'[9]

29. The Master said, 'It is Man who is capable of broadening the Way. It is not the Way that is capable of broadening Man.'

30. The Master said, 'Not to mend one's ways when one has erred is to err indeed.'

31. The Master said, 'I once spent all day thinking without taking food and all night thinking without going to bed, but I found that I gained nothing from it. It would have been better for me to have spent the time in learning.'

32. The Master said, 'The gentleman devotes his mind to attaining the Way and not to securing food. Go and till the land and you will end up by being hungry, as a matter of course; study, and you will end up with the salary of an official, as a matter of course. The gentleman worries about the Way, not about poverty.'

33. The Master said, 'What is within the reach of a man's understanding but beyond the power of his benevolence to keep is something he will lose even if he acquires it. A man may be wise enough to attain it and benevolent enough to keep it, but if he does not rule over them with dignity, then the common people will not be reverent. A man may be wise enough to attain it, benevolent enough to keep it and may govern the people with dignity, but if he does not set them to work in accordance with the rites, he is still short of perfection.'

34. The Master said, 'The gentleman cannot be appreciated in small things but is acceptable in great matters. A small man is not acceptable in great matters but can be appreciated in small things.'

35. The Master said, 'Benevolence is more vital to the common

9. cf. XIII.24.

people than even fire and water. In the case of fire and water, I have seen men die by stepping on them, but I have never seen any man die by stepping on benevolence.'

36. The Master said, 'When faced with the opportunity to practise benevolence do not give precedence even to your teacher.'

37. The Master said, 'The gentleman is devoted to principle but not inflexible in small matters.'

38. The Master said, 'In serving one's lord, one should approach one's duties with reverence and consider one's pay as of secondary importance.'

39. The Master said, 'In instruction there is no separation into categories.'

40. The Master said, 'There is no point in people taking counsel together who follow different ways.'

41. The Master said, 'It is enough that the language one uses gets the point across.'

42. Mien, the Master Musician,[10] called. When he came to the steps, the Master said, 'You have reached the steps,' and when he came to the mat, the Master said, 'You have reached the mat.' When everyone was seated, the Master told him, 'This is So-and-so and that is So-and-so over there.'

After the Master Musician had gone, Tzu-chang asked, 'Is that the way to talk to a musician?' The Master said, 'Yes. That is the way to assist a musician.'

10. In this period the musical profession was confined to the blind.

BOOK XVI

1. The head of the Chi Family was going to launch an attack on Chuan Yü. Jan Yu and Chi-lu went to see Confucius and said, 'The Chi are going to take action against Chuan Yü.'

Confucius said, 'Ch'iu, surely it is you who are at fault? Formerly, a royal ancestor of ours gave Chuan Yü the responsibility of sacrificing to the Tung Meng Mountain; moreover, their territory now lies within our boundaries. Thus they are a bulwark of the state. What reason can there be to attack them?'

Jan Yu said, 'It is what our master wishes. Neither of us is in favour of it.'

Confucius said, 'Ch'iu, there is a saying of Chou Jen's which goes: let men who have strength to display join the ranks, let those who lack the strength give up their places. What use to a blind man is the assistant who does not steady him when he totters or support him when he falls. Moreover, what you said is quite wrong. Whose fault is it when the tiger and the rhinoceros escape from their cages or when the tortoise shell and the jade are destroyed in their caskets?'

Jan Yu said, 'But Chuan Yü is strongly fortified and close to Pi. If it is not taken now, it is sure to be a source of trouble for the descendants of our master in the future.'

Confucius said, 'Ch'iu, the gentleman detests those who, rather than saying outright that they want something, can be counted on to gloss over their remarks. What I have heard is that the head of a state or a noble family worries not about underpopulation but about uneven distribution, not about poverty but about instability.[1] For where there is even distribution there is no such thing as poverty, where there is harmony there is no such thing as underpopulation and where there is stability there is no such thing as

1. The text is corrupt here. In the light of what follows, this passage should, probably, read: ' . . . worries not about poverty but about uneven distribution, not about underpopulation but about disharmony, not about overturning but about instability'.

overturning. It is for this reason that when distant subjects are unsubmissive one cultivates one's moral quality in order to attract them, and once they have come one makes them content. But you and Yu have not been able either to help your master to attract the distant subjects when they are unsubmissive or to preserve the state when it is disintegrating. Instead, you propose to resort to the use of arms within the state itself. I am afraid that Chi-sun's worries lie not in Chuan Yü but within the walls of his palace.'

2. Confucius said, 'When the Way prevails in the Empire, the rites and music and punitive expeditions are initiated by the Emperor. When the Way does not prevail in the Empire, they are initiated by the feudal lords. When they are initiated by the feudal lords, it is surprising if power does not pass from the Emperor within ten generations. When they are initiated by the Counsellors, it is surprising if power does not pass from the feudal lords within five generations. When the prerogative to command in a state is in the hands of officials of the Counsellors it is surprising if power does not pass from the Counsellors within three generations. When the Way prevails in the Empire, policy does not rest with the Counsellors. When the Way prevails in the Empire, the Commoners do not express critical views.'

3. Confucius said, 'It is five generations since patronage passed out of the control of the Ducal House. It is four generations since government came under the control of the Counsellors. For this reason the descendants of the three houses of Huan are on the decline.'[2]

4. Confucius said, 'He stands to benefit who makes friends with three kinds of people. Equally, he stands to lose who makes friends with three other kinds of people. To make friends with the straight, the trustworthy in word and the well-informed is to benefit. To make friends with the ingratiating in action, the pleasant in appearance and the plausible in speech is to lose.'

2. The logic that leads to this conclusion is somewhat obscure in the light of the previous chapter.

5. Confucius said, 'He stands to benefit who takes pleasure in three kinds of things. Equally, he stands to lose who takes pleasure in three other kinds of things. To take pleasure in the correct regulation of the rites and music, in singing the praises of other men's goodness and in having a large number of excellent men as friends is to benefit. To take pleasure in showing off, in a dissolute life and in food and drink is to lose.'

6. Confucius said, 'When in attendance upon a gentleman one is liable to three errors. To speak before being spoken to by the gentleman is rash; not to speak when spoken to by him is to be evasive; to speak without observing the expression on his face is to be blind.'

7. Confucius said, 'There are three things the gentleman should guard against. In youth when the blood and *ch'i* [3] are still unsettled he should guard against the attraction of feminine beauty. In the prime of life when the blood and *ch'i* have become unyielding, he should guard against bellicosity. In old age when the blood and *ch'i* have declined, he should guard against acquisitiveness.'

8. Confucius said, 'The gentleman stands in awe of three things. He is in awe of the Decree of Heaven. He is in awe of great men. He is in awe of the words of the sages. The small man, being ignorant of the Decree of Heaven, does not stand in awe of it. He treats great men with insolence and the words of the sages with derision.'

9. Confucius said, 'Those who are born with knowledge are the highest. Next come those who attain knowledge through study. Next again come those who turn to study after having been vexed by difficulties. The common people, in so far as they make no effort to study even after having been vexed by difficulties, are the lowest.'

10. Confucius said, 'There are nine things the gentleman turns his thought to: to seeing clearly when he uses his eyes, to hearing acutely

3. *Ch'i* is the basic constituent of the universe. The refined *ch'i* fills the human body and, amongst other things, circulates with the blood.

when he uses his ears, to looking cordial when it comes to his countenance, to appearing respectful when it comes to his demeanour, to being conscientious when he speaks, to being reverent when he performs his duties, to seeking advice when he is in doubt, to the consequences when he is enraged, and to what is right at the sight of gain.'

11. Confucius said, '"Seeing what is good I act as if I were in danger of being left behind; seeing what is not good I act as if I were testing hot water." I have met such a man; I have heard such a claim.

'"I live in retirement in order to attain my purpose and practise what is right in order to realize my way." I have heard such a claim, but I have yet to meet such a man.'

12. Duke Ching of Ch'i had a thousand teams of four horses each, but on his death the common people were unable to find[12] anything to praise him for, whereas Po Yi and Shu Ch'i starved under Mount Shou Yang and yet to this day the common people still sing their praises. This is probably what is meant.[4]

13. Ch'en Kang asked Po-yü, 'Have you not been taught anything out of the ordinary?'

'No, I have not. Once my father was standing by himself. As I crossed the courtyard with quickened steps,[5] he said, "Have you studied the *Odes*?" I answered, "No." "Unless you study the *Odes* you will be ill-equipped to speak." I retired and studied the *Odes*.

'Another day, my father was again standing by himself. As I crossed the courtyard with quickened steps, he said, "Have you studied the rites?" I answered, "No." "Unless you study the rites you will be ill-equipped to take your stand." I retired and studied the rites. I have been taught these two things.'

4. This chapter is obviously defective. The beginning seems missing. Hence no speaker is mentioned. Neither is there any saying to which the final sentence can refer.

5. as a sign of respect.

Ch'en Kang retired delighted and said, 'I asked one question and got three answers. I learned about the *Odes*, I learned about the rites and I learned that a gentleman keeps aloof from his son.'

14. The lord of a state uses the term 'lady' for his wife. She uses the term 'little boy' for herself. The people of the state refer to her by the term 'the lady of the lord', but when abroad they use the term 'the little lord'. People of other states also refer to her by the term 'the lady of the lord.'[6]

6. This is probably a ritual text which was copied into the blank space at the end of this scroll, and has nothing to do with the rest of the book.

BOOK XVII

1. Yang Huo wanted to see Confucius, and when Confucius refused to go and see him he sent Confucius a present of a piglet.[1]

Confucius had someone keep watch on Yang Huo's house, and went to pay his respects during his absence. On the way he happened to meet Yang Huo who said to him, 'Come now. I will speak with you.' Then he went on, 'Can the man be said to be benevolent who, while hoarding his treasure, allows the state to go astray? I should say not. Can the man be said to be wise who, while eager to take part in public life, constantly misses the opportunity? I should say not. The days and the months slip by. Time is not on our side.' Confucius said, 'All right. I shall take office.'

2. The Master said, 'Men are close to one another by nature. They diverge as a result of repeated practice.'

3. The Master said, 'It is only the most intelligent and the most stupid who are not susceptible to change.'

4. The Master went to Wu Ch'eng. There he heard the sound of stringed instruments and singing. The Master broke into a smile and said, 'Surely you don't need to use an ox-knife to kill a chicken.'

Tzu-yu answered, 'Some time ago I heard it from you, Master, that the gentleman instructed in the Way loves his fellow men and that the small man instructed in the Way is easy to command.'

The Master said, 'My friends, what Yen says is right. My remark a moment ago was only made in jest.'

5. Kung-shan Fu-jao, using Pi as a stronghold, staged a revolt.[2] He summoned the Master and the Master wanted to go.

---

1. According to a version of this story in the *Mencius*, III.B.7, it was 'a steamed piglet' (p. 112).

2. against the Chi Family, perhaps under the pretext of restoring power to the Duke of Lu.

Tzu-lu was displeased and said, 'We may have nowhere to go, but why must we go to Kung-shan?'

The Master said, 'The man who summons me must have a purpose. If his purpose is to employ me, can I not, perhaps, create another Chou in the east?'

6. Tzu-chang asked Confucius about benevolence. Confucius said, 'There are five things and whoever is capable of putting them into practice in the Empire is certainly "benevolent".'

'May I ask what they are?'

'They are respectfulness, tolerance, trustworthiness in word, quickness and generosity. If a man is respectful he will not be treated with insolence. If he is tolerant he will win the multitude. If he is trustworthy in word his fellow men will entrust him with responsibility. If he is quick he will achieve results. If he is generous he will be good enough to be put in a position over his fellow men.'

7. Pi Hsi summoned the Master and the Master wanted to go.

Tzu-lu said, 'Some time ago I heard it from you, Master, that the gentleman does not enter the domain of one who in his own person does what is not good. Now Pi Hsi is using Chung Mou as a stronghold to stage a revolt. How can you justify going there?'

The Master said, 'It is true, I did say that. But has it not been said, "Hard indeed is that which can withstand grinding"? Has it not been said, "White indeed is that which can withstand black dye"? Moreover, how can I allow myself to be treated like a gourd which, instead of being eaten, hangs from the end of a string?'

8. The Master said, 'Yu, have you heard about the six qualities and the six attendant faults?'

'No.'

'Be seated and I shall tell you. To love benevolence without loving learning is liable to lead to foolishness. To love cleverness without loving learning is liable to lead to deviation from the right path. To love trustworthiness in word without loving learning is liable to lead to harmful behaviour. To love forthrightness without loving learning is liable to lead to intolerance. To love courage without loving learning is liable to lead to insubordination. To love unbending strength without loving learning is liable to lead to indiscipline.'[3]

9. The Master said, 'Why is it none of you, my young friends, study the *Odes*? An apt quotation from the *Odes* may serve to stimulate the imagination, to show one's breeding, to smooth over difficulties in a group and to give expression to complaints.

'Inside the family there is the serving of one's father; outside, there is the serving of one's lord; there is also the acquiring of a wide knowledge of the names of birds and beasts, plants and trees.'[4]

10. The Master said to Po-yü, 'Have you studied the *Chou nan* and *Shao nan*?[5] To be a man and not to study them is, I would say, like standing with one's face directly towards the wall.'[6]

11. The Master said, 'Surely when one says "The rites, the rites," it is not enough merely to mean presents of jade and silk. Surely when one says "Music, music," it is not enough merely to mean bells and drums.'[7]

12. The Master said, 'A cowardly man who puts on a brave front is, when compared to small men, like the burglar who breaks in or climbs over walls.'

13. The Master said, 'The village worthy is the ruin of virtue.'[8]

3. cf. VIII.2.
4. To these activities the study of the *Odes* must, presumably, be relevant, but the point is not explicitly made. This is very likely due to some corruption in the text.
5. These are the opening sections of the *Book of Odes*.
6. cf. XVI.13.
7. cf. III.3.
8. For Mencius' elaboration on this saying, see the *Mencius*, VII.B.37 (p. 203).

14. The Master said, 'The gossip-monger is the outcast of virtue.'

15. The Master said, 'Is it really possible to work side by side with a mean fellow in the service of a lord? Before he gets what he wants, he worries lest he should not[12] get it. After he has got it, he worries lest he should lose it, and when that happens he will not stop at anything.'

16. The Master said, 'In antiquity, the common people had three weaknesses, but today they cannot be counted on to have even these. In antiquity, in their wildness men were impatient of restraint; today, in their wildness they simply deviate from the right path. In antiquity, in being conceited, men were uncompromising; today, in being conceited, they are simply ill-tempered. In antiquity, in being foolish, men were straight; today, in being foolish, they are simply crafty.'

17. The Master said, 'It is rare, indeed, for a man with cunning words and an ingratiating face to be benevolent.'9

18. The Master said, 'I detest purple for displacing vermillion. I detest the tunes of Cheng for corrupting classical music.10 I detest clever talkers who overturn states and noble families.'

19. The Master said, 'I am thinking of giving up speech.' Tzu-kung said, 'If you did not speak, what would there be for us, your disciples, to transmit?' The Master said, 'What does Heaven ever say? Yet there are the four seasons going round and there are the hundred things coming into being. What does Heaven ever say?'

20. Ju Pei wanted to see Confucius. Confucius declined to see him on the grounds of illness. As soon as the man conveying the message

9. This forms part of I.3.
10. According to the traditional interpretation, vermillion is a pure colour while purple is a mixed colour, but by Confucius' time the practice of using purple in place of vermillion was becoming widespread. For Confucius' condemnation of the music of Cheng see V.11.

had stepped out of the door, Confucius took his lute and sang, making sure that he heard it.

21. Tsai Wo asked about the three-year mourning period, saying, 'Even a full year is too long. If the gentleman gives up the practice of the rites for three years, the rites are sure to be in ruins; if he gives up the practice of music for three years, music is sure to collapse. A full year's mourning is quite enough. After all, in the course of a year, the old grain having been used up, the new grain ripens, and fire is renewed by fresh drilling.'[11]

The Master said, 'Would you, then, be able to enjoy eating your rice[12] and wearing your finery?'

'Yes. I would.'

'If you are able to enjoy them, do so by all means. The gentleman in mourning finds no relish in good food, no pleasure in music, and no comforts in his own home. That is why he does not eat his rice and wear his finery. Since it appears that you enjoy them, then do so by all means.'

After Tsai Wo had left, the Master said, 'How unfeeling Yü is. A child ceases to be nursed by his parents only when he is three years old. Three years' mourning is observed throughout the Empire. Was Yü not given three years' love by his parents?'

22. The Master said, 'It is no easy matter for a man who always has a full stomach to put his mind to some use. Are there not such things as *po* and *yi*?[13] Even playing these games is better than being idle.'

23. Tzu-lu said, 'Does the gentleman consider courage a supreme quality?' The Master said, 'For the gentleman it is morality that is

11. A different kind of wood is used for each of the four seasons so that the same wood is used again after a full year. This practice, presumably, had a ritual significance.

12. Rice was a luxury with millet being the staple food.

13. While *yi* is the game known as *wei ch'i* (*go* in Japanese) in later ages, *po* is believed to have been a board game in which the moves of the pieces are decided by a throw of dice.

supreme. Possessed of courage but devoid of morality, a gentleman will make trouble while a small man will be a brigand.'

24. Tzu-kung said, 'Does even the gentleman have dislikes?' The Master said, 'Yes. The gentleman has his dislikes. He dislikes those who proclaim the evil in others. He dislikes those who, being in inferior positions, slander their superiors. He dislikes those who, while possessing courage, lack the spirit of the rites. He dislikes those whose resoluteness is not tempered by understanding.'

The Master added, 'Do you, Ssu, have your dislikes as well?'

'I dislike those in whom plagiarizing passes for wisdom. I dislike those in whom insolence passes for courage. I dislike those in whom exposure of others passes for forthrightness.'

25. The Master said, 'In one's household, it is the women and the small men that are difficult to deal with. If you let them get too close, they become insolent. If you keep them at a distance, they complain.'

26. The Master said, 'If by the age of forty a man is still disliked there is no hope for him.'

BOOK XVIII

1. The Viscount of Wei left him, the Viscount of Chi became a slave on account of him and Pi Kan lost his life for remonstrating with him.[1] Confucius commented, 'There were three benevolent men in the Yin.'

2. Liu Hsia Hui was dismissed three times when he was judge. Someone said, 'Is it not time for you to leave?' 'If, in the service of another, one is not prepared to bend the Way, where can one go without being dismissed three times? If, in the service of another, one is prepared to bend the Way, what need is there to leave the country of one's father and mother?'

3. In considering the treatment he should accord Confucius, Duke Ching of Ch'i said, 'I am unable to accord him such exalted treatment as the Chi Family receives.'[2] So he placed him somewhere between the Chi and the Meng,[3] saying, 'I am getting old. I am afraid I will not be able to put his talents to use.' Confucius departed.

4. The men of Ch'i made a present of singing and dancing girls. Chi Huan Tzu accepted them and stayed away from court for three days. Confucius departed.

5. Chieh Yü, the Madman of Ch'u, went past Confucius, singing,

> Phoenix, oh phoenix!
> How thy virtue has declined!
> What is past is beyond help,
> What is to come is not yet lost.
> Give up, give up!
> Perilous is the lot of those in office today.

1. i.e., the tyrant Chou.
2. in Lu.
3. Both the Chi and the Meng were noble families in Lu.

Confucius got down from his carriage with the intention of speaking with him, but the Madman avoided him by hurrying off, and in the end Confucius was unable to speak with him.

6. Ch'ang Chü and Chieh Ni were ploughing together yoked as a team. Confucius went past them and sent Tzu-lu to ask them where the ford was. Ch'ang Chü said, 'Who is that taking charge of the carriage?'[4] Tzu-lu said, 'It is K'ung Ch'iu.' 'Then, he must be the K'ung Ch'iu of Lu.' 'He is.' 'Then, he doesn't have to ask where the ford is.'

Tzu-lu asked Chieh Ni. Chieh Ni said, 'Who are you?' 'I am Chung Yu.' 'Then, you must be the disciple of K'ung Ch'iu of Lu?' Tzu-lu answered, 'I am.' 'Throughout the Empire men are all the same. Who is there for you[5] to change places with? Moreoever, for your own sake, would it not be better if, instead of following a Gentleman who keeps running away from men,[6] you followed one who runs away from the world altogether?'[7] All this while he carried on harrowing without interruption.

Tzu-lu went and reported what was said to Confucius.

The Master was lost in thought for a while and said, 'One cannot associate with birds and beasts. Am I not a member of this human race? Who, then, is there for me to associate with? While the Way is to be found in the Empire, I will not change places with him.'

7. Tzu-lu, when travelling with [Confucius], fell behind. He met an old man, carrying a basket on a staff over his shoulder.

Tzu-lu asked, 'Have you seen my Master?'

The old man said, 'You seem neither to have toiled with your limbs nor to be able to tell one kind of grain from another. Who may your Master be?' He planted his staff in the ground and started weeding.

Tzu-lu stood, cupping one hand respectfully in the other.

4. The expression *chih yü* is obscure and is likely to be corrupt.
5. taking *erh* as 'you'.
6. meaning Confucius.
7. meaning himself.

The old man invited Tzu-lu to stay for the night. He killed a chicken and prepared some millet for his guest to eat, and presented his two sons to him.

The next day, Tzu-lu resumed his journey and reported this conversation. The Master said, 'He must be a recluse.' He sent Tzu-lu back to see him again. When he arrived, the old man had departed.

Tzu-lu commented, 'Not to enter public life is to ignore one's duty. Even the proper regulation of old and young cannot be set aside. How, then, can the duty between ruler and subject be set aside? This is to cause confusion in the most important of human relationships simply because one desires to keep unsullied one's character. The gentleman takes office in order to do his duty. As for putting the Way into practice, he knows all along that it is hopeless.'[8]

8. Men who withdrew from society: Po Yi, Shu Ch'i, Yü Chung, Yi Yi, Chu Chang, Liu Hsia Hui, Shao Lien. The Master commented, 'Not to lower their purpose or to allow themselves to be humiliated describes, perhaps, Po Yi and Shu Ch'i.' Of Liu Hsia Hui and Shao Lien he said, 'They, indeed, lowered their purpose and allowed themselves to be humiliated, but their words were consistent with their station, and their deeds with circumspection. That was all.' Of Yü Chung and Yi Yi he said, 'They gave free rein to their words while living as recluses, but they were unsullied in character and showed sound judgement in accepting their dismissal. I, however, am different. I have no preconceptions about the permissible and the impermissible.'

9. Chih, the Grand Musician, left for Ch'i; Kan, musician for the second course, left for Ch'u; Liao, musician for the third course, left for Ts'ai; Ch'üeh, musician for the fourth course, left for Ch'in; Fang Shu the drummer crossed the River; Wu, player of the hand-drum, crossed the River Han; Yang, the Grand Musician's deputy, and Hsiang who played the stone chimes crossed the sea.

8. cf. XIV.38.

10. The Duke of Chou said to the Duke of Lu,[9] 'The gentleman does not treat those closely related to him casually[*13*], nor does he give his high officials occasion to complain because their advice was not heeded. Unless there are grave reasons, he does not abandon officials of long standing. He does not look for all-round perfection in a single person.'[10]

11. There were eight Gentlemen in Chou: Po Ta, Po K'uo, Chung T'u, Chung Hu, Shu Yeh, Shu Hsia, Chi Sui and Chi K'uo.

9. his son.
10. cf. XIII.25.

BOOK XIX

1. Tzu-chang said, 'One can, perhaps, be satisfied with a Gentleman who is ready to lay down his life in the face of danger, who does not forget what is right at the sight of gain,[1] and who does not forget reverence during a sacrifice nor sorrow while in mourning.'

2. Tzu-chang said, 'How can a man be said either to have anything or not to have anything who fails to hold on to virtue with all his might[14] or to believe in the Way with all his heart.'

3. Tzu-hsia's disciples asked Tzu-chang about friendship. Tzu-chang said, 'What does Tzu-hsia say?' 'Tzu-hsia says, "You should make friends with those who are adequate and spurn those who are inadequate."'
   Tzu-chang said, 'That is different from what I have heard. I have heard that the gentleman honours his betters and is tolerant towards the multitude and that he is full of praise for the good while taking pity on the backward. If I am greatly superior, which among men need I be intolerant of? If I am inferior, then others will spurn me, how can there be any question of my spurning them?'

4. Tzu-hsia said, 'Even minor arts are sure to have their worthwhile aspects, but the gentleman does not take them up because the fear of a man who would go a long way is that he should be bogged down.'

5. Tzu-hsia said, 'A man can, indeed, be said to be eager to learn who is conscious, in the course of a day, of what he lacks and who never forgets, in the course of a month, what he has mastered.'

6. Tzu-hsia said, 'Learn widely and be steadfast in your purpose, inquire earnestly and reflect on what is at hand, and there is no need for you to look for benevolence elsewhere.'

1. cf. XIV.12.

7. Tzu-hsia said, 'The artisan, in any of the hundred crafts, masters his trade by staying in his workshop; the gentleman perfects his way through learning.'

8. Tzu-hsia said, 'When the small man makes a mistake, he is sure to gloss over it.'

9. Tzu-hsia said, 'In the three following situations the gentleman gives a different impression. From a distance he appears formal; when approached, he appears cordial; in speech he appears stern.'

10. Tzu-hsia said, 'Only after he has gained the trust of the common people does the gentleman work them hard, for otherwise they would feel themselves ill-used. Only after he has gained the trust of the lord does the gentleman advise him against unwise action, for otherwise the lord would feel himself slandered.'

11. Tzu-hsia said, 'If one does not overstep the bounds in major matters, it is of no consequence if one is not meticulous in minor matters.'

12. Tzu-yu said, 'The disciples and younger followers of Tzu-hsia can certainly cope with sweeping and cleaning, with responding to calls and replying to questions put to them, and with coming forward and withdrawing, but these are only details. On what is basic they are ignorant. What is one to do with them?'
   When Tzu-hsia heard this, he said, 'Oh! how mistaken Yen Yu is! In the way of the gentleman, what is to be taught first and what is to be put last as being less urgent? The former is as clearly distinguishable from the latter as grasses are from trees. It is futile to try to give such a false picture of the way of the gentleman. It is, perhaps, the sage alone who, having started something, will always see it through to the end.'[2]

2. Tzu-hsia's point seems to be this. If a student is taught, step by step, from the superficial to the basic, then he would have gained something even if he does not, in pursuing his studies, attain his final goal. At any rate, the final goal is something only the sage is supposed to be capable of attaining.

13. Tzu-hsia said, 'When a man in office finds that he can more than cope with his duties, then he studies; when a student finds that he can more than cope with his studies, then he takes office.'

14. Tzu-yu said, 'When mourning gives full expression to grief nothing more can be required.'

15. Tzu-yu said, 'My friend Chang is difficult to emulate. All the same he has not, as yet, attained benevolence.'

16. Tseng Tzu said, 'Grand, indeed, is Chang, so much so that it is difficult to work side by side with him at the cultivation of benevolence.'

17. Tseng Tzu said, 'I have heard the Master say that on no occasion does a man realize himself to the full, though, when pressed, he said that mourning for one's parents may be an exception.'

18. Tseng Tzu said, 'I have heard the Master say that other men could emulate everything Meng Chuang Tzu did as a good son with the exception of one thing: he left unchanged both his father's officials and his father's policies, and this was what was difficult to emulate.'³

19. The Meng Family appointed Yang Fu as judge and he sought the advice of Tseng Tzu. Tseng Tzu said, 'Those in authority have lost the Way and the common people have, for long, been rootless. If you succeed in extracting the truth from them, do not congratulate yourself on this but have compassion on them.'

20. Tzu-kung said, 'Chou was not as wicked as all that. That is why the gentleman hates to dwell downstream for it is there that all that is sordid in the Empire finds its way.'

21. Tzu-kung said, 'The gentleman's errors are like an eclipse of the sun and moon in that when he errs the whole world sees

3. cf. I.11.

him doing so and when he reforms the whole world looks up to him.'

22. Kung-sun Ch'ao of Wei asked Tzu-kung, 'From whom did Chung-ni[4] learn?' Tzu-kung said, 'The way of King Wen and King Wu has not yet fallen to the ground but is still to be found in men. There is no man who does not have something of the way of Wen and Wu in him. Superior men have got hold of what is of major significance while inferior men have got hold of what is of minor significance. From whom, then, does the Master not learn? Equally, how could there be such a thing as a constant teacher for him?'

23. Shu-sun Wu-shu said to the Counsellors at court, 'Tzu-kung is superior to Chung-ni.' This was reported to Tzu-kung by Tzu-fu Ching-po.

Tzu-kung said, 'Let us take outer walls as an analogy. My walls are shoulder high so that it is possible to peer over them and see the beauty of the house. But the Master's walls are twenty or thirty feet high so that, unless one gains admittance through the gate, one cannot see the magnificence of the ancestral temples or the sumptuousness of the official buildings. Since those who gain admittance through the gate are, shall we say, few, is it any wonder that the gentleman should have spoken as he did?'

24. Shu-sun Wu-shu made defamatory remarks about Chung-ni. Tzu-kung said, 'He is simply wasting his time. Chung-ni cannot be defamed. In other cases, men of excellence are like hills which one can climb over. Chung-ni is like the sun and the moon which one has no way of climbing over. Even if someone wanted to cut himself off from them, how could this detract from the sun and the moon? It would merely serve the more to show that he did not know his own measure.'

25. Ch'en Tzu-ch'in said to Tzu-kung, 'You are just being respectful, aren't you? Surely Chung-ni is not superior to you.'

4. i.e., Confucius.

Tzu-kung said, 'The gentleman is judged wise by a single word he utters; equally, he is judged foolish by a single word he utters. That is why one really must be careful of what one says. The Master cannot be equalled just as the sky cannot be scaled. Were the Master to become the head of a state or a noble family, he would be like the man described in the saying: he only has to help them stand and they will stand, to guide them and they will walk, to bring peace to them and they will turn to him, to set them tasks and they will work in harmony. In life he is honoured and in death he will be mourned. How can he be equalled?'

BOOK XX

1. Yao said,

> Oh! Shun,
> The succession, ordained by Heaven, has fallen on thy person.
> Hold thou truly to the middle way.
> If the Empire shoud be reduced to dire straits
> The honours bestowed on thee by Heaven will be terminated
> for ever.

It was with these same words that Shun commanded Yü.

[T'ang] said, 'I, Lü, the little one, dare to offer a black bull and to make this declaration before the great Lord. I dare not pardon those who have transgressed. I shall present thy servants as they are so that the choice rests with Thee alone. If I transgress, let not the ten thousand states suffer because of me; but if the ten thousand states transgress, the guilt is mine alone.'

The Chou was greatly blessed and the good men abounded.

> I may have close relatives,
> But better for me to have benevolent men.
> If the people transgress
> Let it be on my head alone.[1]

* * *

Decide on standard weights and measures after careful consideration, and re-establish official posts fallen into disuse, and government measures will be enforced everywhere. Restore states that

---

1. It has been suggested that these are the words used by King Wu in enfeoffing feudal lords, and may have been used, in particular, in the enfeoffment of T'ai Kung of Ch'i.

This whole passage consists of advice to kings or declarations by them. These kings all founded new dynasties. Shun founded the Yü, Yü founded the Hsia, T'ang founded the Yin, and King Wu founded the Chou. The language of this account of ancient history is strongly reminiscent of the *Book of History*. It is very unlikely that this passage has much to do with Confucius except that it may constitute teaching material used in the Confucian school.

have been annexed, revive lines that have become extinct, raise men who have withdrawn from society and the hearts of all the common people in the Empire will turn to you.

What was considered of importance: the common people, food, mourning and sacrifice.

If a man is tolerant, he will win the multitude. If he is trustworthy in word, the common people will entrust him with responsibility. If he is quick he will achieve results.[2] If he is impartial the common people will be pleased.[3]

2. Tzu-chang asked Confucius, 'What must a man be like before he can take part in government?'

The Master said, 'If he exalts the five excellent practices and eschews the four wicked practices he can take part in government.'

Tzu-chang said, 'What is meant by the five excellent practices?'

The Master said, 'The gentleman is generous without its costing him anything, works others hard without their complaining, has desires without being greedy, is casual without being arrogant, and is awe-inspiring without appearing fierce.'

Tzu-chang said, 'What is meant by "being generous without its costing him anything"?'[4]

The Master said, 'If a man benefits the common people by taking advantage of the things around them that they find beneficial, is this not being generous without its costing him anything? If a man, in working others hard, chooses burdens they can support, who will complain? If, desiring benevolence, a man obtains it, where is the greed? The gentleman never dare neglect his manners whether he be dealing with the many or the few, the young or the old. Is this not being casual without being arrogant? The gentle-

2. The paragraph up to this point is also found in XVII.6 where instead of *min* (common people) the text reads *jen* (fellow men).

3. This passage is not attributed to any speaker. It seems to consist of a number of unconnected parts on various aspects of government. Although one of these parts, as we have just pointed out, is, indeed, attributed to Confucius in XVII.6, it would be rash to infer from this that Confucius must be responsible for everything else as well.

4. In the light of the answer, the question should cover all five excellent practices instead of only the first.

man, with his robe and cap adjusted properly and dignified in his gaze, has a presence which inspires people who see him with awe. Is this not being awe-inspiring without appearing fierce?'

Tzu-chang said, 'What is meant by the four wicked practices?'

The Master said, 'To impose the death penalty without first attempting to reform is to be cruel; to expect results without first giving warning is to be tyrannical; to insist on a time limit when tardy in issuing orders is to cause injury. When something has to be given to others anyway, to be miserly in the actual giving is to be officious.'

3. Confucius said, 'A man has no way of becoming a gentleman unless he understands Destiny; he has no way of taking his stand unless he understands the rites; he has no way of judging men unless he understands words.'

Appendix 1

EVENTS IN THE LIFE OF CONFUCIUS

Compared to other thinkers in ancient China about most of whom hardly anything at all is known, Confucius seems to have fared very well. The standard source of his life is the biography forming chapter 47 of the *Shih chi* (*Records of the Historian*) written at the beginning of the first century B.C. by Ssu-ma Ch'ien. It is a biography of some length and seems, at first sight, to be full of information, but this impression turns out to be deceptive. The greater part of this information is unreliable. Indeed, Ts'ui Shu (1740–1816), who examined meticulously the evidence for the events in Confucius' life in his *Chu Ssu k'ao hsin lu* which is still the standard work on the subject, quite rightly summed up the matter by saying, 'In the *Shih chi* [biography] what is unfounded amounts to seventy or eighty per cent.'[1] This, when one comes to think of it, is hardly surprising.

Because Confucius gained the reputation of a sage, perhaps even in his lifetime, apocryphal stories about him abounded from very early times. For instance, the *Kuo yü*, a miscellaneous collection of accounts of the various states in the Spring and Autumn (*ch'un ch'iu*) period, already includes a number of stories about Confucius which can only be looked upon as inventions prompted by his reputation as a savant. On one occasion he was able to identify an unusual animal that looked like a sheep.[2] On another he identified a giant skeleton as that of Fang Feng Shih who was said to have been executed by Yü, the founder of the Hsia Dynasty, for arriving late at a conference.[3] On yet another occasion an eagle which fell dying had an arrow on it with a stone head more than a foot long. Confucius was able to tell that the bird had come from the far-off land of the northern barbarians of Su Shen as this type of arrow

1. *K'ao hsin lu*, p. 418.
2. *Kuo yü*, 5.7a.
3. op. cit., 5.10b–11a.

was peculiar to them.[4] Besides this type of story which was meant to show how immensely erudite Confucius was, there were also stories circulated by rival schools either to discredit the sage by ridiculing him or to lend respectability to their own ideas. There are, for instance, numerous stories illustrating Taoist ideas in the *Chuang tzu* in which Confucius figures prominently. Again, there are stories in the *Han fei tzu* where Confucius is made the mouth-piece of Legalist ideas.

If the *Kuo yü*, let alone the *Chuang tzu* and the *Han fei tzu*, already abounded in apocryphal stories, we should not be sur-prised if a great deal of such material found its way into the *Shih chi*. Nor should we blame the author of the *Shih chi* for his credulity. Ssu-ma Ch'ien was exceedingly cautious in the way he dealt with his source material: nothing was to be rejected unless he could satisfy himself of its unreliability. Where there was room for doubt he would rather preserve the tradition and leave the reader to judge for himself. This attitude is summed up in the words he used to praise Confucius as a historian. 'He showed his caution when he transmitted what was doubtful as something doubtful' (*Shih chi*, p. 487). But this caution does pose a problem for the modern reader. There is, it seems to me, no way out of this problem but to adopt the austere principle that whatever is not vouched for by a handful of early works has to be subjected to careful scrutiny, and tradition has to be rejected where there is sufficient grounds for doubt. In my opinion, the early sources which are to be relied upon include no more than the *Analects*, supplemented by the *Mencius*, and the *Tso chuan* (the *Tso commentary on the Spring and Autumn Annals*). The *Analects* we have to rely on as it is the earliest authoritative source concerning Confucius, although even here there are passages which are open to doubt. The *Mencius* can be used as a supplementary source which sometimes confirms in greater detail what is found in the *Analects*. It is likely to be reliable because of the immense respect Mencius showed Confucius and the healthy scepticism he showed towards apocryphal traditions concerning great men of the past.[5] The *Tso chuan* is slightly more

4. op. cit., 5.11b–12a.
5. See, for instance, *Mencius*, V.A.7,8,9 (p. 146–48).

problematical. Although it is the only reliable account we have of the history of the Spring and Autumn period, there are, nevertheless, cases where a prophetic element is introduced which can only mean that extraneous material had been introduced after the event. For this reason, such material should be isolated and treated with scepticism.

We shall now attempt to reconstruct a chronological account of all the events in Confucius' life that have the authority of the three early works. We shall also use this opportunity to take all the datable passages from the *Analects* and put them in the appropriate place in the chronology with the hope that this will give them a historical background which may be of help to the reader. We shall, then, conclude by examining some of the more important events attributed to Confucius' life in the *Shih chi* and other works and showing them to be ill-founded.

I. CONFUCIUS' FORBEARS

According to the *Tso chuan* (Duke Chao 7), in his dying words Meng Hsi Tzu said that Confucius was descended from Fu Fu He who, though he was the eldest son of Duke Min of Sung, yielded the succession to his younger brother who became Duke Li (r. 9th c. B.C.). Meng Hsi Tzu then went on to mention Cheng K'ao Fu[6] who served under three dukes in Sung between 799 and 729 B.C. and was known for his respectful attitude. Meng Hsi Tzu also mentioned that Confucius was descended from a sage who was killed in Sung. This, according to Tu Yü's commentary, was K'ung Fu Chia.[7] Elsewhere in the *Tso chuan* (Duke Yin 3) there is an account of Duke Mu (r. 728–720), just before he died, entrusting his baby son to K'ung Fu Chia[8] who was then murdered by Hua Tu in 710 B.C. together with the young duke.[9]

Confucius' father is not mentioned in any of the early sources.

6. According to commentators, the great grandson of Fu Fu He.
7. *Tso chuan chu shu*, 44.16b–17a.
8. op. cit., 3.7b–8a.
9. op. cit., 5.5a–b.

The *Tso chuan* (Duke Hsiang 10), however, mentions one Shu He of Tsou who demonstrated his immense physical strength by holding up the portcullis with his bare hands while his comrades made their getaway.[10] The *Shih chi*, in an account of the same incident, gives his name as Shu Liang He and identifies him as Confucius' father.[11] Nothing is known about his mother, though there were later traditions about her in keeping with her status as the mother of a sage.

2. BIRTH AND EARLY LIFE

After the murder of K'ung Fu Chia by Hua Tu in 710 B.C., his descendents, according to later tradition, fled to Lu. Whatever the truth of this tradition, Confucius was without doubt a native of Lu. A recluse, in conversation with Tzu-lu, referred to him as 'K'ung Ch'iu of Lu' (*Analects* XVIII.6), and he referred to Lu as 'the state of my father and mother' (*Mencius*, VII.B.17).

None of our three sources gives the date of the birth of Confucius, but the *Ku Liang chuan* and the *Kung Yang chuan*, both commentaries to the *Spring and Autumn Annals*, agree in giving the year of his birth as the twenty-first year of Duke Hsiang, i.e., 552 B.C. The *Shih chi*, however, gives it as a year later.

In his youth, Confucius held minor offices. This is clear from the *Analects* where Confucius is recorded as saying,

> I was of humble station when young. That is why I am skilled in many menial things. (IX.6)

Mencius, too, says,

> Confucius was once a minor official in charge of stores. He said, 'All I have to do is to keep correct records.' He was once a minor official in charge of sheep and cattle. He said, 'All I have to do is to see to it that the sheep and cattle grow up to be strong and healthy.' (*Mencius*, V.B.5)

10. op. cit., 31.3b.
11. *Shih chi*, p. 1905.

3. ENTRY INTO OFFICIAL LIFE

According to the *Tso chuan* (Duke Chao 17) in 525 B.C. Confucius presented himself to the Viscount of T'an, then on a visit to Lu, in order to be instructed about the system in use in the time of Shao Hao of naming offices after birds.[12] At this time Confucius was twenty-seven and it is probable that he already held some junior post at the Lu court. Otherwise, he would hardly have had access to a visiting dignitary.

In 522 B.C. it is recorded in the *Tso chuan* (Duke Chao 20) that Confucius commented on the gamekeeper who would rather die than answer to a wrong form of summons.[13] This same incident is also mentioned in the *Mencius* (V.B.7) where Confucius' comment, somewhat different, was

> A man whose mind is set on high ideals never forgets that he may end in a ditch; a man of valour never forgets that he may forfeit his head.

In the same year Tzu-ch'an, the distinguished statesman of Cheng, died and Confucius wept and said, 'A benevolent man from a past age'.[14]

In 518 B.C., before he died, Meng Hsi Tzu, still smarting from his miserable showing when he assisted at a ceremony many years ago, expressed the wish that his two sons should go and receive instructions from Confucius on the rites.[15]

In 517, when the *ti* sacrifice[16] was performed in the temple of Duke Hsiang of Lu, only two teams of eight *wan* dancers took part while the rest of the dancers were at the Chi Family.[17] This may be the incident which prompted Confucius' reaction recorded in the *Analects*,

12. *Tso chuan chu shu*, 48.3b–9a.
13. op. cit., 49.13b–14a.
14. *Tso chuan chu shu*, 49.21b.
15. op. cit., 44.16b–17b.
16. In *Analects* III.10 and III.11 the *ti* sacrifice is also mentioned.
17. *Tso chuan chu shu*, 51.17a.

Confucius said of the Chi Family, 'They use eight rows of eight dancers each to perform in their courtyard. If this can be tolerated, what cannot be tolerated?' (III.1)

4. VISIT TO CH'I

That Confucius visited Ch'i is clear from the early sources. In the *Analects* we find

> The Master heard the *shao* in *Ch'i* and for three months did not notice the taste of the meat he ate. He said, 'I never dreamt that the joys of music could reach such heights.' (VII.14)

and

> Duke Ching of Ch'i asked Confucius about government. Confucius said, 'Let the ruler be a ruler, the subject a subject, the father a father, the son a son.' The Duke said, 'Splendid! Truly, if the ruler be not a ruler, the subject not a subject, the father not a father, the son not a son, then even if there be grain, would I get to eat it?' (XII.11)

and finally,

> In considering the treatment he should accord Confucius, Duke Ching of Ch'i said, 'I am unable to accord him such exalted treatment as the Chi Family receives [in Lu].' So he placed him somewhere between the Chi and the Meng, saying, 'I am getting old. I am afraid I will not be able to put his talents to use.' Confucius departed. (XVIII.3)

The *Mencius* also records Confucius' departure from Ch'i.

> Mencius said, 'When he left Lu, Confucius said, "I proceed as slowly as possible. This is the way to leave the state of one's father and mother." When he left Ch'i he started after emptying the rice from the steamer. This is the way to leave a foreign state.' (VII.B.17. See also V.B.1)

Neither the *Analects* nor the *Mencius* gives any date for the visit to Ch'i, but as Duke Ching of Ch'i reigned from 547 to 490 B.C. Confucius could have been in Ch'i any time before 490, but, in fact, his visit is likely to have been much earlier than 490, for, as we shall see, he was back in Lu some time before 502.

5. RETURN TO LU FROM CH'I

Whatever the date of Confucius' return to Lu, some time must have elapsed before he took office, as we find him being urged from various quarters to take part in public life. In the *Analects* we find

> Someone said to Confucius, 'Why do you not take part in government?'
>
> The Master said, 'The *Book of History* says, "Oh! Simply by being a good son and friendly to his brothers a man can exert an influence upon government." In so doing a man is, in fact, taking part in government. How can there be any question of his having actively to "take part in government"?' (II.21)

and

> Yang Huo wanted to see Confucius, and when Confucius refused to go and see him he sent Confucius a present of a piglet.
>
> Confucius had someone keep watch on Yang Huo's house, and went to pay his respects during his absence. On the way he happened to meet Yang Huo who said to him, 'Come now. I will speak with you.' Then he went on, 'Can the man be said to be benevolent who, while hoarding his treasure, allows the state to go astray? I should say not. Can the man be said to be wise who, while eager to take part in public life, constantly misses the opportunity? I should say not. The days and the months slip by. Time is not on our side.' Confucius said, 'All right. I shall take office.' (XVII.1)

The Yang Huo in this passage has traditionally been identified as Yang Hu, an official in the household of the Chi Family who managed not only to usurp the power in the Chi Family but also the power in the state of Lu. In the end he overreached himself and had to flee the country in 501 B.C. If the identification of Yang Huo with Yang Hu is accepted, then the conversation recorded in XVII.1 must have taken place before 501, but unfortunately the identification is by no means certain. An account of this incident is also to be found in the *Mencius*.

Yang Huo wanted to see Confucius, but disliked acting in a manner contrary to the rites. When a Counsellor made a gift to a Gentleman, the Gentleman, if he was not at home to receive it, had to go to the Counsellor's home to offer his thanks. Yang Huo waited until Confucius was out before presenting him with a steamed piglet. But Confucius also waited until Yang Huo went out before going to offer his thanks. At that time if Yang Huo had taken the initiative in showing courtesy to Confucius, how could Confucius have refused to see him.[18]

There is difficulty in identifying the Yang Huo here with Yang Hu. First, Yang Huo is referred to as 'Counsellor'. If he was, indeed, Yang Hu, then he was merely an official in the household of the Chi Family. Even if it was common practice to accord such officials the courtesy title of Counsellor, it is doubtful if Mencius, a stickler for etiquette, would have acceded to such a practice. Second, Yang Huo is said to have 'disliked acting in a manner contrary to the rites'. This does not sound like Yang Hu at all. Third, in *Mencius* III.A.3. a saying of Yang Hu's is quoted. It is difficult to see why the same person should be referred to differently in the two places. Fourth, in the *Tso chuan* there are numerous references to Yang Hu but none to Yang Huo. Thus, we have no positive evidence for the identification of Yang Huo with Yang Hu, but, of course, this is not to say that the identification may not in fact be correct.

In the *Tso chuan* (Duke Ting 1) there is a reference to Confucius in the office of *ssu k'ou* (police commissioner) at a date after 502 B.C.[19] This is supported by the *Mencius* (VI.B.6). According to the *Mencius* (V.B.4) Confucius took office under Chi Huan Tzu, and this must, then, be between 505 and 492 B.C., the period when the latter was in power. It is possible that it was while Confucius was *ssu k'ou* that Yüan Ssu was his Steward (*Analects*, VI.5). It is also

18. *Mencius*, III.B.7. In my translation of the *Mencius* (p. 112) I substituted 'Yang Hu' for 'Yang Huo' throughout this passage because, having accepted at that time the identification of Yang Huo with Yang Hu I followed the practice of using only one name for one person in order to avoid confusion in view of the fact that Yang Hu appears in III.A.3.

19. *Tso chuan chu shu*, 54.6b.

possible that it was to this period that the conversation in the *Mencius* refers:

> 'When Confucius held office in Lu, the people of Lu were in the habit of fighting over the catch in a hunt to use as sacrifice, and Confucius joined in the fight. If even fighting over the catch is permissible, how much more the acceptance of a gift.'
>
> 'In that case, did not Confucius take office in order to further the Way?'
>
> 'Yes he did.'
>
> 'If he did, why did he join in the fight over the catch?'
>
> 'The first thing Confucius did was to lay down correct rules governing sacrificial vessels, ruling out the use of food acquired from the four quarters in such vessels.'
>
> 'Why did he not resign his office?'
>
> 'He wanted to make a beginning. When this showed that a ban was practicable, and in spite of this it was not put into effect, he resigned.' (V.B.4)

During the time Confucius was *ssu k'ou*, there were two noteworthy events. First, he assisted at the ceremony during a meeting between Duke Ting of Lu and Duke Ching of Ch'i in Chia Ku in 500 B.C. This is recorded in the *Tso chuan* (Duke Ting 10).[20] The second was the attempt to demolish the three strongholds of the Three Families in 498 B.C., which ended in failure.[21] The next year Confucius left Lu for Wei. It would seem that the departure of Confucius was directly the consequence of the failure of this attempt, but both the *Analects* and the *Mencius* give as reasons something totally different. In the *Analects*, it is said:

> The men of Ch'i made a present of singing and dancing girls. Ch Huan Tzu accepted them and stayed away from court for three days. Confucius departed. (XVIII.4)

Mencius, however, says,

> Confucius was the police commissioner of Lu, but his advice was not followed. He took part in a sacrifice, but, afterwards, was not given a share of the meat of the sacrificial animal. He left the state

20. *Tso chuan chu shu*, 56.2a–4a.
21. op. cit., 56.9b–10b.

without waiting to take off his ceremonial cap. Those who did not understand him thought he acted in this way because of the meat, but those who understood him realized that he left because Lu failed to observe the proper rites. For his part, Confucius preferred to be slightly at fault in thus leaving rather than to leave for no reason at all. The doings of a gentleman are naturally above the under-standing of the ordinary man. (VI.B.6)

Perhaps the reason given in the *Analects*, too, is no more than a pretext.

There is one other passage in the *Analects* which definitely be-longs to this period and is of some interest.

The Master said, 'Grant me a few more years so that I may study the *Changes* at the age of fifty and I shall be free from major errors.' (VII.17)

503 B.C. was the year Confucius reached the age of fifty and the date of this saying must be before that year. This passage has been adduced as evidence that Confucius made a profound study of the *Book of Changes*. But for *yi* (change) there is an alternative reading *yi* which is a grammatical particle. If one follows this reading, then the rendering is:

Grant me a few more years so that I may study at the age of fifty and I shall be free from major errors.

The tradition that links Confucius with the authorship of the so-called 'Ten Wings' in the *Book of Changes* is by no means founded on firm evidence.

6. TRAVEL ABROAD (497–484 B.C.)

After he left Lu, Confucius travelled abroad visiting a number of states, but nowhere is it stated when he started on his travels nor the order in which he visited these states. There is, however, some help to be derived from the *Mencius*.

When Confucius met with disfavour in Lu and Wei, there was the incident of Huan Ssu-ma of Sung who was about to waylay and kill him, and he had to travel through Sung in disguise. At that time

Confucius was in trouble, and he had as host Ssu-ch'eng Chen-tzu and took office with Chou, Marquis of Ch'en. (*Mencius*, V.A.8)

This would seem to indicate that after he left Lu, Confucius first went to Wei and then from Wei to Ch'en by way of Sung. Now Ch'en and Ts'ai are mentioned together both in the *Analects* and in the *Mencius*.

The Master said, 'None of those who were with me in Ch'en and Ts'ai ever got as far as my door.' (*Analects*, XI.2)

Mencius said, ' That the gentleman [i.e. Confucius] was in difficulties in the region of Ch'en and Ts'ai was because he had no friends at court.' (*Mencius*, VII.B.18)

As Ts'ai is mentioned after Ch'en the visit to Ts'ai most probably came after Confucius took office in Ch'en. This is entirely reasonable, as Ts'ai, then part of Ch'u, was to the southwest of Ch'en, and Ch'en in turn, was to the southwest of Sung. If we remember that Confucius passed Sung in order to get to Ch'en, then he must have got to Ch'en before he could go to Ts'ai.

On Confucius' return to Lu, we are more fortunate. We know when and from which state he returned. According to the *Tso chuan* (Duke Ai 11) in 484 B.C. when consulted by K'ung Wen Tzu on military matters, Confucius said, 'It is the bird that should choose the tree. How can the tree choose the bird?' Although he was persuaded not to leave Wei, it so happened that he was summoned by the men of Lu so he returned to Lu.[22] The *Tso chuan* then goes on to record that the head of the Chi Family consulted Confucius through Jan Yu on matters of taxation.[23] This means that Confucius was certainly back in Lu by the end of 484 B.C. at the latest.

Now that we have settled the itinerary, we can take a look at the events that took place during these years of foreign travel.

a. First Visit to Wei

The first visit to Wei must have taken place before 493 B.C. as Duke Ling died that year and there are conversations between the Duke and Confucius recorded in the *Analects*. In XIII.9 we find

22. *Tso chuan chu shu*, 58.27a–b.
23. ibid, 58.27b.

When the Master went to Wei, Jan Yu drove for him. The Master
said, 'What a flourishing population!'

Jan Yu said, 'When the population is flourishing, what further
benefit can one add?'

'Make the people rich.'

'When the people have become rich, what further benefit can
one add?'

'Train them.'

This sounds like the kind of conversation likely to take place on
a first visit.

According to the *Mencius*, while in Wei Confucius had, as host,
Yen Ch'ou-yu. Mencius added,

> The wife of Mi Tzu[24] was a sister of the wife of Tzu-lu. Mi Tzu said
> to Tzu-lu, 'If Confucius will let me act as host to him, the office
> of Minister in Wei is his for the asking.' Tzu-lu reported this to
> Confucius who said, 'There is the Decree.' Confucius went forward
> in accordance with the rites and withdrew in accordance with what
> was right, and in matters of success or failure said, 'There is the
> Decree.' (V.A.8)

While in Wei, Confucius is said to have had a meeting with
Nan Tzu, the notorious wife of Duke Ling, which displeased
Tzu-lu. According to the *Analects* Confucius had to placate him.

> The Master went to see Nan Tzu. Tzu-lu was displeased. The Master
> swore, 'If I have done anything improper, may Heaven's curse be
> on me, may Heaven's curse be on me!' (VI.28)

That Duke Ling of Wei was not a particularly good man can be
seen from the following passage in the *Analects*:

> When the Master spoke of the total lack of moral principle on the
> part of Duke Ling of Wei, K'ang Tzu commented, 'That being the
> case, how is it he did not lose his state?'
>
> Confucius said, 'Chung-shu Yü was responsible for foreign
> visitors, Priest T'uo for the ancestral temple and Wang-sun Chia
> for military affairs. That being the case, what question could there
> have been of his losing his state?' (XIV.19)

24. A favourite of Duke Ling.

Duke Ling being the kind of man he was, it is easy to understand why Mencius describes Confucius' taking office under him as a case of doing so because one is treated with decency (*Mencius*, V.B.4).

Concerning the reason why Confucius left Wei after his first visit, there is this passage in the *Analects*:

> Duke Ling of Wei asked Confucius about military formations. Confucius answered, 'I have, indeed, heard something about the use of sacrificial vessels, but I have never studied the matter of commanding troops.' The next day he departed. (XV.1)

It is too much of a coincidence that Confucius' first visit to Wei terminated when Duke Ling asked him a question about military matters while his second visit to the same state nearly terminated when he was asked the same question by K'ung Wen Tzu.[25] It is possible that these are different versions of the same story. If that is the case, we have to accept the above version from the *Analects* in preference to the one in the *Tso chuan*.

b. Passing Through Sung

Of Confucius passing through Sung, Mencius said, 'There was the incident of Huan Ssu-ma of Sung who was about to waylay and kill him, and he had to travel through Sung in disguise' (*Mencius*, V.A.8). That there was such an incident is confirmed in the *Analects* where Confucius said, 'Heaven is author of the virtue that is in me. What can Huan T'ui do to me?' (VII.23). The Huan Ssu-ma in the *Mencius* is the Huan T'ui of the *Analects*.

c. In Ch'en and Ts'ai

According to Mencius, Confucius took office under Chou, Marquis of Ch'en. There is also a reference to this period in the *Tso chuan* (Duke Ai 3). In 492 B.C. there was a fire in Lu and the temples of both Duke Huan and Duke Hsi suffered in the conflagration. Confucius, it is said, on learning of the news of the fire in Ch'en, proclaimed that it must have been the temples of Huan and Hsi that suffered.[26] This is just the kind of story most probably

---

25. See p. 171 above.
26. *Tso chuan chu shu*, 57.18a.

invented to show the ominiscience of the sage and little credence
can be given it, but it does show that Confucius was in Ch'en.

The *Mencius* mentions the difficulty the gentleman met with in
Ch'en and Ts'ai (VII.B.18). More about this incident is to be found
in the *Analects*:

> In Ch'en when provisions ran out the followers had become so
> weak that none of them could rise to their feet. Tzu-lu, with resent-
> ment written all over his face, said, 'Are there times when even
> gentlemen are brought to such extreme straits?' The Master said,
> 'It comes as no surprise to the gentleman to find himself in extreme
> straits. The small man finding himself in extreme straits would
> throw over all restraint.' (XV.2)

In 489 B.C. Wu invaded Ch'en. It is very likely that Confucius
experienced difficulty when travelling from Ch'en to Ts'ai during
this time. This would account for the remark Mencius made about
Confucius being in difficulties 'in the region of Ch'en and Ts'ai'.

It must have been in Ts'ai that Confucius met the Governor
of She. According to the *Tso chuan* (Duke Ai 2) in 493 B.C. the
state of Ts'ai moved to Chou Lai.[27] As this was far removed from
Ch'en, it was unlikely that Confucius visited it. But in 491 Chu
Liang, the Governor of She, collected together in Fu Han[28] former
inhabitants of Ts'ai who had not gone to Chou Lai. It must have
been in Fu Han, in 489, that Confucius met the Governor of She,
a man of outstanding ability through whose efforts the insurrection
in Ch'u by Po Kung in 479 was put down. In the *Analects* there
are two passages in which the Governor of She figures.

> The Governor of She asked about government. The Master said,
> 'Ensure that those who are near are pleased and those who are
> far away are attracted.' (XIII.16)

> The Governor of She asked Tzu-lu about Confucius. Tzu-lu did
> not answer. The Master said, 'Why did you not simply say something
> to this effect: he is the sort of man who forgets to eat when he tries
> to solve a problem that has been driving him to distraction, who is

27. See *Tso chuan chu shu*, 57.8b. Chou Lai is in modern Anhwei.
28. in modern Honan.

so full of joy that he forgets his worries and who does not notice the onset of old age.' (VII.19)

From Ts'ai Confucius must have returned to Ch'en and it was in Ch'en that he felt nostalgic for Lu. In the *Analects* we find

When he was in Ch'en, the Master said, 'Let us go home. Let us go home. Our young men at home are wildly ambitious, and have great accomplishments for all to see, but they do not know how to prune themselves.' (V.22)

In the *Mencius*, we find one of Mencius' disciples asking a question about this.

Wan Chang asked, 'When Confucius was in Ch'en, he exclaimed, "Let us go home. The young men of my school are wild and unconventional, rushing forward while not forgetting their origins." As Confucius was in Ch'en what made him think of the wild Gentlemen of Lu?' (VII.B.37)

d. Return to Wei

In 496 B.C. Prince K'uai K'ui, the son of Duke Ling of Wei attempted to kill Nan Tzu, the wife of his father, because he was ashamed of her notoriety, but had to flee to Chin when the attempt failed. In 493 Duke Ling died and Che, the son of Prince K'uai K'ui, succeeded him. With the help of the Chin army Prince K'uai K'ui managed to install himself in the city of Ch'i in the outlying region of Wei, and waited for an opportunity to regain the throne by ousting his son. It was against this background that the following conversation in the *Analects* must have taken place.

Jan Yu said, 'Is the Master on the side of the Lord of Wei [i.e. Che]?' Tzu-kung said, 'Well, I shall put the question to him.'

He went in and said, 'What sort of men were Po Yi and Shu Ch'i?'

'They were excellent men of old.'

'Did they have any complaints?'

'They sought benevolence and got it. So why should they have any complaints?'

When Tzu-kung came out, he said, 'The Master is not on his side.' (VII.15)

In antiquity, Po Yi and Shu Ch'i were the sons of the lord of Ku Chu. The father intended Shu Ch'i, the younger of the two sons, to succeed him, but when he died neither of his sons was willing to deprive the other of the succession and they both fled to the mountains. By asking about Po Yi and Shu Ch'i, Tzu-kung was able to interpret Confucius' answer as indicating his disgust at the unseemly struggle between father and son. Prince K'uai K'ui eventually succeeded in ousting his son in 480 B.C. It was on this occasion that Tzu-lu who was in the service of K'ung K'ui, the son of K'ung Wen Tzu, died resisting the invasion, but by that time Confucius had left Wei.

There is a conversation between Tzu-kung and Confucius concerning the posthumous title of K'ung Wen Tzu.

> Tzu-kung asked, 'Why was K'ung Wen Tzu called "wen"?'
> The Master said, 'He was quick and eager to learn: he was not ashamed to seek the advice of those who were beneath him in station. That is why he was called "wen".' (V.15)

As K'ung Wen Tzu, according to the *Tso chuan*, must have died some time between 484 and 480 B.C., and Confucius was back in Lu by the end of 484 at the latest, it is just possible that this conversation took place in Wei before Confucius left for home, though it is more likely that it took place in Lu after Confucius' return.

Belonging to the period before Confucius left Wei is the passage in the *Analects*:

> Tzu-lu said, 'If the Lord of Wei left the administration of his state to you, what would you put first?'
> The Master said, 'If something has to be put first, it is, perhaps, the rectification of names.'
> Tzu-lu said, 'Is that so? What a roundabout way you take! Why bring rectification in at all?'
> The Master said, 'Yu, how boorish you are. Where a gentleman is ignorant, one would expect him not to offer any opinion. When names are not correct, what is said will not sound reasonable; when what is said does not sound reasonable, affairs will not culminate in success; when affairs do not culminate in success, rites and music will not flourish; when rites and music do not flourish,

punishments will not fit the crimes; when punishments do not fit the crimes, the common people will not know where to put hand and foot. Thus when the gentleman names something, the name is sure to be usable in speech, and when he says something, this is sure to be practicable. The thing about the gentleman is that he is anything but casual where speech is concerned.' (XIII.3)

Perhaps from this insistence on the rectification of names one can detect a covert reference to the struggle in which the father did not behave like a father and the son not like a son.

In the *Mencius* it is said that Confucius took office under Duke Hsiao of Wei and Mencius describes this as an instance of taking office because the Prince wished to keep good people at his court (V.B.4). There is no Duke Hsiao in Wei according either to the *Spring and Autumn Annals* or to the *Shih chi*. Chu Hsi suggested that Duke Hsiao was in fact Che.[29] Ts'ui Shu pointed out that it was very probable that the Ousted Duke (*Ch'u Kung*) was not his proper posthumous title and that he could well have been given the title of *hsiao* (filial) in view of his obedience to the wishes of his grandfather in resisting his own father.[30]

7. RETURN TO LU AND LAST YEARS

We have already seen that Confucius returned to Lu from Wei towards the end of 484 B.C. at the latest. Now, Duke Ai of Lu came to the throne in 494 while Chi K'ang Tzu succeeded to his father's position as powerful minister in Lu in 493. Confucius, however, had left Lu in 497. Thus, all conversations with Duke Ai and Chi K'ang Tzu must have taken place after his return to Lu in 484 and before his death in 479. The views Confucius expressed in these conversations are particularly important as the views of a philosopher matured in the course of a long and eventful life.

According to the *Tso chuan*, as we have seen, in 484 Chi K'ang Tzu consulted Confucius, through Jan Yu, on matters of taxation.

29. In his commentary on the passage in question in the *Mencius* (*Meng tzu chi chu*, 10.9b).

30. *K'ao hsin lu*, p. 488.

There is one passage in the *Analects* concerning Jan Yu which is, perhaps, connected with this incident.

> The wealth of the Chi Family was greater than that of the Duke of Chou, and still Ch'iu helped them add further to that wealth by raking in the taxes. The Master said, 'He is no disciple of mine. You, my young friends, may attack him openly to the beating of drums.' (XI.17)

Mencius, in quoting the words of Confucius, added a comment of his own:

> While he was steward to the Chi Family, Jan Ch'iu doubled the yield of taxation without being able to improve their virtue. Confucius said, 'Ch'iu is no disciple of mine. You, my young friends, may attack him openly to the beating of drums.' From this it can be seen that Confucius rejected those who enrich rulers not given to the practice of benevolent government. (IV.A.14)[31]

In 481 B.C. Ch'en Heng murdered Duke Chien of Ch'i. This event referred to in the *Tso chuan* (Duke Ai 14)[32] is recorded in the *Analects*.

> Ch'en Ch'eng Tzu killed Duke Chien. After washing himself ceremonially, Confucius went to court and reported to Duke Ai, saying, 'Ch'en Heng killed his lord. May I request that an army be sent to punish him?' The Duke answered, 'Tell the three noble lords.' Confucius said, 'I have reported this to you simply because I have a duty to do so, seeing that I take my place after the Counsellors, and yet you say "Tell the three noble lords."'
>
> He went and reported to the three noble lords, and they refused his request. Confucius said, 'I have reported this to you simply because I have a duty to do so, seeing that I take my place after the Counsellors.' (XIV.21)

This seems to indicate that after his recall to Lu, Confucius was made a Counsellor of the lowest rank.

In the same year, according to the *Tso chuan*[33] a *ch'i lin* (unicorn)

31. *Mencius*, p. 123–4. The wording of the quotation from Confucius has been slightly emended to bring it in line with the present translation.
32. *Tso chuan chu shu*, 59.19a–b.
33. *Tso chuan chu shu*, 59.11a.

was caught in a hunt and it was Confucius who identified it as such. As the *Ch'un ch'iu* (*Spring and Autumn Annals*) ends with the capture of the *ch'i lin* and Confucius is credited with its authorship (*Mencius*, III.B.9), it seems likely to have been finished by 481 B.C.

Not only was Confucius concerned with the *Ch'un ch'iu*, but he was also deeply concerned with music and the *Odes*. In the *Analects* we find

> The Master said, 'It was after my return from Wei to Lu that the music was put right, with the *ya* and *sung* being assigned their proper places.' (IX.15)

As the *ya* and *sung* are two sections of the *Odes* it would seem to support the tradition that Confucius edited the *Odes* though the tradition that he reduced the number of *Odes* from three thousand to three hundred is almost certainly an exaggeration.

Apart from the single conversation with Duke Ai quoted above which can be dated exactly, there are other passages in the *Analects* in which the Duke or Chi K'ang Tzu figures that cannot be dated exactly. Here are the passages in which the Duke figures:

> Duke Ai asked, 'What must I do before the common people will look up to me?'
>
> Confucius answered, 'Raise the straight and set them over the crooked and the common people will look up to you. Raise the crooked and set them over the straight and the common people will not look up to you.' (II.19)

> Duke Ai asked Tsai Wo about the altar to the god of earth. Tsai Wo replied, 'The Hsia used the pine, the Yin used the cedar, and the men of Chou used the chestnut (*li*), saying that it made the common people tremble (*li*).'
>
> The Master, on hearing of this reply, commented, 'One does not explain away what is already done, one does not argue against what is already accomplished, and one does not condemn what has already gone by.' (III.21)

> When Duke Ai asked which of his disciples was eager to learn, Confucius answered, 'There was one Yen Hui who was eager to learn. He did not vent his anger upon an innocent person, nor did he make the same mistake twice. Unfortunately, his allotted span

was a short one and he died. Now there is no one. No one eager to
learn has come to my notice.' (VI.3)

Here are the passages in which Chi K'ang Tzu figures:

Chi K'ang Tzu asked, 'How can one inculcate in the common people
the virtue of reverence, of doing their best and of enthusiasm?'
    The Master said, 'Rule over them with dignity and they will be
reverent; treat them with kindness and they will do their best;
raise the good and instruct those who are backward and they will
be imbued with enthusiasm.' (II.20)

Chi K'ang Tzu asked, 'Is Chung Yu good enough to be given
office?'
    The Master said, 'Yu is resolute. What difficulties could there
be for him in taking office?'
    'Is Ssu good enough to be given office?'
    'Ssu is a man of understanding. What difficulties could there be
for him in taking office?'
    'Is Ch'iu good enough to be given office?'
    'Ch'iu is accomplished. What difficulties could there be for him
in taking office?' (VI.8)

When K'ang Tzu sent a gift of medicine, [Confucius] bowed his head
to the ground before accepting it. However, he said, 'Not knowing
its properties, I dare not taste it.' (X.16)

Chi K'ang Tzu asked which of his disciples was eager to learn.
Confucius answered, 'There was one Yen Hui who was eager to
learn, but unfortunately his allotted span was a short one and he
died. Now there is no one.' (XI.7. This is very similar to VI.3
quoted above.)

Chi K'ang Tzu asked Confucius about government. Confucius
answered, 'To govern is to correct. If you set an example by being
correct, who would dare to remain incorrect?' (XII.17).

The prevalence of thieves was a source of trouble to Chi K'ang Tzu
who asked the advice of Confucius. Confucius answered, 'If you
yourself were not a man of desires, no one would steal even if
stealing carried a reward.' (XII.18)

Chi K'ang Tzu asked Confucius about government, saying,
'What would you think if, in order to move closer to those who
possess the Way, I were to kill those who do not follow the Way?'

Confucius answered, 'In administering your government, what need is there for you to kill? Just desire the good yourself and the common people will be good. The virtue of the gentleman is like wind; the virtue of the small man is like grass. Let the wind blow over the grass and it is sure to bend.' (XII.19)

According to the *Tso chuan*,[34] Confucius died in the fourth month of the sixteenth year of Duke Ai (479 B.C.).

TRADITIONS IN THE *Shih chi* AND OTHER WORKS

The traditions concerning Confucius in the *Shih chi*, most of which are to be found in other works, fall under two main categories. The first consists of stories showing Confucius the sage as somehow different from ordinary mortals. The second concerns the attainment of high office by Confucius and what he did when in office. Neither category deserves much credence, but it may be instructive to examine some of these stories.

Of the first category, we have already seen the stories in the *Kuo yü* designed to show that Confucius displayed extraordinary knowledge of rare creatures and objects. All of these are incorporated in the *Shih chi* biography.

Another type of story attempts to show that Confucius was different from other men. For instance, his birth was of the kind one would expect of a sage. The *Shih chi* says,

[Shu Liang] He and a girl of the Yen family had an illicit union and Confucius was born. [She] prayed at Mount Ni (Ni Ch'iu) and had Confucius. In the twenty-second year of Duke Hsiang of Lu, Confucius was born. He was born with the top of his head sunken in. Hence he was named Ch'iu.[35] His *tzu* was Chung-ni, and his clan name was K'ung. (p. 1905)

This passage sets out to show that Confucius had an unusual birth, the result of an illicit union between Shu Liang He and a girl of

34. *Tso chuan chu shu*, 60.2a.
35. The word *ch'iu* is supposed to mean a mound high all round and sunken in the middle.

the Yen family. It also shows that Confucius was physically different from ordinary men. The top of his head was sunken like a valley. Hence he was named Ch'iu. Here Ssu-ma Ch'ien seems to have preserved two different traditions. According to the first, Confucius was named Ch'iu because the top of his head was like a mound sunken in the middle (*ch'iu*). According to the second, his name was Ch'iu and his *tzu* was *Chung-ni* because it was to Mount Ni (*Ni Ch'iu*) that his mother prayed.

Of Confucius' physical peculiarities, there is another story in the *Shih Chi*,

> Confucius went to Cheng and got separated from his disciples. He stood alone by the eastern gate of the outer walls. Someone from Cheng said to Tzu-kung, 'By the eastern gate there is a man. In his forehead he looks like Yao, in his neck like Kao Yao, in his shoulders like Tzu-ch'an, and from his waist downwards he is shorter than Yü by three inches. He looks downcast like a dog from a bereaved family.' Tzu-kung recounted this to Confucius who smiled cheerfully and said, 'What one looks like is not of the slightest importance, but to say that I am like a dog from a bereaved family, that is so indeed, that is so indeed.' (p. 1921–2)

This must have originated as a story meant to ridicule Confucius' ungainly appearance, though it seems to have undergone a transformation in the hands of some Confucian editor into a story showing Confucius' lack of concern for appearances by the introduction of the final remark. Whatever the case, it is certainly founded on the popular belief that a sage ought to look very different from ordinary men.

There is yet another type of story which was invented to show that very early in life Confucius was already showing the promise of the sage that he was to be. For instance, in the *Shih chi* it is said,

> When Confucius played as a child, he would set out sacrificial vessels and practise the proper ritual. (p. 1966)

The *Shih chi* goes on to say,

> When Confucius was seventeen, Meng Hsi Tzu said to his sons, 'K'ung Ch'iu is the descendant of a sage killed in Sung . . . I have heard that from among the descendants of a sage, though not

necessarily from his immediate descendants, will arise a man who will distinguish himself. Now K'ung Ch'iu is young and fond of the rites. He is probably the one who will distinguish himself. If I die, you must make him your teacher.' When Hsi Tzu died, Yi Tzu and Nan-kung Ching-shu, the man of Lu, went to study the rites with him. (p. 1908)

We have seen that Meng Hsi Tzu did not die until the twenty-fourth year of Duke Chao (518 B.C.) although in the *Tso chuan* the speech is recorded under the seventh year of Duke Chao (535 B.C.) because it was his failure when he assisted at a ceremony that year which prompted his dying words. Ssu-ma Ch'ien had apparently misread the *Tso chuan* and took 535 B.C. as the year Meng Hsi Tzu died. Ts'ui Shu has pointed out that in 535 'not only was Confucius too young to be a teacher, but neither of Hsi Tzu's two sons was as yet born'.[36] The mistake must have been made easier by the belief, to begin with, that Confucius showed early promise as a teacher of the rites.

In this connection it is worthwhile to take a look at the story concerning Confucius receiving instructions from Lao Tzu.

Nan-kung Ching-shu of Lu said to the Lord of Lu, 'May your servant be granted permission to go to Chou with Confucius.' The Lord of Lu gave him a carriage and two horses, together with one servant, and he went [with Confucius] to Chou to ask about the rites. It was probably then that they met Lao Tzu. When they departed, Lao Tzu saw them off and said, 'I have heard that men of wealth and rank make gifts of money while benevolent men make gifts of words. I have not been able to win either wealth or rank, but I have been undeservedly accorded the name of a benevolent man. These words are my parting gift: "There are men with clever and penetrating minds who are never far from death. This is because they expose the evil deeds of others. Neither a son nor a subject should look upon his person as his own." ' (*Shih chi*, p. 1909)

Although no date is attached to this incident, the passage obviously was originally continuous with the passage containing Meng Hsi Tzu's dying words. In between the two are interposed two separate items. The first records the death of Chi Wu Tzu and the suc-

36. *K'ao hsin lu*, p. 427.

cession by P'ing Tzu to his position. The second is a paragraph summarizing the whole of Confucius' career from the time he was a minor official to the time he returned from his travels to Lu in 484 B.C. when he was sixty-eight.

Now if the account of the meeting between Confucius and Lao Tzu was meant to be in 535 B.C., then there is the same absurdity that Nan-kung Ching-shu was as yet unborn. But even if the date of the meeting is not meant to have been 535, it could not have been intended to be later than 522, as the biography resumes its chronological order from this passage onwards and the next event recorded is the visit to Lu of Duke Ching of Ch'i in the twentieth year of Duke Chao (522 B.C.). Even in 522, Nan-kung Ching-shu would be no more than ten. It would have been absurd for a boy of that age, whose father was still alive, to approach the Lord of Lu for permission to go to Chou with Confucius. This shows that the story about a meeting between Confucius and Lao Tzu, as found in the *Shih chi*, is riddled with inconsistencies.

As Confucius was greatly interested in music, there were natur-ally stories about him in this connection. One of these stories found in the *Han shih wai chuan* and the reconstituted *K'ung tzu chia yü* is also to be found in the *Shih chi*. Confucius learned to play a piece of music from Music Master Hsiang. He made steady progress until in the end he was able to see the composer in his mind's eye. He described what he saw and said, 'Who else could this be but King Wen?' The music master was astonished at this and con-fessed that his teacher did say that the piece was by King Wen (*Shih chi*, p. 1925). The fantastic nature of the story needs no comment.

We can now turn to traditions about Confucius' official career. The *Shih chi* says,

> Subsequently, Duke Ting made Confucius the steward of Chung Tu. After a year, the four quarters took him as a model. From steward of Chung Tu he became *ssu k'ung* and from *ssu k'ung* he became *ta ssu k'ou*. (p. 1915)

All this is supposed to have happened in one year, the ninth year of Duke Ting (501). It is possible that Confucius did hold the office of steward of Chung Tu, as this is supported by the *T'an kung* chapter of the *Li chi*,[37] but as the stewardship of Chung Tu was, presumably, a modest position, it is difficult to see how he could have been made *ssu k'ung* immediately afterwards and then *ta ssu k'ou*. Now, there are other difficulties. The position of *ssu k'ung*, an office in charge of construction work in Lu, was, according to the *Tso chuan*, of Upper Ministerial rank and held without a break by the Meng Family, and it is difficult to see how Confucius could have been appointed to the post. That he was *ta ssu k'ou* is also problematical. Both the *Tso chuan* and the *Mencius* only said that Confucius was *ssu k'ou*, not *ta ssu k'ou*.[38] It is possible that whoever fabricated the story about Confucius being made *ta ssu k'ou* was vaguely aware that *ssu k'ou* was of a modest status, say, that of a Counsellor of the lower rank and that a transfer from the exalted position of *ssu k'ung* to *ssu k'ou* would, in fact, be a demotion, this would run contrary to the purpose of the fabrication which was to endow Confucius with a position of greater importance, so he added the epithet *ta* – great – to the title *ssu k'ou*. This is, of course, mere conjecture, but, whatever the case, Confucius' rapid rise as an official is more likely to be the doing of his later admirers than of Duke Ting.

The promotion of Confucius in the *Shih chi* does not end with *ta ssu k'ou*. It goes on to say,

> In the fourteenth year of Duke Ting [496 B.C.] when Confucius was fifty-six, from *ta ssu k'ou* he [went on] to discharge the duties of prime minister. (p. 1917)

Although here Confucius is said 'to discharge the duties of prime minister', elsewhere the *Shih chi* dispenses with this periphrastic expression and simply describes him as 'prime minister of Lu'.[39] It is instructive to trace the change in wording with which Confucius' official position is described. We begin with the *Tso chuan*

37. *Li chi chu shu*, 8.7b.

38. See p. 168 ff. above.

39. See ch. 31, *Hereditary House of Wu* (p. 1467); ch. 32, *Hereditary House of Ch'i* (p. 1505); ch. 39, *Hereditary House of Chin* (p. 1685); ch. 40, *Hereditary House of Ch'in* (p. 1717); ch. 44, *Hereditary House of Wei* (p. 1837); ch. 66, *Biography of Wu Tzu-hsü* (p. 2178).

(Duke Ting 10) which simply says, 'In the summer the Duke met
the Marquis of Ch'i at Chu Ch'i, in other words, at Chia Ku.
K'ung Ch'iu assisted [at the ceremony] (*hsiang*).'[40] The *Shih chi*
biography, in recording the same event, says, 'Confucius dis-
charged the duties of assisting [at the ceremony] (*she hsiang shih*)'
(p. 1915). The single word *hsiang* is expanded into the phrase *she
hsiang shih*, but because of the context, the meaning has not notice-
ably changed. Further on in the biography we find

> In the fourteenth year of Duke Ting when Confucius was fifty-six,
> from *ta ssu k'ou* he [went on] to discharge the duties of prime
> minister (*hsing she hsiang shih*). (p. 1917)

Here yet another word *hsing* is added and, because of the context,
the meaning of the word *hsiang* slides imperceptibly from 'assisting' to 'prime minister', and the phrase quite naturally means
'discharging the duties of prime minister'. The transformation is
complete, when, as we have seen, elsewhere in the *Shih chi* Confucius is simply described as prime minister of Lu (*hsiang Lu*).
From having assisted, on one occasion, at the ceremony during a
meeting of the Duke of Lu and the Duke of Ch'i, Confucius'
position was gradually inflated until he was the prime minister of
Lu. It would seem that the later the tradition the more exalted
Confucius' position.

There are, however, difficulties for the theory that Confucius
was ever prime minister. First, as Ts'ui Shu has pointed out,[41]
in the *ch'un ch'iu* period the word *hsiang* was not yet used for
prime minister. Second, by 496 B.C. Confucius had left Lu. We
have Mencius' authority who said, 'Confucius was *ssu k'ou*, but
his advice was not followed. He took part in a sacrifice, but, afterwards, was not given a share of the meat of the sacrificial animal.
He left the state without waiting to take off his cap' (VI.B.6).
According to this, not only did Confucius leave before 496, but he
was still only *ssu k'ou* when he left. Again, the *Lü shih ch'un ch'iu*
says that Confucius, in spite of the number of rulers he presented
himself to in his extensive travels, 'attained merely the position

40. *Tso chuan chu shu*, 56.2a.
41. *K'ao hsin lu*, p. 455.

of *ssu k'ou* of Lu'.[42] This, in fact, is an unambiguous statement that in his whole life Confucius never attained a position higher than that of *ssu k'ou* of Lu. There is a further point which is important. As the *Lü shih ch'un ch'iu* was finished in 240 B.C., it shows that even at that date there was no generally accepted tradition that Confucius was ever prime minister or even *ssu k'ung*, and we should be sceptical about such traditions.

Having made Confucius prime minister, the *Shih chi* goes on to say,

> Thereupon he killed Shao Cheng Mao, a Counsellor of Lu, who caused disorder in the government. (p. 1917)

Although this entry in the *Shih chi*, probably of Legalist provenance, is of little significance in itself because of the inherent improbability of the event, it is necessary to deal with it in some detail as it was, a few years ago, widely used in ill-informed attacks on Confucius for ulterior political motives. The account in the *Shih chi* is excessively brief, but, fortunately, accounts are to be found in other works. Some of these accounts are equally brief, but others are in fuller form. The works in which a fuller form of the story is to be found are the *Hsün tzu*,[43] the *Shuo yüan*,[44] the *K'ung tzu chia yü*[45] and the *Yin wen tzu*.[46] There is a short quotation from what must have been a longer account in the *Han shih nei chuan* to be found in the *Po hu t'ung*.[47] The *Huai nan tzu*[48] also contains a reference to the incident.

Now although Hsün Tzu lived in the period from the last quarter of the 4th c. to the first half of the 3rd c. B.C. and the greater part of the *Hsün tzu* was most probably by him, the Shao Cheng Mao story is to be found in chapter 28, *Tso yu*, which is in the final section of the book (chapters 27 to 32), a section largely consisting of miscellaneous material and most likely to be of a date later than the bulk of the work. The *Han shih nei chuan*, no longer extant,

42. *Lü shih ch'un ch'iu*, 14.18b.
43. *Hsün tzu*, 20.2a–3a.
44. *Shuo yüan*, 15.14b–15b.
45. *K'ung tzu chia yü*, 1.4b–5b.
46. *Yin wen tzu*, 11b–12a.
47. *Po hu t'ung*, 4.5b.
48. *Huai nan tzu*, 13.17b.

was by Han Ying who was a *po shih* (professor) in the time of Emperor Wen (r. 179–157 B.C.) of the Western Han. The *Huai nan tzu* was finished probably in the middle of the 2nd c. B.C. The *Shuo yüan*, a miscellaneous collection, was compiled by Liu Hsiang who lived in the 1st c. B.C. The *K'ung tzu chia yü*, as we have it, is a reconstituted work, generally believed to have been compiled by Wang Su[49] (195–256 A.D.). The present *Yin wen tzu* is generally believed to be a forgery not earlier than the 3rd c. A.D.

Let us begin with the *Han shih nei chuan* and the *Shuo yüan*. The *Han shih nei chuan* is no longer extant, but the *Han shih wai chuan* by the same author is. In the present *Shuo yüan* there are some eighty passages which are close parallels to passages in the *Han shih wai chuan* and it can be shown that the *Shuo yüan* passages were, in many cases, taken verbatim from the *Han shih wai chuan*. That being the case, the likelihood is that there are passages taken verbatim from the *Han shih nei chuan* as well. The quotation from the *Han shih nei chuan* preserved in the *Po hu t'ung* is very short and possibly abbreviated but otherwise exactly what we would expect if it were a fragment of a longer passage which came to be incorporated without attribution into the *Shuo yüan*. The *Po hu t'ung* quotation is as follows:

> The *Han shih nei chuan* [says], 'Confucius was the *ssu k'ou* of Lu and his initial act of punishment (*hsien chu*) fell on Shao Cheng Mao. (4.5b)

For our purpose, the significant point is that in both the *Han shih nei chuan* and the *Shuo yüan* Confucius is referred to as *ssu k'ou* of Lu. While the *Huai nan tzu* does not mention his official position, the *Shih chi* and the *K'ung tzu chia yü* both say 'from *ta ssu k'ou* Confucius [went on] to discharge the duties of prime minister'.[50] In the *Hsün tzu* Confucius had become the 'acting prime

49. The original *K'ung tzu chia yü* must have been one of the sources used by Ssu-ma Ch'ien and was still extant when Pan Ku wrote the 'Bibliographical Chapter' of the *Han shu*. The present *K'ung tzu chia yü* was mainly compiled out of ancient sources extant in Wang Su's time but it may also contain material forged by Wang Su.

50. The *Shih chi* (p. 1917) has *hsing she hsiang shih* while the *K'ung tzu chia yü* (1.4b) has *she hsing hsiang shih*. This slight difference in word order does not make any substantial difference in the meaning.

minister (*she hsiang*)', but by the *Yin wen tzu* he was simply 'prime minister of Lu (*Lu hsiang*)'. As we have seen, the later the tradition, the more exalted the position of Confucius became. Seen in this light, the *Han shih nei chuan* and, by implication, the *Shuo yüan* would seem to represent the earliest stage of the tradition when Confucius was still only *ssu k'ou*. The *Shih chi* and the *K'ung tzu chia yü* represent a transitional stage when he was still only *ta ssu k'ou* discharging the duties of prime minister. The *Hsün tzu* represents the next stage when he was acting prime minister. The *Yin wen tzu* represents the final stage when he was simply the prime minister of Lu. That the *Yin wen tzu* should describe Confucius as prime minister of Lu comes as no surprise as it was a forgery of a date long after the tradition had been established. But that the *Hsün tzu* should describe Confucius as acting prime minister is surprising, since the tradition seemed, as we have seen, not to have been generally accepted even as late as 240 B.C. by which time Hsün Tzu was probably dead; but as the story is found in a chapter which is of late date, then this is compatible with its being a late invention.

Since the *Shuo yüan* version represents the earliest stage of the tradition, let us quote it in full.

Confucius was *ssu k'ou* in Lu for seven days and he executed (*chu*) [51] Shao Cheng Mao under the Eastern tower flanking the palace gate. None of the disciples who, on hearing the news, hastened to come forward spoke, though they were of one mind. Tzu-kung hastened to come forward, saying, 'Now Shao Cheng Mao is a well-known figure in the state of Lu. Why is it, Master, that your initial act of punishment (*hsien chu*) after assuming the responsibility of government falls on him?' Confucius said, 'Ssu, this is not within your understanding. Now there are five things a true King punishes, and thieving is not one of them. First comes the mind that is treacherous while discerning; second come words that are eloquent while false; third comes conduct that is unswerving while perverse; fourth comes memory that is wide in scope but stupid; fifth comes following what is

51. The word *chu* has either the more general sense of 'to punish' or the more specific sense of 'to execute', but there is little doubt that in the present story it is meant to be understood that Confucius executed Shao Cheng Mao. As these meanings are not mutually exclusive, in the translation both 'punish' and 'execute' are used, depending on the demands of the context.

wrong while giving it a gloss. These five all enjoy the name of discernment, intelligence, cleverness and understanding, but are in fact not the genuine thing. If such a one should go in for practising deception, then his intelligence is sufficient to sway the multitude and his strength is sufficient to enable him to stand alone. He will, then, outshine other evil men and has to be punished. Now a man having one of the five qualities mentioned above will not escape punishment. Here is Shao Cheng Mao who has them all. That is why my initial act of punishment falls on him. Formerly, T'ang punished Chu Mu, T'ai Kung punished P'an Chih, Kuan Chung punished Shih Fu Li, Tzu-ch'an punished Teng Hsi. These five [52] gentlemen never hesitated to punish. What is described as "punishment" is so described not because the men punished attack and rob in the day and drill holes through walls in the night, but because they are all the likes of men who engineer the downfall of those who oppose them. They are naturally the object of suspicion to the gentleman and the cause of bewilderment over right and wrong to the stupid. The *Odes* say,

> How I am worried in my heart!
> I am hated by the crowd of small men.

This describes well what I have said.' (15.14b–16a)

The first thing to notice about this story is that it belongs to the category of illustrative story. In an illustrative story, the identity of the characters is unimportant and can vary, but the tendency is to use well-known figures in order to lend credence to the point. The question to ask about such stories is, 'What is the point it is supposed to illustrate?' In the present case, the answer is quite straightforward. The point is the punishment and suppression of any man who wins over the multitude by his eloquence, intelligence and strength of character, in other words, what would today be described as a charismatic figure. The earlier cases cited as precedent, though not very promising at first sight, turn out, on closer examination, to be of some help. In three of the four cases, the culprit, like Shao Cheng Mao, is otherwise unknown to us and, most probably, totally fictitious. The fourth, however, is historical. Teng Hsi was, according to the *Hsün tzu*, [53] a sophist like Hui

52. In fact four only are listed.
53. *Hsün tzu*, 2.2a.

Shih. Apart from the present story, he is also said, in the *Lü shih ch'un ch'iu*,[54] to have been put to death by Tzu-ch'an. This, however, is at odds with the account of the *Tso chuan* where Teng Hsi was said to have been executed by Ssu Ch'uan in the ninth year of Duke Ting (501 B.C.), some twenty years after Tzu-ch'an's death.

> Ssu Ch'uan of Cheng killed Teng Hsi and appropriated for his own use Teng Hsi's bamboo criminal code. (*Tso chuan chu shu*, 55.19a–b)

Thus it would seem that Teng Hsi had inscribed his own criminal code on bamboo, and this was likely to have been in opposition to Tzu-ch'an who had had a tripod cast in 536 B.C. with the criminal code inscribed on it. Given what we know of Tzu-ch'an, it is as unlikely for him, as for Confucius, to have resorted to killing in order to suppress an opponent, but whatever the historical fact, the story of the killing of Teng Hsi is likely to be a story used for Legalist purposes. The major principle of Legalist philosophy was the supreme authority of the state in pronouncing on what is right and wrong, and it would be in keeping with this philosophy to advocate the execution of any man who takes it upon himself to tamper with the criminal code.

Of the other cases cited, the one concerning the execution of P'an Chih by T'ai Kung of Ch'i is interesting. Although P'an Chih is otherwise unknown, there is another similar story about T'ai Kung. In the *Han fei tzu* there are two versions side by side of this story. Here is the shorter version:

> T'ai Kung Wang was enfeoffed in Ch'i in the East. By the sea there lived an excellent man, Mad Chüeh. T'ai Kung Wang, hearing of this, went to call on him three times. Three times he left his horse at the door, but Mad Chüeh made no attempt to reciprocate the courtesy. T'ai Kung Wang killed him. At that time Tan, the Duke of Chou, was in Lu. He went post-haste to stop it, but by the time he arrived, T'ai Kung Wang had already killed Mad Chüeh. Tan, the Duke of Chou, said, 'Mad Chüeh is counted an excellent man in the whole Empire. Why did you, sir, kill him?' T'ai Kung Wang answered, 'Mad Chüeh expressed the view that he would not be a subject to the Emperor nor a friend to the feudal lords. I feared that he

54. *Lü shih ch'un ch'iu*, 18.10a.

would throw the law into confusion and supplant the teachings of the
state. That is why I made him the object of my initial act of punishment (*shou chu*). Suppose there is a horse here, which resembles, in
appearance, a steed and yet it neither goes off when driven nor comes
forward when led. Even a slave would not entrust himself to such a
horse and have it turn a cart round.' (*Han fei tzu*, 13.4a)

This story is used by Han Fei Tzu to illustrate the point that the
ruler should get rid of anyone beyond his power to control.
According to Legalist theory, reward and punishment are 'the two
handles' by which a ruler can control his subjects. If a man does not
respond to either, there is nothing the ruler can do either to encourage or to deter him. Such a person is what the world admires,
but in the eyes of the Legalist ruler, he only resembles an excellent
man but is not the genuine thing. Mad Chüeh was precisely such a
person and that is why he had to be made an example of.

What is interesting for us in this story is that the expression *shou
chu* is used. This is very like the *hsien chu* in the *Shuo yüan* and the
shih chu in the *K'ung tzu chia yü*. They all mean 'the initial act of
punishment'. That the expression constitutes the crucial element in
the story is shown by the fact that it appears even in the brief
quotation from the *Han shih nei chuan*.[55] The sharing in common of
this expression shows that the story about the punishment of Shao
Cheng Mao by Confucius and that about the punishment of
Mad Chüeh by T'ai Kung Wang belong to the same type. They
both serve to illustrate points in Legalist philosophy. Seen in this
light, the story of Shao Cheng Mao is merely another of the stories
found in Legalist literature in which Confucius is made the mouth-
piece of Legalist ideas. Here, for instance, is a blatant example from
the *Han fei tzu* of Legalist sentiments being put into the mouth of
Confucius:

Duke Ai of Lu asked Chung-ni, 'The *Ch'un ch'iu* records, "Winter,
the twelfth month, frost fell but did not kill the pulse." Why does
it record this?'

Chung-ni answered, 'What this means is that what can be killed

55. It is interesting to note that in the *K'ung tzu chia yü* the chapter in which
the story is found is entitled '*Shih chu*'. This shows, at least, that in Wang
Su's view, that constituted the point of the story.

is not killed. Now if what ought to be killed is not killed, then peaches and plums will bear fruit in winter. Now if Heaven is defied by plants when it fails to follow its way, how much more so would it be with a ruler of men?' (op. cit., 9.5b–6a)

This, like the Shao Cheng Mao story, illustrates the point that the ruler should be ruthless when the situation calls for severity.

That the Shao Cheng Mao story is of Legalist provenance is supported from yet another quarter. In chapter 14 of the *Kuan tzu* which deals with what should be prohibited by the law we find

Conduct that is firm while perverse, words that are eloquent while crafty, the transmission of what is wrong with erudition, the following of what is evil while giving it a gloss – these are prohibited by the sage king. (*Kuan tzu*, 5.7b)

Allowing for insignificant variants, this indisputably Legalist piece of writing is almost identical in wording with the relevant part in the Shao Cheng Mao story.[56]

Once we see that the story of Shao Cheng Mao is of Legalist provenance, we can see why Confucius is depicted there as advocating the suppression and execution of a potential trouble maker, an act which contradicts everything he stood for. To show the story for what it is we can do no better than to remind ourselves once more where Confucius stood on the question of the killing of wicked men.

Chi K'ang Tzu asked Confucius about government, saying, 'What would you think if, in order to move closer to those who possess the Way, I were to kill those who do not follow the Way?'

Confucius answered, 'In administering your government what need is there for you to kill? Just desire the good yourself and the common people will be good. The virtue of the gentleman is like

56. This resemblance was first noted by Yin T'ung-yang in his *Kuan tzu hsin shih* published in 1917, (quoted in Kuo Mo-juo et al., *Kuan tzu chi chiao*, Peking, 1956, p. 221), but the significance of the resemblance was first pointed out by Professor Hsü Fu-kuan in a postscript, dated 26 November 1959, to his *Yi ke li shih ku shih te hsing ch'eng chi ch'i yen chin* (*Chung kuo ssu hsiang shih lun chi*, Taipei, 1974, p. 132). Anyone familiar with Professor Hsü's article will know how much I am indebted to him in my treatment of the Shao Cheng Mao story.

wind; the virtue of the small man is like grass. Let the wind blow over the grass and it will bend.' (XII.19)

This examination of the traditions in the *Shih chi* unsupported by early sources serves to confirm Ts'ui Shu's verdict that in the *Shih chi* biography 'what is unfounded amounts to seventy or eighty per cent,'[57] and to show that we were right to have adhered to the austere principle of subjecting to close scrutiny whatever is not vouched for by the three early sources.

57. See p. 161 above.

Chronology

551 (or 552)	Confucius born.
525	Presented himself to the Viscount of T'an then on a visit to Lu.
522	Commented on gamekeeper who would rather die than answer wrong form of summons.
517	Commented on the number of *wan* dancers taking part in a performance in the courtyard of the Chi Family.
	First brief visit to Ch'i.
502	Became *ssu k'ou* in Lu some time after this date.
500	Assisted at ceremony during meeting between Duke Ting of Lu and Duke Ching of Ch'i in Chia Ku.
498	Unsuccessful attempt to demolish strongholds of the Three Families in Lu.
497	Left Lu and started on his travels.
	First visit to Wei.
?	Passes through Sung on way to Ch'en when Huan T'ui was said to have made an attempt on his life.
492	While in Ch'en commented on fire in the temples of Duke Huan and Duke Hsi in Lu.
489	Probably travelling in the region of Ch'en and Ts'ai during the invasion of Ch'en by Wu.
	Visited Ts'ai and met the Governor of She in Fu Han.
?488	Return to Wei.
484	Return from Wei to Lu.
481	Requested Duke Ai to send punitive expedition against Ch'en Heng who had assassinated Duke Chien of Ch'i.
479	Died.

Appendix 2

THE DISCIPLES AS THEY APPEAR
IN THE *ANALECTS*

In the 'Biography of Confucius' in the *Shih chi* it is said

> Confucius taught the *Odes*, the *Book of History*, the rites and music, and his disciples were said to have numbered three thousand, while those who were versed in the six arts numbered seventy-two. (p. 1938)

It is not clear what authority Ssu-ma Ch'ien had for the exaggerated number of 'three thousand', but there must have been an early tradition that Confucius' disciples were round seventy in number. This is the number mentioned in the *Mencius* (II.A.3), the *Lü shih ch'un ch'iu* (ch. 14, pt. 7),[1] the *Han fei tzu* (ch. 49),[2] the *Ta Tai li chi* (ch. 60)[3] and the *Huai nan tzu* (ch. 21).[4] These are all works earlier in date than the *Shih chi*. But even this number is probably exaggerated. In the 'Biography of Confucius' Disciples' which forms chapter 67 of the *Shih chi* where the number is given as seventy-seven (p. 2185), we can see that Ssu-ma Ch'ien was hard put to it to substantiate this claim. He has to admit that apart from the first thirty-five, the rest are not recorded anywhere. No indication is given where, if that is the case, he found these names either. Even amongst the first thirty-five, six at the end of the list are not mentioned in the *Analects*. If one examines the *Analects* one finds that the number is approximately twenty-five, and this includes some who appear only once and some who never speak at all.

Of all the disciples who appear in the *Analects*, there is a later group of five who deserve special mention at the outset. These are Tseng Tzu, Tzu-hsia, Tzu-yu, Tzu-chang and Yu Tzu. They

1. *Lü shih ch'un ch'iu*, 14.18b.
2. *Han fei tzu*, 19.3a.
3. *Ta Tai li chi*, 6.2b–3a.
4. *Huai nan tzu*, 21.7a.

played a very important role in the propagation of the teachings of Confucius after the Master's death. That this is so can be seen from two facts. First, in the *Analects*, they are the only disciples with their own sayings recorded. Other disciples appear mainly in conversation, mostly with Confucius. There are some sayings recorded of some of the other disciples, for instance, Tzu-kung, but these tend to be about Confucius and were recorded, presumably, because they constituted material about the Master. Second, the five figure very prominently as a group in certain chapters of the *Li chi* and the *Ta Tai li chi*, two collections of Confucian writings containing valuable material about Confucianism in the period immediately after the death of Confucius.

In Book XI of the *Analects* there is a passage in which a number of disciples are grouped under four heads:

> Virtuous conduct: Yen Yüan, Min Tzu-ch'ien, Jan Po-niu and Chung-kung; speech: Tsai Wo and Tzu-kung; government: Jan Yu and Chi-lu; culture and learning: Tzu-yu and Tzu-hsia. (XI.3)

This seems to have been written at an early date as Tzu-yu and Tzu-hsia are the only two from the later group who are mentioned. That this classification of the disciples is important can be seen from the fact that Mencius, in conversation with Kung-sun Ch'ou, echoed it,

> Tsai Wo and Tzu-kung excelled in rhetoric; Jan Niu, Min Tzu and Yen Hui excelled in the exposition of virtuous conduct.

Kung-sun Ch'ou then said,

> I have heard that Tzu-hsia, Tzu-yu and Tzu-chang each had one aspect of the Sage while Jan Niu, Min Tzu and Yen Hui were replicas of the Sage in miniature. (*Mencius*, II.A.2)

We can see that, apart from the omission of Jan Yu and Chi-lu, the names listed in the *Mencius* are virtually the same as in *Analects* XI.3, except that Kung-sun Ch'ou added the name of Tzu-chang. This only serves to underline the point that the original passage in the *Analects* must have been written at a time when Tzu-chang was not yet prominent among Confucius' disciples.

Apart from the later group of five, let us assume that the disciples who do not figure in the list in *Analects* XI.3 and who put in only the occasional appearance are of lesser importance, and we shall deal with them first.

First, there are those who, though they are considered to be disciples of Confucius in the *Shih chi* and elsewhere, are, in fact, unlikely to be so. For instance, there is no reason to believe that Kung Po-liao who is only mentioned once as having 'spoken ill of Tzu-lu to Chi-sun' (XIV.36) was a disciple. T'an-t'ai Mieh-ming is said to have been one of Tzu-yu's discoveries when he was steward of Wu Ch'eng (VI.14) but this is hardly sufficient grounds for including him amongst the disciples. Yen Lu, the father of Yen Yüan, is mentioned only once when he asked to be given the Master's carriage 'to pay for an outer coffin for his son' (XI.8). He is included amongst the disciples, perhaps because Tseng Hsi, the father of Tseng Tzu, seemed to have been one. Finally, there is Shen Ch'eng who is said to be 'full of desires' (V.11). The only reason in favour of his being a disciple is that Confucius' remark is found in a part of the *Analects* dealing exclusively with disciples. The case of Tzu-ch'in is somewhat different. He is universally considered a disciple of Confucius'. He appears three times in the *Analects*. On one occasion (XVI.3) he asked Confucius' son whether he had been taught anything special by his father. On the other two occasions (I.10, XIX.25) he discussed Confucius with Tzu-kung. It is inconceivable that any disciple should say to Tzu-kung, 'You are just being respectful, aren't you? Surely Chung-ni is not superior to you' (XIX.25), and he did not even take the trouble to refer to Confucius as 'the Master'.

Next come those who are mentioned only once or twice but who have never spoken in the *Analects*. Although there may be doubts about some of them, they are, nevertheless, likely to be disciples. There is Wu-ma Ch'i who reported a criticism of Confucius by Ch'en Ssu-pai to the Master (VII.31). As this is the only mention of him in the *Analects* and he did not in fact say anything of his own, it is difficult to be sure of his relationship to Confucius. There is Kung-yeh Ch'ang who was considered by Confucius a worthy choice as husband for his own daughter, because, though he was in gaol, it was through no fault of his own (V.1). Similarly, Nan Jung was given the daughter of Confucius' elder brother as wife (V.2). Of Nan Jung, we know a little more. He 'repeated over and over again the lines about the white jade sceptre' (XI.6), and he was not cast aside when the Way prevailed in the state, nor did he suffer the humiliation of punishment when the Way fell into disuse (V.2). He is generally identified with Nan-kung K'uo who asked a question about Yi and Ao who were known for their physical strength in antiquity and Yü and Chi who were sages of old, on which Confucius commented, 'How gentlemanly that man is! How he reveres virtue!' (XIV.5). In the same category is Tzu-chien who was said to be such a gentleman (V.3). When Tzu-kao was made prefect of Pi by Tzu-lu, Confucius, presumably considering him not yet ready for office, commented, 'He is ruining another man's son' (XI.25). It is therefore no surprise to find Confucius being pleased with Ch'i-tiao K'ai for refusing to take office on the grounds that he was not ready (V.6). Lao who reported a saying of Confucius (IX.7) is of uncertain identity. Yüan Ssu, when he became Confucius' steward, refused a gift of grain (VI.5). It is, perhaps, fitting that a man of such scruples should ask about the shameful (XIV.1). Tseng Hsi, the father of Tseng Tzu, is mentioned only once when Confucius expressed approval of what he enjoyed doing in life (XI.26).

There are three disciples who, though they appear a number of times in the *Analects*, do not figure in XI.3. First, there is Ssu-ma Niu, whose questions are recorded in three consecutive chapters in Book XII. He asked about benevolence and was told that a benevolent man was loath to speak. When he pressed the question, Confucius answered, 'When to act is difficult, is it any wonder that one is loath to speak?' (XII.3). When he asked about the gentleman, he was told that 'the gentleman is free from worries and fears'. He again pressed the question and Confucius answered, 'If, on examining himself, a man finds nothing to reproach himself for, what worries and fears can he have?' (XII.4). In XII.5 we find, 'Ssu-ma Niu appeared worried, saying, "All men have brothers. I alone have none."' In the *Tso chuan* (Duke Ai 14)[5] Ssu-ma

5. *Tso chuan chu shu*, 59.17a–19a.

Niu is said to be the brother of Huan T'ui[6] of whose insubordination he was ashamed. This would account for his remark. But it is interesting that Confucius' characterization of the gentleman seemed to have been directed against Ssu-ma Niu's proneness to worry. If this is the case, then it is very likely that he was a man who was more given to words than to action. Hence Confucius' remark about the benevolent man.

Kung-hsi Hua must have been quite well-known amongst Confucius' disciples, as he figures in Meng Wu Po's question (V.8) in the company of Jan Ch'iu and Tzu-lu. Confucius' answer shows that he was a person versed in court ceremonies and could be given diplomatic responsibility. This is confirmed by his own modest claim that he would like 'on ceremonial occasions in the ancestral temple or in diplomatic gatherings', to be 'a minor official in charge of protocol' (XI.26). On one occasion he went on a mission to Ch'i 'drawn by well-fed horses, and wearing light furs' (VI.4). When Confucius denied any claim to be either a sage or a benevolent man, and said that the only thing that might be said of him was that he learned without flagging and taught without growing weary, Kung-hsi Hua's comment was, 'This is precisely where we disciples are unable to learn from your example' (VII.34). This shows something of his flair for diplomatic language. Finally, he found an apparent contradiction in Confucius' answers to the same question put to him by two disciples and asked for an explanation. This is the kind of ability to think for oneself that Confucius valued.

Fan Ch'ih asked questions about benevolence and wisdom (XII.22, XIII.19) and 'the exaltation of virtue, the reformation of the depraved and the recognition of misguided judgement' (XII.21). He could not have been too bright, for twice he failed to understand the answer, and on one occasion Confucius had to give him further explanation (II.5) and on the other Tsu-hsia had to interpret for him Confucius' reply (XII.22). He once asked about growing crops and vegetables and this brought Confucius' comment, 'How petty Fan Hsü is!' (XIII.4).

We can now turn to the disciples listed in XI.3. Four of them

6. For Huan T'ui see *Analects* VII.23.

are listed under the head of 'virtuous conduct'. They are Yen Yüan, Min Tzu-ch'ien, Jan Po-niu and Chung-kung.

Amongst all Confucius' disciples, pride of place must go to Yen Yüan who was undoubtedly Confucius' favourite. That his conduct was exemplary is borne out by what Confucius said of him. Benevolence is something Confucius very rarely granted anyone, including himself, yet he said, 'In his heart for three months at a time Hui does not lapse from benevolence,' while in contrast, 'the others attain benevolence merely by fits and starts' (VI.7). He was a poor man. Confucius said of his poverty, 'Hui is perhaps difficult to improve upon; he allows himself constantly to be in dire poverty' (XI.19). Again, he said, 'How admirable Hui is! Living in a mean dwelling on a bowlful of rice and a ladleful of water is a hardship most men would find intolerable, but Hui does not allow this to affect his joy. How admirable Hui is!' (VI.11). He really was able to live up to Confucius' precept, 'Poor yet delighting in the Way' (I.15). Confucius considered Yen Yüan as an equal. He said to him, 'Only you and I have the ability to go forward when employed and to stay out of sight when set aside' (VII.11).

Although praised for his virtuous conduct, Yen Yüan was equally outstanding in his eagerness to learn. When asked which of his disciples was eager to learn, Confucius answered, 'There was one Yen Hui who was eager to learn but unfortunately his allotted span was a short one and he died. Now there is no one' (XI.7, also VI.3). Since in Confucius' teaching, ability to think and eagerness to learn are two sides to the same activity, we should not be surprised that Yen Yüan was also the most intelligent of the disciples. Once Confucius commented, 'Hui is no help to me at all. He is pleased with everything I say' (XI.4). This passiveness was only apparent. Elsewhere Confucius said, 'I can speak to Hui all day without his disagreeing with me in any way. Thus he would seem to be stupid. However, when I take a closer look at what he does in private after he has withdrawn from my presence, I discover that it does, in fact, throw light on what I said. Hui is not stupid after all' (II.9). This is an understatement. There is a conversation between Confucius and Tzu-kung on another occasion when the Master asked Tzu-kung – a man of no mean intelligence – 'Who is the better

man, you or Hui?' 'How dare I compare myself with Hui? When
he is told one thing he understands ten. When I am told one thing
I understand only two.' The Master said, 'You are not as good as he
is. Neither of us is as good as he is' (V.9). The high praise is not
surprising since, for Confucius, the intelligent student when told
something should be able to 'see its relevance to what he has not
been told' (I.15). Because he died young, Confucius said of him,
'I watched him make progress, but I did not see him realize his
capacity to the full. What a pity!' (IX.21). The sorrow Confucius
showed at the death of Yen Yüan is recorded in the *Analects*:

> When Yen Yüan died, the Master said, 'Alas! Heaven has bereft me!
> Heaven has bereft me!' (XI.9)

> When Yen Yüan died, in weeping for him, the Master showed
> undue sorrow. His followers said, 'You are showing undue sorrow.'
> 'Am I? Yet if not for him, for whom should I show undue sorrow?'
> (IX.10)

Given Confucius' high regard for Yen Yüan, it is perhaps somewhat surprising that he should have refused a request from Yen
Yüan's father to be given his carriage to provide for an outer
coffin (XI.8), but this is perhaps explained by another passage:

> When Yen Yüan died, the disciples wanted to give him a lavish
> burial. The Master said, 'It would not be proper.' All the same, they
> gave him a lavish burial. The Master said, 'Hui treated me as a
> father, yet I have been prevented from treating him as a son. This
> was none of my choice. It was the doing of these others.' (XI.11)

It was not proper to give Yen Yüan a lavish burial, presumably
because it was above his station. If this was so, it might well have
been equally improper for him to have had an outer coffin, particularly seeing that Confucius said of his own son that he did not
have one either.

That Yen Yüan had great affection for Confucius can be seen
from this passage:

> When the Master was under siege in K'uang, Yen Yüan fell behind.
> The Master said, 'I thought you had met your death.' 'While you,
> Master, are alive, how would I dare die?' (XI.23)

Yen Yüan left an imaginative description of Confucius as a teacher:

Yen Yüan, heaving a sigh, said, 'The more I look up at it the higher it appears. The more I bore into it the harder it becomes. I see it before me. Suddenly it is behind me.

'The Master is good at leading one on step by step. He broadens me with culture and brings me back to essentials by means of the rites. I cannot give up even if I wanted to, but, having done all I can, it seems to rise sheer above me and I have no way of going after it, however much I want to.' (IX.11)

Perhaps we can best round off this sketch of Yen Yüan by a remark Confucius made about him and one made by himself. According to Confucius, 'he did not vent his anger upon an innocent person, nor did he make the same mistake twice' (VI.3). In describing what he would like to be, Yen Yüan said, 'I should like never to boast of my own goodness and never to impose onerous tasks on others' (V.26). These are very down-to-earth qualities of a man who, even in the critical eyes of Confucius, came near to attaining perfection.

Min Tzu-ch'ien was highly thought of by Confucius, and is said to have been a very good son (XI.5). He once made a remark which prompted Confucius to comment, 'Either this man does not speak or he says something to the point' (XI.14). His refusal to take office with the Chi Family (VI.9) shows that he was a man of principle.

Of Jan Po-niu little is known. When he was ill, the Master visited him and, holding his hand through the window, said, 'We are going to lose him. It must be Destiny. Why else should such a man be stricken with such a disease? Why else should such a man be stricken with such a disease?' (VI.10). From the tone of Confucius' remark one can imagine that his illness must have been a particularly horrible one. This might have been what led later generations to speculate that it was leprosy he suffered from.

Chung-kung probably came from humble origins, as Confucius said of him, 'Should a bull born of plough cattle have a sorrel coat and well-formed horns, would the spirits of the mountains and rivers allow it to be passed over even if we felt it was not good enough to be used?' (VI.6). When someone said that Chung-kung

was benevolent but did not have a facile tongue, Confucius with-
held judgement on his benevolence but said there was no need for
him to have a facile tongue (V.5). He may not have had a facile
tongue, but his occasional remark received the approval of the
Master (VI.2). He was once steward to the Chi Family, though he
was worthy of much better things. What higher praise could
Confucius have bestowed than the remark, 'Yung could be given
the seat facing south (i.e., the seat of the ruler)'? (VI.1).

Under the head of 'speech' are listed only two disciples, Tsai Wo
and Tzu-kung.

Tsai Wo enjoys the dubious distinction of having been criticized
by Confucius on more occasions than any other disciple. When
Duke Ai asked him about the altar to the god of earth, Tsai Wo
answered that the men of Chou used the chestnut, saying that it
made the common people tremble. This brought from Confucius
the comment that what is past should be left alone (III.21). When
Tsai Wo took a nap in the daytime, Confucius said, 'A piece of
rotten wood cannot be carved, nor can a wall of dried dung be
trowelled. As far as Yü is concerned what is the use of condemning
him?' and added for good measure, 'I used to take on trust a man's
deeds after having listened to his words. Now having listened to a
man's words I go on to observe his deeds. It was on account of
Yü that I have changed in this respect' (V.10). When Tsai Wo
wanted to shorten the mourning period from three years to one,
Confucius said, 'How unfeeling Yü is' (XVII.21). Perhaps Tsai Wo,
for his part, harboured a secret contempt for benevolent men
whom he thought of as simpletons. He asked, 'If a benevolent
man was told that there was another benevolent man in the well,
would he, nevertheless, go and join him?' (VI.26). In spite of all
these strictures, Tsai Wo's admiration for Confucius remained
unbounded. 'In my view,' he said, 'the Master surpassed greatly
Yao and Shun' (*Mencius*, II.A.2).

Next to Yen Yüan, Tzu-kung was the most distinguished of
Confucius' early group of disciples. He was a man of the world,
successful as a diplomat and as a merchant, according to the *Shih
chi*. When Chi K'ang Tzu asked whether Tzu-kung was good
enough to be given office, Confucius answered, 'Ssu is a man of

understanding. What difficulties could there be for him in taking office?' (VI.8). When Tzu-kung asked what Confucius thought of him, the answer was, 'You are a vessel' (V.4). This is, at first sight, a somewhat surprising answer, seeing that Confucius also said that the gentleman was no vessel (II.12). But there Confucius probably meant by gentleman someone who was suitable to be a ruler, and the remark meant only that a ruler should not be a specialist. If that is the case, all Confucius was saying was that Tzu-kung did not possess the qualities of the ruler, but simply those of the specialist. This contrasts markedly with his remarks about Jan Yung, 'Yung could be given the seat facing south' (VI.1).

As to his success as a merchant, there is a remark of Confucius which is relevant. 'Ssu,' he said, 'refuses to accept his lot and indulges in money making, and is frequently right in his conjectures' (XI.19). Perhaps it was because he was so good with money that he could not tolerate unnecessary expenditure. 'Tzu-kung wanted to do away with the sacrificial sheep at the announcement of the new moon. The Master said, "Ssu, you are loath to part with the price of the sheep, but I am loath to see the disappearance of the rite"' (III.17). That Tzu-kung was, both morally and intellectually, not the equal of Yen Yüan was obvious from a passage quoted above.[7] As we have seen, Confucius associated himself with Tzu-kung by saying, 'Neither of us is as good as he is' (V.9). In fact Confucius had a high opinion of Tzu-kung's intelligence. He said once, 'Ssu, only with a man like you can one discuss the *Odes*. Tell such a man something and he can see its relevance to what he has not been told' (I.15).

If Confucius thought highly of Tzu-kung's intelligence, he was not quite so complimentary on his moral qualities.

> Tzu-kung said, 'While I do not wish others to impose on me, I also wish not to impose on others.'
> The Master said, 'Ssu, that is quite beyond you.' (V.12)

This comment may sound harsh, but if we look more closely at Tzu-kung's wish it is only to be expected. Elsewhere, we find,

7. See pp. 201-2 above.

Tzu-kung asked, 'Is there a single word which can be a guide to conduct throughout one's life?' The Master said, 'It is perhaps the word "*shu*". Do not impose on others what you yourself do not desire.' (XV.24)

Putting the two together we can see that it is the practice of '*shu*' that Confucius thought was beyond Tzu-kung. Elsewhere, Tseng Tzu describes the way of the Master as consisting in *chung* and *shu* (IV.15), and Confucius also remarked, 'a benevolent man helps others to take their stand in so far as he himself wishes to take his stand, and gets others there in so far as he himself wishes to get there. The ability to take as analogy what is near at hand (viz., oneself) can be called the method of benevolence' (VI.30). From these sayings we can see that '*shu*' is in fact the way to put benevolence into practice. As Confucius so rarely granted that anyone was benevolent, there is little wonder that he did not think Tzu-kung capable of it. When on another occasion Tzu-kung asked about the practice of benevolence, Confucius' advice was, 'You should . . . make friends with the most benevolent Gentlemen in the state where you happen to be staying' (XV.10). Perhaps Tzu-kung was more given to protesting about his desire for benevolence than to the actual practice of it, for when he asked about the gentleman, the Master said, 'He puts his words into action before allowing his words to follow his action' (II.13).

There is another shortcoming of Tzu-kung's which Confucius pointed out:

Tzu-kung was given to grading people. The Master said, 'How superior Ssu is! For my part I have no time for such things.' (XIV.29)

This tendency of Tzu-kung's can be seen in some passages in the *Analects*. For instance, he asked whether Tzu-chang or Tzu-hsia was superior (XI.16). Again, he asked whether Kuan Chung was a benevolent man (XIV.17).

Perhaps it is because of his eloquence that Tzu-kung has left more remarks about Confucius than any other disciple. He described the Master as 'cordial, good, respectful, frugal and deferential' (I.10). He said, 'One can get to hear about the Master's accomplishments, but one cannot get to hear about his views on human nature and the Way of Heaven' (V.13). When someone said that the Master must have been a sage, otherwise why should he be skilled in so many things, Tzu-kung's answer was, 'It is true, Heaven set him on the path to sagehood. However, he is skilled in many things besides' (IX.6). When Confucius said, 'There are three things constantly on the lips of the gentleman none of which I have succeeded in following: "A man of benevolence never worries; a man of wisdom is never in two minds; a man of courage is never afraid," ' Tzu-kung's comment was, 'What the Master has just quoted is a description of himself' (XIV.28). When Confucius said he was thinking of giving up speech, Tzu-kung said, 'If you did not speak, what would there be for us, your disciples, to transmit?' (XVII.19). But above all, Tzu-kung left the panegyric at the end of Book XIX,[8] which was probably meant to be a fitting conclusion to the *Analects* as Book XX was, in all probability, a late addition.

Under the head of 'government' are listed Jan Yu and Tzu-lu. That Jan Yu was gifted in this direction is fully borne out by the passages concerning him in the *Analects*. In answer to a question from Meng Wu Po whether Jan Yu was benevolent, Confucius said he did not know but 'Ch'iu can be given the responsibility as a steward in a town with a thousand households or a noble family with a hundred chariots' (V.8). Again, when Chi K'ang Tzu asked, 'Is Ch'iu good enough to be given office?' Confucius' answer was, 'Ch'iu is accomplished. What difficulties could there be for him in taking office?' (VI.8). Judging by the answers Confucius gave about him, Jan Yu had administrative ability. He must have started his career in Confucius' household. He acted as driver on Confucius' first visit to Wei which must have taken place before 493 B.C. Jan Yu was most probably quite a young man then, but we can see from his questions that he was interested in matters of government. When Confucius remarked that Wei had a flourishing population, Jan Yu asked what further benefit could be added and he was told that one should make the people rich. He again asked what further benefit could be added and he was told that the people should then be given training, presumably, in warfare (XIII.9). On

8. quoted above on pp. 52-3.

another occasion, Jan Yu asked for grain for the mother of Tzu-
hua who was away on a mission to Ch'i (VI.4). He must have been,
then, in charge of the affairs of Confucius' household. Subsequently
he became a member of the household of Chi K'ang Tzu. When
asked what he wanted to do, Jan Yu said, 'If I were to administer
an area measuring sixty or seventy *li* square, or even fifty or sixty
li square, I could, within three years, bring the size of the population
up to an adequate level. As to the rites and music, I would leave that
to abler gentlemen' (XI.26). This confirms everything that we have
learned so far from other chapters in the *Analects*. His interests
were not in the rites and music but in the administration of the
state, in the question of increasing the population and, presumably, in bringing prosperity to the common people.

Jan Yu, however, was probably lacking in drive. This comes out
in the passage where he asked whether one should immediately
put into practice what one had heard and was told by Confucius
that one should when precisely the opposite answer had been given
to the same question from Tzu-lu. Asked by Kung-hsi Hua
to explain the discrepancy between the two answers, Confucius
said, 'Ch'iu holds himself back. It is for this reason that I tried to
urge him on' (XI.22). This lack of drive also manifests itself in
quiescence to action that should be resisted on moral grounds.
When he and Tzu-lu were supposed to have reported to Confucius that the Chi Family was going to take military action against
a dependency,[9] Confucius blamed him for not stopping this, and
Jan Yu said that his Master, i.e., Chi K'ang Tzu, wished it. Confucius replied that if that was the case he should resign. Only then
did Jan Yu come out with the true motive. Unless annexed, the
dependency will constitute a source of trouble for the Chi Family
in future generations. This called forth Confucius' acid remark,
'Ch'iu, the gentleman detests those who, rather than saying outright that they want something, can be counted on to gloss over
their remarks' (XVI.1).

9. It is interesting that throughout the conversation Tzu-lu remained silent.
The fact is, Tzu-lu and Jan Yu were never in the service of Chi K'ang Tzu
at the same time. This conversation must have been between Confucius and
Jan Yu alone, and Tzu-lu's name was added by someone who was unaware
of the facts.

On another occasion, Confucius was even more outspoken in his criticism.

> The wealth of the Chi Family was greater than that of the Duke of Chou, and still Ch'iu helped them add further to that wealth by raking in the taxes. The Master said, 'He is no disciple of mine. You, my young friends, may attack him openly to the beating of drums.' (XI.17)

Confucius' considered judgement was that Jan Yu could be described as a minister 'appointed to make up the full quota'. However, he added that he would not do as he was told 'when it comes to patricide or regicide' (XI.24).

Tzu-lu, Yen Yüan and Tzu-kung make up the group of the best known of Confucius' early disciples. Tzu-lu was the oldest and we have a clearer picture of him as a man than of any of the other disciples. He figures in more than thirty chapters in the *Analects*. Of these some two-thirds have to do with his character. He was resolute and courageous and a man of action, impetuous in nature and not over fond of learning. When Chi K'ang Tzu asked whether Tzu-lu was good enough to be given office, Confucius answered, 'Yu is resolute. What difficulties could there be for him in taking office?' (VI.8). Confucius criticized him a number of times for his courage. Once when Tzu-lu appeared overjoyed on hearing Confucius say that if he were to put to sea on a raft, the one to follow him would be Tzu-lu. The Master, then, added, 'Yu has a greater love for courage than I, but is lacking in judgement' (V.7). When Tzu-lu asked Confucius whom he would take with him were he leading the Three Armies, the Master said, 'I would not take with me anyone who would try to fight a tiger with his bare hands or to walk across the River and die in the process without regrets' (VII.11). Once, Tzu-lu asked whether the gentleman considered courage a supreme quality, the Master pointedly answered, 'For the gentleman it is morality that is supreme. Possessed of courage but devoid of morality, a gentleman will make trouble while a small man will be a brigand' (XVII.23).

Once Confucius remarked, 'A man like Yu will not die a natural death' (XI.13). It is not clear what occasioned the remark, but it proved to be prophetic. Tzu-lu, in fact, died fighting for his lord in Wei in 480 B.C.

Being a man of courage, Tzu-lu was probably versed in military matters. Thus when asked whether Tzu-lu was benevolent, Confucius, instead of answering the question, said, 'Yu can be given the responsibility of managing the military levies in a state of a thousand chariots' (V.8). Nevertheless, Confucius, as we have seen, impressed upon Tzu-lu that courage alone was not enough even in war.

Tzu-lu was a man of action rather than of words. 'Before he could put into practice something he had heard the only thing Tzu-lu feared was that he should be told something further' (V.14). It is perhaps because of this that Confucius warned him against acting too rashly:

> Tzu-lu asked, 'Should one immediately put into practice what one has heard?' The Master said, 'As your father and elder brothers are still alive, you are hardly in a position immediately to put into practice what you have heard.'

To the same question put by Jan Yu, Confucius, as we have seen, gave the opposite answer. His explanation of why he did so is this. 'Ch'iu holds himself back. It is for this reason that I tried to urge him on. Yu has the energy of two men. It is for this reason that I tried to hold him back' (XI.22).

When he made Tzu-kao the prefect of Pi, Tzu-lu was reproached by Confucius for ruining another man's son, presumably because Tzu-kao was too young and had much to learn. In his retort, Tzu-lu showed his contempt for learning. 'There are the common people and one's fellow men, and there are the altars to the gods of earth and grain. Why must one have to read books before one is said to learn?' Confucius commented, 'It is for this reason that I dislike men who are plausible' (XI.25).

On another occasion we find this conversation:

> The Master said, 'Yu, have you heard about the six qualities and the six attendant faults?'
> 'No.'
> 'Be seated and I shall tell you. To love benevolence without

loving learning is liable to lead to foolishness. To love cleverness without loving learning is liable to lead to deviation from the right path. To love trustworthiness in word without loving learning is liable to lead to harmful behaviour. To love forthrightness without loving learning is liable to lead to intolerance. To love courage without loving learning is liable to lead to insubordination. To love unbending strength without loving learning is liable to lead to indiscipline.' (XVII.8)

This was certainly said with Tzu-lu's special shortcomings in mind.

Confucius was often critical of Tzu-lu. On one occasion when Confucius asked a group of disciples who were in attendance what they would like to do given the opportunity, Tzu-lu leapt in with an answer and Confucius smiled at him. When asked afterwards by another disciple why he smiled at Tzu-lu, Confucius answered that Tzu-lu showed a lack of modesty (XI.26). During the time when Confucius was seriously ill, Tzu-lu told his disciples to act as retainers. When he recovered, Confucius rebuked Tzu-lu, saying, 'Yu has long been practising deception. In pretending that I had retainers when I had none, who would we be deceiving? Would we be deceiving Heaven?' (IX.12). On one occasion we find,

The Master said, 'If anyone can, while dressed in a worn-out gown padded with old silk floss, stand beside a man wearing fox or badger fur without feeling ashamed, it is, I suppose, Yu.

> Neither envious nor covetous,
> How can he be anything but good?'

Thereafter, Tzu-lu constantly recited these verses. The Master commented, 'The way summed up in these verses will hardly enable one to be good.' (IX.27)

There are, however, qualities in Tzu-lu that Confucius admired. He said, 'If anyone can arrive at the truth in a legal dispute on the evidence of only one party, it is perhaps Yu' (XII.12). In the same passage, it is also said that Tzu-lu never put off the fulfilment of a promise to the next day.

Being closer to Confucius in age than the rest of the disciples and more outspoken by nature, Tzu-lu often criticized Confucius for actions that appeared to him to be wrong. This is probably the reason Tzu-lu is the one credited with reproaching Confucius in apocryphal stories. For instance, he was supposed to have protested when Confucius was said to have been twice tempted to accept invitations from rebellious subjects. On the one occasion he is supposed to have said, 'We may have nowhere to go, but why must we go to Kung-shan?' (XVII.5), and on the other, 'Sometime ago I heard this from you, Master, that the gentleman does not enter the domain of one who in his own person does what is not good. Now Pi Hsi is using Chung Mou as a stronghold to stage a revolt. How can you justify going there?' (XVII.7). Again, when Confucius had an audience with Nan Tzu, the notorious wife of Duke Ling of Wei, Tzu-lu was said to have been displeased. In the end Confucius had to swear, 'If I have done anything improper, may Heaven's curse be on me, may Heaven's curse be on me!' (VI.28). As these stories are likely to be apocryphal, they tell us more about the popular conception of Tzu-lu than about events in Confucius' life.

If Confucius looked upon Yen Yüan as a son, he must have looked upon Tzu-lu as a friend. When he took Tzu-lu to task, one can detect a great deal of affection behind his words.

Of the later group of five disciples, only Tzu-yu and Tzu-hsia figure in the list in *Analects* XI.3 and both come under the head of 'culture and learning'.

Tzu-yu appears in seven chapters in the *Analects*, only in three of these is he recorded as having a conversation with the Master. On one occasion he asked about being filial (II.7); on another when he was the steward of Wu Ch'eng he was asked by Confucius whether he had made any discoveries among his subordinates (VI.14). The third occasion is more interesting:

> The Master went to Wu Ch'eng. There he heard the sound of stringed instruments and singing. The Master broke into a smile and said, 'Surely you don't need to use an ox-knife to kill a chicken.'
>
> Tzu-yu answered, 'Some time ago I heard it from you, Master, that the gentleman instructed in the Way loves his fellow men and that the small man instructed in the Way is easy to command.'

The Master said, 'My friends, what Yen said is right. My remark a moment ago was only made in jest.' (XVII.4)

Followers of the Confucian tradition in subsequent ages placed excessive emphasis on outward conformity to the rites. We can see a beginning here where Tzu-yu identifies the Way with music and the rites.

In the other four chapters in the *Analects* in which Tzu-yu figures, it is his own sayings which are recorded. One remark concerns the way to serve a ruler and to behave towards friends (IV.26); another concerns the way to mourn (XIX.14). The remaining two are, however, directed against his fellow disciples. He said of Tzu-chang, 'My friend Chang is difficult to emulate. All the same he has not, as yet, attained benevolence' (XIX.15). He also criticized the disciples and younger followers of Tsu-hsia for concentrating on menial duties like 'sweeping and cleaning, responding to calls and replying to questions put to them' and 'coming forward and withdrawing', to such an extent that 'on what is basic they are ignorant' (XIX.12).

It is said in the *Han fei tzu* (ch. 50) that after Confucius' death, the Confucian school split into eight sects.[10] If that is true, we can see signs of such a split with this final group of disciples.

In subsequent tradition, Tzu-hsia has been credited with a major role in the transmission of the Classics, with the exception of the *Book of History*. It comes out quite clearly in the *Analects* that, more than any other disciple, he was given to learning, particularly book learning. Of eleven sayings of Tzu-hsia's six are concerned with learning. These include the following:

Tsu-hsia said, 'A man can, indeed, be said to be eager to learn who is conscious, in the course of a day, of what he lacks and who never forgets, in the course of a month, what he has mastered.' (XIX.5)

Tzu-hsia said, 'Learn widely, and be steadfast in your purpose, inquire earnestly and reflect on what is at hand, and there is no need for you to look for benevolence elsewhere.' (XIX.6)

Tzu-hsia said, 'The artisan, in any of the hundred crafts, masters his trade by staying in his workshop; the gentleman perfects his way through learning.' (XIX.7)

10. *Han fei tzu*, 19.7b.

Tzu-hsia said, 'When a man in office finds that he can more than cope with his duties, then he studies; when a student finds that he can more than cope with his studies, then he takes office.' (XIX.13)

That he was an apt student of the *Odes* is shown by his question on the meaning of some verses which elicited, in the end, the remark from Confucius, 'It is you, Shang, who have thrown light on the text for me. Only with a man like you can one discuss the *Odes*' (III.8). This, together with his reputation for learning, may well be responsible for the tradition that he was the author of the Preface to the *Odes*.

Though Tzu-hsia was given to book learning, he did not place it above virtuous conduct. One of his remarks is, 'I would grant that a man has received instruction who appreciates men of excellence where other men appreciate beautiful women, who exerts himself to the utmost in the service of his parents and offers his person to the service of his lord, and who, in his dealings with his friends, is trustworthy in what he says, even though he may say he has never been taught' (I.7). There is, nevertheless, a danger that Tzu-hsia might err on the side of pedantry. Once Confucius said to him, 'Be a gentleman *ju*, not a petty *ju*' (VI.13). When, on becoming the prefect of Chü Fu, Tzu-hsia asked about government, he was told by Confucius, 'Do not be impatient. Do not see only petty gains. If you are impatient, you will not reach your goal. If you see only petty gains, the great tasks will not be accomplished' (XIII.17). Perhaps it was because he took Confucius' admonitions to heart that Tzu-hsia said, 'Even minor arts are sure to have their worthwhile aspects, but the gentleman does not take them up because the fear of a man who would go a long way is that he should be bogged down' (XIX.4). When Tzu-kung asked about the relative merits of Tzu-chang and Tzu-hsia, Confucius replied, 'Shih (i.e., Tzu-chang) overshoots the mark; Shang (i.e., Tzu-hsia) falls short' (XI.16). This may be pointing to the same tendency on the part of Tzu-hsia to pay too much attention to the petty at the expense of the great tasks.

Tseng Tzu and Yu Tzu occupied a very special position amongst the disciples of Confucius. There are only four disciples who enjoyed the distinction in the *Analects* of the epithet *tzu* – master.

While Min Tzu-ch'ien is referred to as Min Tzu in one passage (XI.13) and Jan Ch'iu as Jan Tzu in two (VI. 4, XIII.14),[11] Tseng Tzu and Yu Tzu are invariably referred to as Tseng Tzu and Yu Tzu.

Tseng Tzu is once described by Confucius as slow (XI.18). This he made up for by possessing great steadfastness. He said,

> A Gentleman must be strong and resolute, for his burden is heavy and the road is long. He takes benevolence as his burden. Is that not heavy? Only with death does the road come to an end. Is that not long? (VIII.7)

There is an account of his last moments.

> When he was seriously ill Tseng Tzu summoned his disciples and said, 'Take a look at my hands. Take a look at my feet. The *Odes* say,
>
> > In fear and trembling,
> > As if approaching a deep abyss,
> > As if walking on thin ice.
>
> Only now am I sure of being spared, my young friends.' (VIII.3).

Only with death was he sure that he had preserved intact the body he inherited from his parents by escaping mutilating punishments. This shows the same unrelenting effort to the end.

Again, he said, 'If a man can be entrusted with an orphan six *ch'ih* tall, and the fate of a state one hundred *li* square, without his being deflected from his purpose even in moments of crisis, is he not a gentleman? He is, indeed, a gentleman' (VIII.6).

Traditionally, filial duty is firmly associated with the name of Tseng Tzu. This is borne out by the *Analects*. He said, 'Conduct the funeral of your parents with meticulous care and let not sacrifice to your remote ancestors be forgotten, and the virtue of the common people will incline towards fullness' (I.9). Twice he quoted Confucius on the same subject. He said, 'I have heard the Master say that on no occasion does a man realize himself to the full, though, when pressed, he said that mourning for one's parents

---

11. Of these two passages, in XIII.4 however, there is a variant reading 'Jan Yu' for 'Jan Tzu'.

may be an exception' (XIX.17), and, again, 'I have heard the Master say that other men could emulate everything Meng Chuang Tzu did as a good son with the exception of one thing; he left unchanged both his father's officials and his father's policies, and this was what was difficult to emulate' (XIX.18).

Tseng Tzu shows his conscientiousness in his much-quoted saying,

> Every day I examine myself on three counts. In what I have under-taken on another's behalf, have I failed to do my best? In my dealings with my friends have I failed to be trustworthy in what I say? Have I passed on to others anything that I have not tried out myself? (I.4)

The emphasis on friends is echoed in another saying, 'A gentleman makes friends through being cultivated, but looks to friends for support in benevolence' (XII.24). Tseng Tzu has also left comments on two of his own friends. He said, 'To be able yet to ask the advice of those who are not able. To have many talents yet to ask the advice of those who have few. To have yet to appear to want. To be full yet to appear empty. To be transgressed against yet not to mind. It was towards this that my friend used to direct his efforts' (VIII.5). The object of this praise is traditionally taken to be Yen Yüan, and there is no reason to think otherwise. His remark about another friend is not quite so complimentary. He said, 'Grand, indeed, is Chang, so much so that it is difficult to work side by side with him at the cultivation of benevolence' (XIX.16).

Tzu-chang who is the target of Tseng Tzu's jibe was, as we have seen, also criticized by Tzu-yu. He seemed to be a very different kind of person from the other two. He took a broad view and put much more emphasis on what was basic. He said,

> How can a man be said either to have anything or not to have any-thing who fails to hold on to virtue with all his might or to believe in the Way with all his heart. (XIX.2)

Again,

> One can, perhaps, be satisfied with a Gentleman who is ready to

lay down his life in the face of danger, who does not forget what is right at the sight of gain, and who does not forget reverence during sacrifice nor sorrow while in mourning. (XIX.1)

He shows great awareness that it is the spirit behind a moral principle that is important. In the last resort, it is one's readiness to lay down one's life, one's ability to resist the temptation of gain and one's being imbued with a sense of reverence and sorrow that count. When Tzu-chang heard that the disciples of Tzu-hsia were taught that they should make friends with those who were adequate and spurn those who were inadequate, he commented,

> That is different from what I have heard. I have heard that the gentleman honours his betters and is tolerant towards the multitude and that he is full of praise for the good while taking pity on the backward. If I am greatly superior, which among men need I be intolerant of? If I am inferior, then others will spurn me, how can there be any question of my spurning them? (XIX.3)

When a man who expresses such lofty sentiments becomes the butt of criticisms from his friends, one has to seek the reasons for them below the surface. Perhaps Tzu-chang had a tendency to speak rashly without thinking of the difficulty of living up to his word. That is probably the reason Confucius, in his answers to Tzu-chang's questions, put special emphasis on caution in word and deed and on doing one's best as well as on trustworthiness in one's word. When Tzu-chang was studying with an eye to an official career, Confucius' advice was, 'Use your ears widely but leave out what is doubtful; repeat the rest with caution and you will make few mistakes. Use your eyes widely and leave out what is hazardous; put the rest into practice with caution and you will have few regrets' (II.18). Confucius also said to him, 'Make it your guiding principle to do your best for others and to be trustworthy in what you say' (XII.10), and 'If in word you are conscientious and trustworthy and in deed single-minded and reverent, then even in the lands of the barbarians you will go forward without obstruction' (XV.6). The danger of failure through a lack of single-mindedness and energy is also emphasized in the answer to Tzu-chang's question about government. Confucius said, 'Over daily routine do not show weariness, but when there is action to be taken, give of your best' (XII.14).

Tzu-chang had, perhaps, a tendency to pay more attention to appearances than to the substance. This seems to be the point of the following conversation:

> Tzu-chang asked, 'What must a Gentleman be like before he can be said to have got through?' The Master said, 'What on earth do you mean by getting through?' Tzu-chang answered, 'What I have in mind is a man who is sure to be known whether he serves in a state or in a noble family.' The Master said, 'That is being known, not getting through. Now the term "getting through" describes a man who is straight by nature and fond of what is right, sensitive to other people's words and observant of the expression on their faces, and always mindful of being modest. Such a man is bound to get through whether he serves in a state or in a noble family. On the other hand, the term "being known" describes a man who has no misgivings about his own claim to benevolence when all he is doing is putting up a façade of benevolence which is belied by his deeds. Such a man is sure to be known, whether he serves in a state or in a noble family.' (XII.20)

The description of the man who is known was probably meant to fit Tzu-chang. If so, he must have been rather brash and insensitive, more ready to lay claims to benevolence than to justify such claims.

Finally, there is Yu Tzu. As we have seen, Yu Tzu shares with Tseng Tzu the distinction of being invariably referred to as Yu Tzu except on the occasion when he was in conversation with Duke Ai where etiquette demanded that he should be referred to as Yu Juo (XII.9). Another distinction Yu Tzu enjoys is that he is only recorded as making pronouncements of his own, never asking a question of the Master. In his four recorded sayings a wide range of moral topics are covered.

There is no doubt that Yu Tzu enjoyed a special position in the Confucian school and the *Mencius* gives an explanation of this. One day, after the death of Confucius, 'Tzu-hsia, Tzu-chang and Tzu-yu wanted to serve Yu Juo as they had served Confucius because of his resemblance to the Sage,' but Tseng Tzu refused to join them (*Mencius*, III.A.4). It is not clear in what way Yu Tzu resembled Confucius. It is possible that he looked like Confucius, but it is more likely that it was his words that resembled those of Confucius. In the *T'an kung* chapter of the *Li chi*, Tzu-yu is recorded as saying, 'How extraordinarily Yu Tzu's words resemble those of the Master.'[12] This probably refers less to the words than to the sentiments.

Whether Yu Tzu ever became the successor to the Master, there is little doubt that the later group of five disciples played a major role in the early days of the Confucian school and of these Tseng Tzu and Tzu-hsia were particularly important. It is interesting that the Confucian tradition was shaped by Tseng Tzu who was said by Confucius to be 'slow' and Tzu-hsia who was said to 'fall short of the mark'. As we have seen, Tseng Tzu showed greater moral earnestness than intellectual ability while Tzu-hsia showed greater concern for minutiae in the rites than broad moral principle. It is, perhaps, because of the character of these two disciples that later Confucianism was coloured by a certain staidness and pedantry. One is left wondering what sort of a face Confucianism would have shown had Yen Yüan, whose virtuous character was matched by his intellect, lived to transmit the teachings of the Master.

12. *Li chi chu shu*, 8.7a.

Appendix 3

THE *LUN YÜ*

Of the history of the *Lun yü* there is no early account. The earliest explicit quotation from the work is found in the *Fang chi*, a chapter of the *Li chi*.[1] This shows that a work under the name of *Lun yü* must have existed before the Han Dynasty. The earliest source of information about the *Lun yü* is the chapter on bibliography in the *Han shu* (*History of the Han Dynasty*) by Pan Ku, finished towards the end of the first century A.D. In it are listed three versions of the *Lun yü*: the *Lu lun* (*Lun yü* of the state of Lu) in twenty *p'ien* (books), the *Ch'i lun* (*Lun yü* of the state of Ch'i) in twenty-two *p'ien*, the two extra *p'ien* being 'Wen wang' and 'Chih tao', and the *Ku lun* (the *Lun yü* in ancient script, discovered in the walls of Confucius' house) in twenty-one *p'ien*, with two *p'ien* bearing the identical title of 'T₂u-chang'.

The *Han shu* then gives a short account of the compilation and the transmission of the *Lun yü*. This account is taken over and expanded by Lu Te-ming (556–627 A.D.) in his preface to his *Ching tien shih wen*. The added information is that the *Ch'i lun* not only had two extra *p'ien* but that 'the chapters and verses were considerably more numerous than the *Lu lun* (*chang chü p'o tuo yü Lu lun*)'. This remark is somewhat ambiguous. It may mean that the *Ch'i lun* had extra chapters or it may mean that in the *Ch'i lun*, although there were no extra chapters, the text of the chapters was often longer. It is not possible to be sure which is the meaning, but there is no doubt that, whatever the position with regard to the chapters, the number of variant readings was considerable. Lu Te-ming quotes Huan T'an (24 B.C.–56 A.D.) as saying in his *Hsin lun* that in the *Ku lun* the order of the chapters was different and there were more than four hundred variant readings.[2] Some of the variant readings from the three versions were

1. *Li chi chu shu*, 51.16a–b.
2. *Ching tien shih wen*, 1.30b.

recorded by scholars at a time when these were still extant, and these have been collected assiduously by textual critics in recent centuries, but such readings only very occasionally throw any light on the meaning of the passages.[3]

In the first part of the Western Han it was the practice for scholars to specialize in only one of the three versions of the *Lun yü*. It was not until Chang Yü that this was changed. He received instruction on the *Lun yü* from Wang Yang of Lang Yeh and Yung Sheng of Chiao Tung, both being specialists in the *Ch'i lun* (*Han shu*, p. 3347). But he also received instruction on the *Lu lun* from Hsia-hou Chien (*Ching tien shih wen*, 1.31a). However, he did not follow either tradition exclusively. He used his own discretion in the choice of what readings to follow. The result was an eclectic version which came to be known as the *Chang hou lun* (Marquis Chang's *Lun yü*). In the reign period of Ch'u Yüan (48 B.C.–44 B.C.) Chang Yü, because of his expert knowledge of the *Lun yü*, was appointed tutor to the heir apparent who in 32 B.C. became Emperor Ch'eng. As a result, Chang Yü became prime minister in 25 B.C. Because of the high Imperial esteem he enjoyed, Marquis Chang's version of the *Lun yü* became so popular that it eclipsed all other versions.

The next important version of the *Lun yü* was that of Cheng Hsüan (127 A.D.–200 A.D.), probably the greatest of the commentators on the Confucian classics in the two Han dynasties. Though his text was basically that of the *Lu lun*, he, too, absorbed the better readings of the *Ch'i lun* and the *Ku lun*.[4] The present version of the *Lun yü* that we have was edited by Ho Yen (190 A.D.–249 A.D.). This is based, in the main, on the versions of Chang Yü and Cheng Hsüan and is, therefore, eclectic.

It seems clear that even if we could restore the *Lun yü* to the original form of any of the three versions we would be doing no more than restoring it to what it was in the Western Han and

3. For an example where *yi*, meaning change, has a variant *yi* which is a particle, see p. 170 above.

4. Cheng Hsüan's version is no longer extant, though a partial manuscript copy done by a twelve-year-old schoolboy in 710 A.D. was discovered in Sinkiang in 1969.

that is unlikely to add very much to our knowledge of the work.
If our aim is to find out something about the composition of the
Lun yü, the only possible approach is to examine the text itself.
I propose to do this by dividing the *Lun yü* into two portions, one
comprising the first fifteen books and the other the remaining
five books, and examining each under a number of heads. We shall
start with the last five books.

THE LAST FIVE BOOKS

Ts'ui Shu pointed out that the last five books of the *Lun yü* had
certain features which pointed to a late date,[5] but as his remarks
are somewhat brief, it is worthwhile going over the problem in
greater detail. We shall find that Ts'ui Shu's conclusion is in-
controvertible.

Let us start with Book XIX. The striking thing about this book
is that it consists solely of sayings and dialogues of disciples, with
no mention of Confucius at all. The disciples whose sayings are
included are those of the later group, with the exception of Yu Tzu.
Instead, Tzu-kung who was outside the group is included. If Book
XIX is remarkable for containing only sayings of disciples, Book
XX is no less remarkable. It opens with a passage consisting of
injunctions from the sage kings Yao, Shun, T'ang and King Wu.
This is very reminiscent of the style of the *Book of History*. This
opening passage is followed by a shorter passage dealing with
various aspects of government, the concluding words of which are
as follows:

> If a man is tolerant, he will win the multitude. If he is trustworthy
> in word, the common people will entrust him with responsibility.
> If he is quick he will achieve results. If he is impartial the common
> people will be pleased. (XX.1)

In XVII.6 these words, with slight variations, are to be found
again, this time attributed to Confucius. The interesting point is
that Confucius' words are in answer to a question put to him by

5. *K'ao hsin lu*, pp. 512–13.

Tzu-chang. In XX.2 we find again a question from Tzu-chang.
But this can hardly be a coincidence, for in both cases the formula
'*Tzu-chang wen . . . yü K'ung Tzu*' is used. In order to see the significance of this formula we have to discuss the broader question
of the use of '*K'ung Tzu*' for Confucius in the *Lun yü*.

K'ung Tzu *and* tzu   In the first fifteen books of the *Lun yü* the
practice is invariably to refer to Confucius as *tzu* (the Master) and
not as *K'ung Tzu* (Master K'ung),[6] unless Confucius was conversing with someone superior in station or senior in age.[7] There are,
however, a number of cases that are puzzling at first sight, viz.,
VIII.20, X.1, XI.6 and XIV.5. Take the last two cases first. In
XI.6 when Confucius is said to have given the daughter of his
elder brother to Nan Jung as wife, we find him referred to as
'*K'ung Tzu*'. Since Nan Jung must have been a younger man, it is
difficult to see why '*K'ung Tzu*' was used. In XIV.5 the formula
'. . . *wen yü K'ung Tzu*' is used when the questioner was Nan-
Kung K'uo. It is interesting that there is a tradition according to
which Nan-kung K'uo was the same person as Nan Jung. Judging
by his clan name of Nan-kung, Nan-kung K'uo must have been
descended from the ruling house in Lu. If this is the case, it would
account not only for the use of *K'ung Tzu* in XIV.5, but would at
the same time lend support to the identification of the two men and
account for its use in XI.6 as well. As for the case of X.1, Book X
refers to Confucius as '*chün tzu* (the gentleman)' and '*tzu*' besides
'*K'ung Tzu*'. This only shows that the book contains material from
various sources and has, therefore, no uniform practice in this
matter. Finally, there is the case of VIII.20, but this is a chapter
that concerns the sage kings of old, Shun and King Wu, and
shows affinity with the opening passage in Book XX.

To go back to the formula '*Tzu-chang wen . . . yü K'ung Tzu*'.
If the accepted practice in the bulk of the *Lun yü* was only to refer

6. In the present translation, *tzu* is consistently rendered as 'the Master' and
K'ung Tzu as 'Confucius'.

7. For instance, '*K'ung Tzu*' is used in III.19 because Confucius was speaking with Duke Ting and in XIV.32 because Wei-sheng Kao was an older man
as can be seen from his addressing Confucius as 'Ch'iu'.

to Confucius as '*K'ung Tʒu*' in contexts where a superior or senior person was present, then it is a mode of reference doubly unacceptable when the interlocutor was not even an equal but only a disciple. It is also worth noting that in the *Lun yü* Tzu-chang appears as posing a question to Confucius on more than ten occasions and XVII.6 and XX.2 are the only two occasions where the formula is used. This shows that Book XVII and XX are in a very special category. It is interesting to note that '*K'ung Tʒu*' and '*wen yü K'ung Tʒu*' where the questioner is a disciple are also to be found in certain chapters of the *Li chi*, the *Ta Tai li chi* and the last part of the *Hsün tʒu*, comprising the last six chapters. As we have seen in connection with the Shao Cheng Mao story,[8] this part of the *Hsün tʒu* contains miscellaneous material of a late date. That the last five books of the *Lun yü* should agree with works that are likely to be of a late date rather than with the rest of the *Lun yü* is a sign that these books must have been a subsequent addition to the body of the *Lun yü*.

On the usage of '*K'ung Tʒu*' there is a lack of uniformity within the last five books. Book XVI uses exclusively '*K'ung Tʒu*', Book XVII only lapses into '*K'ung Tʒu*' once (XVII.6), while in Book XVIII the first five chapters use '*K'ung Tʒu*' while chapters 7 and 8 use '*tʒu*', with chapter 6 being a doubtful case.

The Expression fu tzu   As the expression originally meant 'that gentleman', in early usage it was confined to reference to a third person. But by the Warring States period it was commonly used, as, for instance, in the *Mencius*, as a mode of address for the person spoken to. It has been pointed out by Ts'ui Shu that in the *Lun yü* there are three cases of *fu tʒu* being used in this way. These are in XVII.3, XVII.7, and XIX.17. This not only suggests that these two books are late in date but also that there is a link between them.

Numbered Sets   In chapters 2 to 10 of Book XVI things are dealt with in numbered sets: the ten generations, the five generations, the three generations, making friends with three kinds of people,

8. See p. 187 above.

taking pleasure in three kinds of things, the three errors, the three things the gentleman should guard against, the three things the gentleman stands in awe of and the nine things the gentleman turns his thoughts to. Even in XVI.9 where no actual number is mentioned, the number three is implicit, there being three grades of knowledge. Elsewhere in XX.2 we also find Tzu-chang asking about 'the five excellent practices' and 'the four wicked practices', while in XX.3 Confucius' saying is concerned with three things the gentleman must understand: Destiny, the rites and words. This suggests that there is also an underlying connection between Book XVI and Book XX. Numbered sets are also to be found in certain chapters of Book XVII. In XVII.8 Confucius tells Tzu-lu about 'the six qualities and the six attendant faults', while in XVII.16 Confucius talks about 'the three weaknesses' of 'the common people'. By contrast, in the first fifteen books the only number that occurs frequently is three, but it is never used with anything that could be described as a set. It is simply used to mean many. The only case where a numbered set occurs is in II.23 where Tzu-chang used the term 'ten generations'. As we shall see, Book II is possibly late because of its mixed content and chapter 23 is the last but one chapter in the Book and can be a late addition.

Apocryphal Stories In the account of Confucius' life, we pointed out that apocryphal stories existed from the earliest times.[9] Some of these, in fact, found their way into the *Lun yü*. First, there are the stories of encounters with recluses with a strong Taoist flavour. Three such stories are to be found in a block in Book XVIII. The first is the story about Chieh Yü, the Madman of Ch'u, in which Chieh Yü sings a song. There is a similar story about the Madman in chapter 4 of the *Chuang tzu*,[10] where a longer version of the song is given. The wording of the song in the two cases is so close that the two stories must be looked upon as variant versions of the same story.

The other two stories (XVIII.6 and XVIII.7) are about encounters with recluses and are equally Taoist in tone. That all three

9. See p. 161 above.
10. *Nan hua chen ching*, 2.27b–29a.

stories are found together may show that they belong together, though XVIII.7 marks itself off by its use of '*tzu*' instead of '*K'ung Tzu*'.

There is a linguistic feature in the second story which has hitherto escaped the notice of scholars. In XVIII.6 the construction '*x wei shui* (who is x?)' occurs twice. Of all the concordanced works of the Pre-Han period, this construction is found only once, in a slightly different form, in the Kung-yang Commentary to the *Spring and Autumn Annals*.[11] This being the case, we can only conclude that this story is of a date considerably later than the bulk of the work.

Belonging to another category are the apocryphal stories which seek to discredit Confucius morally. Two such stories which concern Confucius being tempted to go to rebels who had summoned him are found in Book XVII. The stories are in such close proximity (XVII.5 and XVII.7) that they probably belong together. Apart from the inherent improbability of the theme, we have seen that in XVII.7 *fu tzu* is used as a mode of address for Confucius and that this was the usage of a later age. As the story must have been composed at a later date, little credence can be placed on it. If this is true of one story, it is probably true of the other story as well.[12]

Accounts of Ancient Personages   We have noted that Book XX opens with a passage about sage kings of old from Yao to King Wu of the Chou. This is not the only place in the last five books where such passages are to be found. Book XVIII opens with two chapters and ends with four on historical personages. XVIII.1 consists of a comment by Confucius on 'the three benevolent men in the Yin', while XVIII.2 records a dialogue of Liu Hsia Hui. XVIII.8 records Confucius' comment on a number of what we would today call 'drop-outs' in the Chou. XVIII.9 gives a catalogue of court musicians who emigrated, and XVIII.10 consists of a saying of the

11. '*Tzu ming wei shui* (What is your name?)' (*Kung-yang chu shu*, 15.14a.)
12. There is a third story which is likely to belong to this category. In VI.28 is an account of Tzu-lu's anger over the audience Confucius had with Nan Tzu, the notorious wife of Duke Ling of Wei. Here, however, we have no positive evidence that the story is apocryphal.

Duke of Chou. The book ends with XVIII.11 which is a list of eight Gentlemen of the Chou. This concern with historical personages, often without relevance to Confucius, shows that some historical texts similar to the *Book of History* must have been used as a textbook by some of Confucius' disciples, if not by Confucius himself.

We have now examined a number of features which link parts of the last five books to one another and which show that they probably shared a common origin, and we have seen that some of these features signify a late date. It is time we turn to the first fifteen books.

THE FIRST FIFTEEN BOOKS

We shall examine the first fifteen books under two heads: (1) the internal organization of individual books, and (2) sayings of disciples.

Internal Organization of Individual Books   The casual reader of the *Lun yü* may come away with the impression that the chapters in the individual books are in a haphazard order. This is because it happens to be so with Books I and II. But this is certainly not true of all the books. Let us take a brief look at the first fifteen books from this point of view. There is, however, a preliminary point we must deal with. The grouping of chapters together, though mainly through the similarity in content, is sometimes done purely on a formalistic basis. If a chapter happens to have a key word in common with some other chapters, it is liable to be placed with them, even though the word may be used with a different meaning or with a different purpose in mind. For instance, III.23 and III.25 both deal with music. III.24, however, contains a remark by the border official of Yi to the effect that Heaven was going to use Confucius to rouse the Empire, but because his actual words are, 'Heaven is about to use the Master as a wooden *tuo*,' this chapter is placed amongst the other two on music, *tuo* being the tongue of a bell and the bell is a musical instrument. Again,

IV.7 is placed at the end of a group of chapters on *jen* (benevolence) because the graph *jen* appears in it, but although the graph is the usual one for benevolence, here it is used for the homophone meaning 'man'. Thus in examining the arrangement of the chapters in individual books we must be prepared to accept a certain latitude.

Books I and II, as we have pointed out, lack any obvious principle of organization, and it is likely that they belong together.

All the chapters in Book III, without any exception, deal with the rites and music.

Book IV falls into a number of parts. The first seven chapters deal with benevolence, though IV.7 as we have seen, deals really with the character of a man. IV.8 and IV.9 deal with the Way, IV.10 to IV.17 deal with the gentleman and the small man. IV.18 to IV.21 deal with filial duty, while the last few chapters seem to deal with the way the gentleman should conduct himself.

Book V is concerned with people. The first half (V.1 to V.14) is concerned with the disciples. The next ten chapters (V.15 to V.24), with the exception of V.22, deal with contemporary and ancient personages. V.22 is about the disciples left behind in Lu. In V.26 Yen Yüan and Tzu-lu talked about what they had set their hearts on, while the last two chapters consist of Confucius' sayings about himself.

The first two thirds (VI.1 to VI.21) of Book VI is similar to Book V. The topic is people. The first fifteen chapters concern the disciples while the next seven chapters deal with contemporaries and men in general. The last nine chapters are mixed.

Book VII is entirely devoted to Confucius. The chapters consist either of Confucius' sayings about himself or what other people had to say about him. Even VII.36 and VII.37 which may seem on the surface to be exceptions, can be interpreted as sayings about the sage himself.

Book VIII consists of sayings on a variety of topics, with the exception of two blocks of chapters. VIII.3 to VIII.7, as we have seen, concern Tseng Tzu, while VIII.18 to VIII.20 are about ancient sage kings.

Of Book IX, the first nineteen chapters are about Confucius, the next three, possibly four, are about Yen Yüan. The rest are rather mixed.

Book X is a record of the daily life of Confucius. We have seen that in its opening words Confucius is referred to as '*K'ung Tzu*', though it uses also the term '*chün tzu* (the gentleman)' for Confucius. X.17 is the only chapter in the whole book where Confucius is referred to as '*tzu*'. The final chapter, as sometimes happens, is an interpolation.

Book XI is entirely devoted to Confucius.

Book XII is interesting, because the principle of organization is not the subject matter but the form. Twenty-two out of twenty-four chapters are questions put to Confucius and they invariably open with the words 'So-and-so *wen* (asked).' The remaining two chapters both deal with the gentleman, for though in XII.15 there is no mention of the gentleman, the parallel in VI.27 shows that it is about the gentleman.

Book XIII falls into two parts. The first part, consisting of seventeen chapters, deals with government. The next eleven (XIII.18 to XIII.28) deal with how one should conduct oneself and with the gentleman (*chün tzu*). XIII.20 and XIII.28, however, deal with the Gentleman (*shih*). This serves to show the close connection between the two expressions. The *shih* is only the *chün tzu* that has taken office. The last two chapters deal with the training of the people for war.

Although the chapters in Book XIV look at first sight somewhat mixed in content, there is, in fact, a central theme. This is, once more, that of how to be a man. A number of chapters are about contemporaries, presumably, held up as concrete examples. The final five chapters seem to be the exception and may be later additions.

In Book XV, too, a large part deals with the theme of how to be a man. The exception seems to be the first five and the last five chapters.

Sayings of Disciples   The *Lun yü* is basically a work devoted to the recording of the words of Confucius and material concerning him as a person. Sayings of disciples are rarely recorded, and when they are, it is for the sake of the comment by the Master rather than for the intrinsic interest of the sayings. Here are some examples:

> The people of Lu were rebuilding the treasury. Min Tzu-ch'ien said, 'Why not simply restore it? Why must it be totally rebuilt?'
> The Master said, 'Either this man does not speak or he says something to the point.' (XI.14)

> Chung-kung asked about Tzu-sang Po-tzu. The Master said, 'It is his simplicity of style that makes him acceptable.'
> Chung-kung said, 'In ruling over the common people, is it not acceptable to hold oneself in reverence and merely to be simple in the measures one takes? On the other hand, is it not carrying simplicity too far to be simple in the way one holds oneself as well as in the measures one takes?'
> The Master said, 'Yung is right in what he says.' (VI.2)

In both cases the saying was recorded obviously because it won approval from the Master. There is one case of a conversation which was recorded for the opposite reason:

> Duke Ai asked Tsai Wo about the altar to the god of the earth. Tsai Wo replied, 'The Hsia used the pine, the Yin used the cedar, and the men of Chou used the chestnut (*li*), saying that it made the common people tremble (*li*).'
> The Master, on hearing of this reply, commented, 'One does not explain away what is already done, one does not argue against what is already accomplished, and one does not condemn what has already gone by.' (III.21)

Here Confucius condemns Tsai Wo for trying to rake up for criticism the past that should be left alone.

In this connection we have noted that the later group of five disciples stand out from the rest in a very conspicuous manner. We have seen that Book XIX consists solely of sayings by this group, with the exception of Tzu-kung. When we look at the first fifteen books, we find that Book VIII has a block of five chapters (VIII.3–VIII.7) which not only consist of sayings of Tseng Tzu, but of these, two chapters (VIII.3, VIII.4) record his dying words. Book I has three sayings of Yu Tzu (I.2, I.12, I.13), two of Tseng

Tzu (I.4, I.9) and one of Tzu-hsia (I.7). Book XII and Book XIV each has one saying of Tseng Tzu (XII.24, XIV.26), while Book IV has one of Tzu-yu (IV.26).

Before we proceed any further, we must deal with Tzu-kung whose position in this matter seems ambivalent. On the one hand, in one or two cases what he said is recorded because of Confucius' comment, for instance,

> Tzu-kung said, 'While I do not wish others to impose on me, I also wish not to impose on others.'
> The Master said, 'Ssu, that is quite beyond you.' (V.12)

> The *t'ai tsai* asked Tzu-kung, 'Surely the Master is a sage, is he not? Otherwise why should he be skilled in so many things?' Tzu-kung said, 'It is true, Heaven set him on the path to sagehood. However, he is skilled in many things besides.'
> The Master, on hearing of this, said, 'How well the *t'ai tsai* knows me! I was of humble station when young. That is why I am skilled in many menial things. Should a gentleman be skilled in many things? No, not at all.' (IX.6)

On the other hand, Tzu-kung shares with the later group the distinction of having a block of chapters devoted to him in Book XIX (XIX.20–XIX.25). There are two points to be made. First, Tzu-kung was the only one of Confucius' three best-known disciples to have survived the death of the Master, and there is no doubt that he associated closely with the disciples of the later group, as can be seen from certain chapters of the *Li chi*. Second, there is a single instance where he said,

> Chou was not as wicked as all that. That is why the gentleman hates to dwell downstream, for it is there that all that is sordid in the Empire finds its way. (XIX.20)

Apart from this all his sayings (V.13, XIX.21–XIX.25) concern the Master. Thus although he associated with the later group of disciples he was something of an outsider. His sayings are, indeed, recorded; but not for any insights of his own but for the picture they give of the Master.

Whether a book contains any sayings of the disciples seems to be a point of some significance. That such sayings were considered worth recording must mean that these disciples had by then already established themselves as teachers in their own right. As the five disciples in the later group were very much younger than Confucius, this would mean that their own sayings could only have been recorded some years after the death of Confucius. Books which contain sayings of disciples are Books I, VIII, and XIX. Books IV, XII and XIV are doubtful cases. Both the saying of Tzu-yu in Book IV and that of Tseng Tzu in Book XII come at the end of the book and could easily have been added at a date later than the date of compilation of that particular book. The case of Book XIV is interesting. Tseng Tzu's saying is in the form of a comment on a saying of Confucius', but this saying of Confucius' appears also in Book VIII. As several sayings of Tseng Tzu are to be found in Book VIII, it is just possible that the comment by Tseng Tzu was originally appended to Confucius' saying in Book VIII and through some accident found its way to Book XIV.

Now we have seen that of the first fifteen books, Books I, II, and VIII are the three that show a lack of internal organization, and of these, Books I and VIII are also books in which sayings of disciples are to be found. Book X, with its use of 'K'ung Tzu', probably belongs to the same group as the last five chapters. Thus we can roughly divide the *Lun yü* into three strata. The first stratum consists of the books which are well ordered and in which no sayings of disciples are included. The next consists of Book I (and possibly Book II) and Book VIII. Although these books show a lack of internal organization of the chapters and contain sayings of disciples, they, nevertheless, do not use 'K'ung Tzu' for Confucius. Finally, there is the stratum consisting of Book X and the last five chapters. These are all interlinked through a number of features and are likely to be much later in date than the bulk of the work.

I shall conclude with some tentative suggestions about the way the *Lun yü* was put into the present form. First, the individual units must have been arranged as chapters in some sort of order according to topic. There would be units that either did not fit into any category or were not thought important enough to be included in the corpus. Second, some of these left over units were gathered together and placed, sometimes with material concerning the disciples, into new books, while other units may have been appended to the end of existing books. This need not have happened all at once. Books I (possibly together with II) and VIII may represent an earlier gathering together of such left over material together with material concerning the disciples. The last five books (possibly together with Book X) may represent a later repeat of the same exercise. The case of Book I is interesting. That a book of such a mixed nature should be placed at the beginning of the whole collection was probably due to the desire on the part of disciples of Yu Tzu, Tseng Tzu and Tzu-hsia to enhance the status of their own teachers in the Confucian school not only by including their sayings but by interspersing them amongst the sayings of the Master.

Textual Notes

1. Read 人 for 仁. (I.2, I.6, IV.7, VI.26)

2. Read 樂道. (I.15)

3. Read 示 for 賓. (III.11)

4. Read 能以禮讓爲國於從政乎何有. (IV.13)

5. Omit 輕. (V.26)

6. Read 亦 for 易. (VII.17)

7. Read 必祭. (X.11)

8. Read 客 for 容. (X.24)

9. Read 之 for 而. (XIV.27)

10. Read 舞 as 武. (XV.11)

11. Read 得 for 德. (XVI.12)

12. Emend to 患不得之. (XVII.15)

13. Read 弛 for 施. (XVIII.10)

14. Read 弘 as 強. (XIX.2)

Works Cited

Ching tien shih wen by Lu Te-ming, SPTK (*Ssu pu ts'ung k'an*) ed.
Chou li chu shu, SSCCS (*Shih san ching chu shu*, Nanchang, 1815) ed.
Ch'ün shu chih yao, SPTK ed.
Han fei tzu, SPTK ed.
Han shu, Chung Hua Shu Chü, Peking, 1962.
Hsün tzu, SPTK ed.
Huai nan tzu, SPTK ed.
K'ao hsin lu by Ts'ui Shu, *Wan yu wen k'u* ed.
Kung-yang chu shu, SSCCS ed.
K'ung tzu chia yü, *Yü hai t'ang ying sung ts'ung shu* ed., 1898.
Kuo yü, *Shih li chü Huang shih ts'ung shu* ed.
Li chi chu shu, SSCCS ed.
Mencius, trans. D. C. Lau, Penguin Books, reprint 1976.
Meng tzu chi chu, 1811 ed.
Meng tzu chu shu, SSCCS ed.
Nan hua chen ching (Chuang tzu), SPTK ed.
Po hu t'ung, SPTK ed.
Shih chi, Chung Hua Shu Chü, Peking, 1959.
Shih ching chu shu, SSCCS ed.
Shu ching chu shu, SSCCS ed.
Ta Tai li chi, SPTK ed.
Tao te ching, trans. D. C. Lau, Penguin Books, 1963.
Yi Chou shu, *Ts'ung shu chi ch'eng* ed.
Yin wen tzu, SPTK ed.

Glossary of Personal and Place Names

ALL DATES GIVEN, UNLESS OTHERWISE STATED, ARE B.C.

For names with an asterisk see also Appendix 2.

Ao, XIV.5. A legendary figure famed for his physical strength.

Ch'ai, XI.18, i.e., Kao Ch'ai. See Tzu-kao.

Chang, XIX.15, XIX.16, i.e., Tzu-chang.

Ch'ang-chü XVIII.6. A recluse.

Chao, XIV.11. A noble family in the state of Chin.

Ch'en, V.22, XI.2, XV.2. After he overthrew the Yin, King Wu of Chou sought out a descendant of Shun (q.v.) and enfeoffed him in Ch'en. It occupied the eastern part of modern Honan and the northern part of modern Anhwei.

Ch'en Ch'eng Tzu, XIV.21. A Counsellor in Ch'i. His name was Ch'en Heng while Ch'eng was his posthumous name. He was a descendant of Prince Huan who, fleeing from Ch'en, settled in Ch'i. Ch'en Heng is also known as T'ien Ch'eng, probably because T'ien and Ch'en were phonetic variants in his time. The Ch'en family became increasingly powerful until Ch'en Ch'eng Tzu who, then, murdered Duke Chien in 481.

Ch'en Heng, XIV.21. See Ch'eng Ch'eng Tzu.

Ch'en Kang, XVI.13. See Tzu-ch'in.

Ch'en Ssu-pai, VII.31. It is not even clear whether 'Ssu-pai' is the name of the person or the office he held.

Ch'en Tzu-ch'in, XIX.25. Commentators have identified him with Tzu-ch'in (q.v.).

Ch'en Wen Tzu, V.19. Ch'en Hsü-wu, a Counsellor in Ch'i who, fleeing from Ch'en, settled in Ch'i. Although he figures in the *Tso chuan*, there is no record there of his leaving Ch'i.

Cheng, XV.11, XVII.18. A small state comprising the central part of modern Honan.

Chi, XIV.5. Ch'i, a minister of Shun. Known to posterity as Chi (grain), because he was in charge of agriculture.

Chi, XVIII.3, i.e., the Chi Family.

Chi Family, III.1, III.6, VI.9, XI.17, XIII.2, XVI.1, XVIII.3. See Three Houses of Huan.

Chi Huan Tzu, XVIII.4. Chi-sun Ssu, who held power in Lu from 505 to 492 when he died.

Chi K'ang Tzu, II.20, VI.8, XI.7, XII.17, XII.18, XII.19. Chi-sun Fei who succeeded his father, Chi Huan Tzu, as Senior Minister in Lu in 492 and held power till his death in 468.

Chi K'uo, XVIII.11.

Chi-lu, V.26, XI.3, XI.12, XVI.1. See Tzu-lu.

Chi Sui, XVIII.11.

Chi-sun, XVI.1. See Three Houses of Huan.

Chi Tzu-ch'eng, XII.8. Said to be a Counsellor in Wei.

Chi Tzu-jan, XI.24. Probably a member of the Chi Family.

Chi Wen Tzu, V.20. Chi-sun Hsing-fu who died in 568, seventeen years before Confucius was born.

Ch'i, III.9. A small state in modern Honan where the descendants of the Hsia were enfeoffed.

Ch'i, VI.24, VII.14, XVIII.4, XVIII.9. A state comprising the northern part of modern Shantung and the south-western part of Hopei.

*Ch'i-tiao K'ai, V.6. A disciple of Confucius. In the *Han fei tzu*, it is said that after the death of Confucius the Confucians divided into eight schools of which one was the School of Ch'i-tiao. There is a work entitled *Ch'i-tiao tzu* listed in the 'Bibliographical Chapter' of the *Han shu* which is no longer extant.

Chieh Ni, XVIII.6. A recluse.

Chieh Yü, the Madman of Ch'u, XVIII.5.

Chih, the Master Musician, VIII.15.

Chih, the Grand Musician, XVIII.9. This is probably the same person as Chih, the Master Musician (q.v.).

Ch'ih, V.8, VI.4, XI.26, i.e., Kung-hsi Ch'ih. See Kung-hsi Hua.

Ch'in, XVIII.9. A state in the north-west, comprising the south east of modern Kansu, part of Shensi and reaching to Honan.

Ch'iu, VII.24, XIV.32, i.e., Confucius.

Ch'iu, V.8, VI.8, XI.17, XI.22, XI.24, XI.26, XVI.1, i.e., Jan Ch'iu. See Jan Yu.

Chou, II.23, III.14, III.21, VIII.20, XV.11, XVII.5, XVIII.11, XX.1. The Chou Dynasty.

Chou, XIX.20. The tyrant Chou, the last Emperor of the Yin Dynasty, overthrown by King Wu of the Chou.

Chou Jen, XVI.1. A wise man in antiquity whose words are quoted more than once by Confucius in the *Analects* and elsewhere.

Chu Chang, XVIII.8.

Ch'u. XVIII.9. A large state in the south, comprising much of the area in the region of the Riven Han, including most of modern Hopei and Honan.

Chuan Yü, XVI.1. A dependency of the state of Lu, north-west of Pi Hsien in modern Shantung.

Chuang Tzu of Pien, XIV.12. A man of valour, mentioned also in the *Hsün tzu* and the *Chan kuo ts'e*.

Chung Hu, XVIII.11.

*Chung-kung, VI.2, VI.6, XI.3, XII.2, XIII.2. Jan Yung who is supposed to be of the same clan as Jan Po-niu (q.v.). In the *Hsün tzu*, the only disciple of Confucius who is given unqualified praise is a man called Tzu-kung. It has been suggested that Tzu-kung is, in fact, the same as Chung-kung.

Chung Mou, XVII.7. A town in Chin, located in modern Hopei.

Chung-ni, XIX.22, XIX.23, XIX.24, XIX.25, i.e., Confucius.

Chung-shu Yü, XIV.19. See K'ung Wen Tzu.

Chung T'u, XVIII.11.

Chung Yu, VI.8, XI.24, XVIII.6. See Tzu-lu.

Chü Fu, XIII.17. A town in Lu.

Ch'ü Po-yü, XIV.25, XV.7. A Counsellor in Wei. As he is mentioned in the *Tso chuan* in the year 559, he must have been in his nineties in 493 when he was supposed to have played host to Confucius according to the *Shih chi*.

Ch'üeh, XVIII.9.

Ch'üeh Tang, XIV.44. The district where Confucius' home was.

Confucius (used to render 'K'ung Tzu'), II.19, II.21, III.1, III.19, VI.3, VII.19, VII.31, VIII.20, IX.2, X.1, XI.6, XI.7, XII.11, XII.17, XII.18, XII.19, XIII.15, XIII.18, XIV.5, XIV.19, XIV.21, XIV.25, XIV.32, XV.1, XVI.1, XVI.2, XVI.3, XVI.4, XVI.5, XVI.6, XVI.7, XVI.9, XVI.10, XVI.11, XVII.1, XVII.6, XVII.20, XVIII.1, XVIII.3, XVIII.4, XVIII.5, XVIII.6, XX.2.

Counsellor Chuan, XIV.18.

Duke Ai, II.19, III.21, VI.3, XII.9, XIV.21. Duke Ai of Lu (r. 494–468) probably succeeded his father Duke Ting (q.v.) at a very early age and power was in the hands of the Three Families (q.v.). Fled the country when he failed in an attempt to regain power. Died soon after his return to Lu.

Duke Chao, VII.31. Duke Chao of Lu, (r. 541–509), rather flippant in nature and slack in the observance of the rites. Fled the country after an unsuccessful conflict with one of his powerful ministers and died in exile.

Duke Chien, XIV.21. Duke Chien of Ch'i (r. 484–481) was murdered by Ch'en Ch'eng Tzu (q.v.).

Duke Ching of Ch'i (r. 547–490), XII.11, XVI.12, XVIII.3. Not a particularly wise ruler, his survival was mainly due to his good fortune in having Yen P'ing-chung (q.v.) as prime minister.

Duke Huan, XIV.16, XIV.17. See Duke Huan of Ch'i.

Duke Huan of Ch'i (r. 685–643), XIV.15. The most illustrious of the feudal lords in the Spring and Autumn period and counted as the first of the so-called Five Leaders of the feudal lords. He owed his position in no small measure to his prime minister, Kuan Chung (q.v.).

Duke Ling of Wei (r. 534–493), XIV.19, XV.1. Succeeded his father at the age of seven and ruled for forty-two years. Doted on Nan Tzu, his wife, thus causing the trouble which ensued between his son, K'uai K'ui, and his grandson, Che, the Ousted Duke. Though an unprincipled ruler, he escaped disaster through having at his court a number of good men. Confucius visited Wei during the last years of his reign.

Duke of Chou, VII.5, VIII.11, XI.17, XVIII.10. The younger brother of King Wu (q.v.), the founder of the Chou Dynasty, he aided his nephew, King Ch'eng, in putting down a rebellion of his two brothers.

Duke of Lu, XVIII.10. Po-ch'in, the son of the Duke of Chou (q.v.).

Duke Ting, III.19, XIII.15. Duke Ting of Lu (r. 509–495) succeeded his brother, Duke Chao. It was during his reign that Confucius was most active in politics. See Appendix 1.

Duke Wen of Chin (r. 636–628), XIV.15. An illustrious ruler, counted as the second of the Five Leaders of the feudal lords.

*Fan Ch'ih, II.5, VI.22, XII.21, XII.22, XIII.4, XIII.19. Said to have been a young man when he went to battle with Jan Yu (q.v.) in 484.

Fan Hsü, XIII.4. See Fan Ch'ih.

Fang, XIV.14. A town close to the Ch'i border, situated to the northeast of Pi Hsien in modern Shantung.

Fang Shu, XVIII.9.

Governor of She, VII.19, XIII.16, XIII.18. Shen Chu-liang, better known as Governor of She, is best remembered for his part in putting down the rebellion of Po Kung Sheng, the grandson of King P'ing of Ch'u in 479.

Hsia, II.23, III.9, III.21, XV.11. The Hsia Dynasty.

Hsiang, XVIII.9.

Hsien, XIV.1, i.e., Yüan Hsien. See Yüan Ssu.

Hsüeh, XIV.11. A small state near Lu, situated to the south-west of T'eng Hsien in modern Shantung.

Hu Hsiang, VII.29. A district the location of which is uncertain.

Huan T'ui, VII.23. Descendant of Duke Huan of Sung and commander of the armed forces in that state. According to the *Shih chi*, during the time Confucius was in Sung, Huan T'ui made an attempt on his life.

Hui, II.9, V.9, VI.7, VI.11, IX.20, XI.4, XI.19, XI.23, i.e., Yen Hui. See Yen Yüan.

Jan Ch'iu, III.6, VI.12, XI.24, XIV.12. See Jan Yu.

*Jan Po-niu, XI.3. Disciple of Confucius.

Jan Tzu, VI.4, XIII.14. See Jan Yu.

*Jan Yu, VII.15, XI.3, XI.13, XI.22, XI.26, XIII.9, XVI.1. Disciple of Confucius.

Ju Pei, XVII.20. Mentioned in the *Li chi* as having been sent by Duke Ai of Lu to Confucius for instruction in funeral rites.

Kan, XVIII.9.

K'ang Tzu, X.16, XIV.19. See Chi K'ang Tzu.

Kao Tsung, XIV.40. Wu Ting, King of the Yin Dynasty (r. 1324–1291), was a distinguished ruler responsible for the revival of the dynasty.

Kao Yao, XII.22. A wise minister of the legendary emperor Shun (q.v.).

King Wen (d. 1027), IX.5, XIX.22. Father of King Wu (q.v.) who founded the Chou Dynasty, said to have been responsible for creating the 64 hexagrams out of the 8 trigrams. Judging by what he said, Confucius considered him responsible for the resplendent culture of the Chou Dynasty.

King Wu (r. 1027–1005), VIII.20, XIX.22. Founded the Chou Dynasty by overthrowing the tyrant Chou of the Yin. Confucius seemed critical of him for having resorted to force.

Kuan Chung, III.22, XIV.9, XIV.16, XIV.17. When Prince Chiu was killed at the instigation of Duke Huan of Ch'i, of his two close advisers, Shao Hu died but Kuan Chung lived to serve the murderer of his lord and, in the process, became a great statesman. It was due to him that Ch'i became a powerful and rich state and Duke Huan became the first of the Leaders of the feudal lords.

K'uang, IX.5, XI.23. Possibly the same as the city of K'uang, a few miles south-west of Ch'ang Yüan Hsien in modern Honan.

Kung-ch'uo, XIV.12. See Meng Kung-ch'uo.

*Kung-hsi Hua, VII.34, XI.22, XI.26. Kung-hsi Ch'ih, a disciple of Confucius. Said in the *T'an kung* chapter of the *Li chi* to have been in charge of the funeral of Confucius.

Kung-ming Chia, XIV.13. Otherwise unknown.

*Kung-po Liao, XIV.36.

Kung-shan Fu-jao, XVII.5. According to the *Tso chuan*, when Confucius attempted to demolish the strongholds of the Three Families in Lu, one Kung-shan Fu-niu led the men of Pi to attack Lu, and Confucius ordered an attack on Pi. If Kung-shan Fu-jao is the same person as Kung-shan Fu-niu, then the story that he summoned Confucius and Confucius was tempted to go is totally unfounded.

Kung-shu Wen Tzu, XIV.13, XIV.18. Kung-shu Fa, a Counsellor of Wei, is mentioned in the *Tso chuan* where his name is given as Kung-shu Pa. A conversation between him and Ch'ü Po-yü (q.v.) is recorded in the *T'an kung* chapter of the *Li chi* where it is also recorded that his son, after his death, requested a posthumous title for him.

Kung-sun Ch'ao, XIX.22. A Counsellor of Wei, mentioned in the *Tso chuan*.

*Kung-yeh Ch'ang, V.1. Disciple of Confucius. There is a tradition, recorded by Huang K'an (488–545 A.D.) in his commentary on the *Analects*, according to which Kung-yeh Ch'ang understood the language of birds.

K'ung, XIV.38.

K'ung Ch'iu, XVIII.6, i.e., Confucius.

K'ung Wen Tzu, V.15. A Counsellor in Wei.

*Lao, IX.7. Identity uncertain.

Li, XI.8. See Po-yü.

Liao, XVIII.9.

Lin Fang, III.4, III.6.

Ling Yin Tzu-wen, V.19. Tou Kou-wu-t'u, a man of great integrity. The *Kuo yü* also records his having relinquished the office of *ling yin* three times. In the *Tso chuan* it is said that in 664 when he was made *ling yin* he ruined his family fortune in an attempt to ease the financial difficulties of the state and in 637 he yielded his position of *ling yin* to Tzu-yü who had just scored a resounding military success as the disaffection of such a prominent military leader would have been a serious matter.

Liu Hsia Hui, XV.14, XVIII.2, XVIII.8. Chan Ch'in, a Counsellor in Lu, is commonly known as Liu Hsia Hui. The reason for this is not very clear, but there is a theory that Hui was his posthumous name and that Liu Hsia was the name of the town which was his fief. His official career seems to have been during the time Tsang Wen-chung (q.v.) was in power in Lu, as the few occasions on which he is mentioned in the *Tso chuan* and the *Kuo yü* it is always in connection with Tsang Wen-chung. Liu Hsia Hui was held in great esteem in the Confucian school. Mencius said, 'The sage is a teacher to a hundred generations' (VII.B.15) and cited him as an example.

Lord of Ch'i, V.19. This refers to Duke Chuang of Ch'i who was assassinated by Ts'ui Chu in 548.

Lord of Wei, VII.15, XIII.3. The reference in VII.15 is certainly to the Ousted Duke (see Duke Ling of Wei) while that in XIII.3 has been taken by commentators as being also to him.

Lu, III.23, V.3, VI.24, IX.15, XI.14, XIII.7, XIV.14. The state in which the Duke of Chou was enfeoffed and the native state of Confucius, comprising mainly the south-eastern part of modern Shantung.

Lü, XX.1. The name of T'ang, the Founder of the Yin Dynasty.

Master, the, (used to render '*tzu*'), passim.

Meng, XVIII.3, i.e., the Meng Family.

Meng chih Fan, VI.15.

Meng Ching Tzu, VIII.4. Son of Meng Wu-po (q.v.) to whose position as Counsellor he suceeded and, according to the *T'an kung* chapter of the *Li chi*, he was still alive at the time of Duke Tao of Lu in 437.

Meng Chuang Tzu, XIX.18. Son of Meng Hsien Tzu and uncle of Meng Yi Tzu (q.v.), he succeeded his father as Counsellor in 554 and died in 550.

Meng Family, XIX.19. See the Three Houses of Huan.

Meng Kung-ch'uo, XIV.11, XIV.12. A Counsellor in Lu, mentioned once in the *Tso chuan* for his sound judgement during an invasion by Ch'i in 548.

Meng-sun, II.5, i.e., Meng Yi Tzu (q.v.).

Meng Wu Po, II.6, V.8. Son of Meng Yi Tzu (q.v.) whom he succeeded as Counsellor in Lu in 481. He is mentioned a number of times in the *Tso chuan*. When Duke Ai had to flee the state after an unsuccessful attempt to oust the three powerful families in 468, Meng Wu Po was head of the Meng Family.

Meng Yi Tzu (531–481), II.5. Father of Meng Wu Po (q.v.), Meng Yi Tzu succeeded his father, Meng Hsi Tzu in 518. In 517 during the conflict between Duke Chao and the Chi Family he allied himself with the latter. When Confucius attempted to demolish the strongholds of the Three Families in 498 it was Meng Yi Tzu who stood out against this plan.

Mien, the Master Musician, XV.42.

Min Tzu, XI.13. See Min Tzu-ch'ien.

*Min Tzu-chien, VI.9, XI.3, XI.5, XI.14. Disciple of Confucius who in subsequent ages became a byword for a good son.

Mount Shou Yang, XVI.12. Exact location unknown.

Mount T'ai, III.6. In the central part of modern Shantung and one of the most revered mountains in China.

*Nan Jung, V.2, XI.6. Disciple of Confucius. See also Nan-kung K'uo.

Nan-kung K'uo, XIV.5. There is no agreement among scholars about the identity of Nan-kung K'uo, but there is a strong tradition identifying him with Nan Jung (q.v.). For a discussion of this question see Appendix 3, p. 223.

Nan Tzu, VI.28. Notorious wife of Duke Ling of Wei. Prince K'uai K'ui, the son of Duke Ling made an unsuccessful attempt on her life and had to flee the country in 494.

Ning Wu Tzu, V.21. A Counsellor in Wei who is mentioned a number of times in the Tso chuan in the period 632 to 623 as a wise man and a loyal subject.

Old P'eng, VII.1. Identity uncertain.

Pi, VI.9, XI.25, XVI.1, XVII.5. Near Pi Hsien in modern Shantung.

Pi Hsi, XVII.7. Not mentioned in the Tso chuan, but said in the Shih chi to be steward of Chung Mou, the fief of Chao Chien Tzu, powerful minister in the state of Chin.

Pi Kan, XVIII.1, i.e., Prince Pi Kan, the uncle of the tyrant Chou (q.v.), who is said to have had him killed and his heart taken out to see if the popular belief that the heart of the sage had seven apertures was true.

P'i Ch'en, XIV.8. A Counsellor in Cheng pictured as a resourceful man in the Tso chuan.

P'ien, XIV.9. In Lin Chü Hsien in modern Shantung.

Po, XIV.9.

Po K'uo, XVIII.11.

Po-niu, VI.10. See Jan Po-niu.

Po Ta, XVIII.11.

Po Yi, V.23, VII.15, XVI.12, XVIII.8. Po Yi and Shu Ch'i were the sons of the Lord of Ku Chu. The father intended Shu Ch'i, the younger son, to succeed him, but when he died neither of his sons was willing to deprive the other of the succession and they both fled to the mountains and when King Wu overthrew the Yin they starved themselves to death on Mount Shou Yang, being ashamed to eat the grain of a dynasty that came to power through the use of force.

Po-yü, XVI.13, XVII.10. Son of Confucius.

Priest T'uo, VI.16, XIV.19. Priest in Wei. He displayed his eloquence on the occasion he was taken by Duke Ling in 504 to a meeting of the feudal lords.

Prince Ching of Wei, XIII.8. Praised by Prince Chi Cha of Wu as a gentleman in the *Tso chuan*.

Prince Chiu, XIV.16, XIV.17. Brother of Duke Huan of Ch'i (q.v.) who had him killed in a struggle for the throne in Ch'i.

River, the, XVIII.9, i.e., the Yellow River.

River Han, XVIII.9.

River Wen, VI.9.

River Yi, XI.26. From its source in the north-west of Tsou Hsien in Shantung it flowed west past Ch'ü Fu and joined with River Chu before entering River Ssu.

Shang, III.8, XI.16, i.e., Pu Shang. See Tzu-hsia.

Shao Hu, XIV.16. See under Kuan Chung.

Shao Lien, XVIII.8.

*Shen Ch'eng, V.11.

Shih, XI.6, XI.18, i.e., Chuan-sun Shih. See Tzu-chang.

Shih-shu, XIV.8. Yu Chi, a Counsellor of Cheng, whose skill in diplomatic language is also evident in the accounts in the *Tso chuan*.

Shih Yü, XV.7. Counsellor in Wei.

Shu Ch'i, V.23, VII.15, XVI.12, XVIII.8. Younger brother of Po Yi (q.v.).

Shu Hsia, XVIII.11.

Shu-sun Wu-shu, XIX.23, XIX.24. A Counsellor in Lu.

Shu Yeh, XVIII.11.

Shun, VI.30, VIII.18, VIII.20, XII.22, XIV.42, XV.5, XX.1. A sage king in antiquity.

Ssu, I.15, III.17, V.12, VI.8, XI.19, XIV.29, XV.3, XVII.24, XIX.23, i.e., Tuan-mu Ssu. See Tzu-kung.

*Ssu-ma Niu, XII.3, XII.4, XII.5. Brother of Huan T'ui (q.v.).

Stone Gate, XIV.38. Said to be the outer gate of the capital of Lu.

Sung, III.9. A state comprising part of Honan and Kiangsu provinces.

Sung Chao, VI.16. Prince Chao of Sung, known for his good looks. Said to have been a lover of Nan Tzu (q.v.).

Ta Hsiang, IX.2. Name of a district.

T'ai Po, VIII.1. Eldest of three sons of Ku Kung Tan Fu. Realizing that his father intended the youngest son, Chi Li, to succeed him, he and his second brother Yü Chung fled to the south among the barbarians where T'ai Po became the founder of the state of Wu. Chi Li was succeeded by his son who is known in history as King Wen (q.v.) of Chou.

*T'an-t'ai Mieh-ming, VI.14. The earliest mention of T'an-t'ai Mieh-ming is in the *Ta Tai li chi* and little credence can be given to later traditions about him.

T'ang, VIII.20. The name of Yao's dynasty.

T'ang, XII.22. Founder of the Yin Dynasty.

T'eng, XIV.11. A small state south-west of T'eng Hsien in modern Shantung.

Three Families, III.2. See Three Houses of Huan.

Three Houses of Huan, XVI.3. The three noble families descended from the three sons of Duke Huan of Lu: Meng-sun, Shu-sun and Chi-sun.

Tien, XI.26. See Tseng Hsi.

*Tsai Wo, III.21, VI.26, XI.3, XVII.21. Disciple of Confucius.

Tsai Yü, V.10. See Tsai Wo.

Ts'ai, XI.2, XVIII.9. A small state originally in Shang Ts'ai Hsien in modern Honan, moved in 493 to Chou Lai which is in Feng T'ai Hsien in modern Anhwei.

Ts'an, IV.15, XI.18, i.e., Tseng Ts'an. See Tseng Tzu.

Tsang Wen Chung, V.18, XV.18. Tsang-sun Ch'en, a Counsellor in Lu who died in 617. Although Confucius' remarks concerning him here and elsewhere are unfavourable, he had, in fact, a reputation for wisdom during and after his life time.

Tsang Wu Chung, XIV.12, XIV.14. Tsang-sun He, a Counsellor in Lu and grandson of Tsang Wen Chung, also known for his wisdom.

Tseng Hsi, XI.26. Father of Tseng Tzu.

*Tseng Tzu, I.4, I.9, IV.15, VIII.3, VIII.4, VIII.5, VIII.6, VIII.7, XII.24, XIV.26, XIX.16, XIX.17, XIX.18, XIX.19. Tseng Ts'an, disciple of Confucius who played a prominent part in early Confucianism. He is mentioned in the *Mencius* and the *Hsün tzu* and there is a good deal of material about him in both the *Li chi* and the *Ta Tai li chi*.

Tso-ch'iu Ming, V.15. Though the identity of Tso-ch'iu ming here is uncertain, it is unlikely to be the same as the Tso-ch'iu Ming who is credited with the authorship of the *Tso chuan*.

Tsou, III.15. Name of a small place near Ch'ü Fu in modern Shantung.

Ts'ui Tzu, V.19. Ts'ui Chu, a Counsellor in Ch'i, who assassinated Duke Chuang of Ch'i in 548.

Tung Li, XIV.8. The native place of Tzu-ch'an (q.v.) of Cheng.

Tung Meng Mountain, XVI.1. South of Meng Hsien in modern Shantung.

Tzu-ch'an (d. 522), V.16, XIV.8, XIV.9. Kung-sun Ch'iao, prime minister of Cheng, a great statesman with enlightened views, much admired by Confucius.

*Tzu-chang, II.18, II.23, V.19, XI.20, XII.6, XII.10, XII.14, XII.20, XIV.40, XV.6, XVII.6, XIX.1, XIX.2, XIX.3, XX.2. Chuan-sun Shih, disciple of Confucius, of whom little is known, though he is mentioned in the *Hsün tzu*, the *Lü shih ch'un ch'iu*, the *Li chi* and the *Ta Tai li chi*.

*Tzu-chien, V.3. Fu Tzu-chien, disciple of Confucius, of whom there is a very popular tradition about him as governor of Shan Fu, according to which he kept it in perfect order without doing anything more than playing the lute. In contrast, Wu-ma Ch'i (q.v.) who, when governor of the same Shan Fu, had to wear himself out in order to achieve the same result.

*Tzu-ch'in, I.10.

Tzu-fu Ching-po, XIV.36. Tzu-fu He, a Counsellor in Lu who figured prominently in the period from 492 to 480 and showed himself to be a man of integrity and courage.

Tzu-hsi, XIV.9. There were three men by this name in the Spring and Autumn period, but this Tzu-hsi is likely to be Kung-sun Hsia, a cousin of Tzu-ch'an who succeeded to his position as the man in charge of the government in Cheng.

*Tzu-hsia, I.7, II.8, III.8, VI.13, XI.3, XII.5, XII.22, XIII.17, XIX.3, XIX.4, XIX.5, XIX.6, XIX.7, XIX.8, XIX.9, XIX.10, XIX.11, XIX.12, XIX.13. Pu Shang, disciple of Confucius. Figured prominently in a number of chapters of the *Li chi* and is credited by tradition with a major role in the transmission of the Confucian classics.

Tzu-hua, VI.4. See Kung-hsi Hua.

*Tzu-kao, XI.15. Kao Ch'ai, disciple of Confucius. As Tzu-lu became steward to the Chi Family in 498 it must have been then that Tzu-kao as a young man was made steward of Pi. He survived the coup in Wei when Tzu-lu died, and is last mentioned in the *Tso chuan* in 478 when he was likely to be holding office in Lu.

*Tzu-kung, I.10, I.15, II.13, III.17, V.4, V.9, V.12, V.13, V.15, VI.30, VII.15, IX.6, IX.13, XI.3, XI.13, XI.16, XII.7, XII.8, XII.23, XIII.20, XIII.24, XIV.17, XIV.28, XIV.29, XIV.35, XV.10, XV.24, XVII.19, XVII.24, XIX.20, XIX.21, XIX.22, XIX.23, XIX.24, XIX.25. Tuan-mu Ssu, disciple of Confucius. First mentioned in 495 when he must have been a young man, he was the only one of the three best known disciples to have survived the Master. He had a distinguished career as a diplomat and a merchant. He is last mentioned in the *Tso chuan* in 468 when he was probably still holding office in Wei.

*Tzu-lu, V.7, V.8, V.14, V.26, VI.28, VII.11, VII.19, VII.35, IX.12, IX.27, X.27, XI.13, XI.15, XI.22, XI.25, XI.26, XII.12, XIII.1, XIII.3, XIII.28, XIV.12, XIV.16, XIV.22, XIV.36, XIV.38, XIV.42, XV.2, XVII.5, XVII.7, XVII.23, XVIII.6, XVIII.7. Chung Yu, disciple of Confucius. He was steward to the Chi Family in 498, and died in Wei in 480 fighting for his lord.

Tzu-sang Po-tzu, VI.2. Identity unknown.

*Tzu-yu, II.7, IV.26, VI.14, XI.3, XVII.4, XIX.12, XIX.14, XIX.15. Yen Yen, disciple of Confucius. Little is known about him, but he must have been one of the younger men who came to study under Confucius after the latter's return from his travels in 484.

Tzu-yü, XIV.8. Kung-sun Hui of Cheng who was Master of Protocol. Praised for his skill in diplomatic language in the *Tso chuan* in the same terms as in the *Analects*.

Viscount of Chi, XVIII.1. Uncle of the tyrant Chou (q.v.) of the Yin.

Viscount of Wei, XVIII.1. Elder brother of the tyrant Chou (q.v.) of the Yin.

Wang-sun Chia, III.13, XIV.19. A Counsellor in Wei, mentioned once in the *Tso chuan* in 502 as an intimate adviser of Duke Ling of Wei (q.v.).

Wei, IX.15, XIII.7, XIII.9, XIV.39, XIX.22. A state in modern Honan.

Wei, XIV.11. A noble family of Chin.

Wei-sheng Kao, V.24. Some commentators identify him with the Wei-sheng Kao who was drowned because he insisted on waiting as he had promised for a woman who failed to keep her appointment at the foot of a bridge.

Wei-sheng Mu, XIV.32.

Wu, VII.31. A semi-barbarian state comprising parts of modern Kiangsu and Chekiang.

Wu, XVIII.9.

Wu Ch'eng, VI.14, XVIII.4. South-west of Pi Hsien in modern Shantung.

*Wu-ma Ch'i, VII.31. See under Tzu-chien.

Wu Meng Tzu, VII.31. The wife of Duke Chao of Lu.

Yang, XVIII.9.

Yang Fu, XIX.19.

Yang Huo, XVII.1. Otherwise unknown, but traditionally identified with Yang Hu, an official in the household of the Chi Family. For a discussion of this question see Appendix 1, pp. 167–8.

Yao, VI.30, VIII.19, XIV.42, XX.1. A sage king in antiquity.

Yen, VI.14, XVII.4, i.e., Yen Yen. See Tzu-yu.

Yen Hui, VI.3, XI.7. See Yen Yüan.

*Yen Lu, XI.8. Father of Yen Yüan.

Yen P'ing-chung, V.17. Yen Ying, a distinguished statesman, who served three rulers in Ch'i: Duke Ling, Duke Chuang and Duke Ching, and in fifty years saw a lot of trouble in the state, but managed to keep his integrity. Even when Ts'ui Chu assassinated Duke Chuang in 548, he was spared in spite of the fact that he refused to make an oath of alliance with Ts'ui Chu. In the reign of Duke Ching he became prime minister and was known for the simple and frugal life he led.

Yen Yu, XIX.12. See Tzu-yu.

*Yen Yüan, V.26, VII.11, IX.11, IX.21, XI.3, XI.8, XI.9, XI.10, XI.11, XI.23, XII.1, XV.11. The most gifted of Confucius' disciples, whose early death saddened Confucius in his last years.

Yi, III.24. A place in Wei.

Yi, XIV.5. There are three men by the same name in antiquity, all known for their skill in archery. The one referred to here is likely to be the ruler of Yu Ch'iung in the Hsia Dynasty.

Yi Yi, XVIII.8.

Yi Yin, XII.22. A wise minister with whose help T'ang gained the Empire.

Yin, II.23, III.9, III.21, VIII.20, XV.11, XVIII.1. The Yin Dynasty.

Yu, II.17, V.7, V.8, VI.8, IX.27, XI.13, XI.15, XI.18, XI.22, XI.24, XI.26, XII.12, XIII.3, XV.4, XVI.1, XVII.7, XVII.8, i.e., Chung Yu. See Tzu-lu.

Yu Juo, XII.9. See Yu Tzu.

*Yu Tzu, I.2, I.12, I.13. Disciple of Confucius. He occupied a very special position in the Confucian school after the death of Confucius.

Yung, V.5, VI.1, i.e., Jan Yung. See Chung-kung.

Yü, V.10, XVII.21, i.e., Tsai Yü. See Tsai Wo.

Yü, VIII.18, VIII.21, XIV.5, XX.1. Founder of the Hsia Dynasty.

Yü, VIII.20. Name of the dynasty of Shun (q.v.).

Yü Chung, XVIII.8. The second son of Ku Kung Tan Fu and younger brother of T'ai Po (q.v.).

Yüan Jang, XIV.43. Said to be an old friend of Confucius in the *T'an kung* chapter of the *Li chi*.

*Yüan Ssu, VI.5. Disciple of Confucius. The description of him in the *Analects* as a man scrupulous in what he was willing to accept must have prompted later writers to invent stories in which he is depicted as a Taoist recluse totally above material attractions of the world.

FOR THE BEST IN PAPERBACKS, LOOK FOR THE

In every corner of the world, on every subject under the sun, Penguin represents quality and variety – the very best in publishing today.

For complete information about books available from Penguin – including Pelicans, Puffins, Peregrines and Penguin Classics – and how to order them, write to us at the appropriate address below. Please note that for copyright reasons the selection of books varies from country to country.

In the United Kingdom: For a complete list of books available from Penguin in the U.K., please write to *Dept E.P., Penguin Books Ltd, Harmondsworth, Middlesex, UB7 0DA*

In the United States: For a complete list of books available from Penguin in the U.S., please write to *Dept BA, Penguin, 299 Murray Hill Parkway, East Rutherford, New Jersey 07073*

In Canada: For a complete list of books available from Penguin in Canada, please write to *Penguin Books Canada Ltd, 2801 John Street, Markham, Ontario L3R 1B4*

In Australia: For a complete list of books available from Penguin in Australia, please write to the *Marketing Department, Penguin Books Australia Ltd, P.O. Box 257, Ringwood, Victoria 3134*

In New Zealand: For a complete list of books available from Penguin in New Zealand, please write to the *Marketing Department, Penguin Books (NZ) Ltd, Private Bag, Takapuna, Auckland 9*

In India: For a complete list of books available from Penguin, please write to *Penguin Overseas Ltd, 706 Eros Apartments, 56 Nehru Place, New Delhi, 110019*

In Holland: For a complete list of books available from Penguin in Holland, please write to *Penguin Books Nederland B.V., Postbus 195, NL–1380 AD Weesp, Netherlands*

In Germany: For a complete list of books available from Penguin, please write to *Penguin Books Ltd, Friedrichstrasse 10 – 12, D–6000 Frankfurt Main 1, Federal Republic of Germany*

In Spain: For a complete list of books available from Penguin in Spain, please write to *Longman Penguin España, Calle San Nicolas 15, E–28013 Madrid, Spain*

PENGUIN CLASSICS

John Aubrey	**Brief Lives**
Francis Bacon	**The Essays**
James Boswell	**The Life of Johnson**
Sir Thomas Browne	**The Major Works**
John Bunyan	**The Pilgrim's Progress**
Edmund Burke	**Reflections on the Revolution in France**
Thomas de Quincey	**Confessions of an English Opium Eater**
	Recollections of the Lakes and the Lake Poets
Daniel Defoe	**A Journal of the Plague Year**
	Moll Flanders
	Robinson Crusoe
	Roxana
	A Tour Through the Whole Island of Great Britain
Henry Fielding	**Jonathan Wild**
	Joseph Andrews
	The History of Tom Jones
Oliver Goldsmith	**The Vicar of Wakefield**
William Hazlitt	**Selected Writings**
Thomas Hobbes	**Leviathan**

Samuel Johnson/
  James Boswell
	**A Journey to the Western Islands of
	    Scotland/The Journal of a Tour to the
	    Hebrides**

Charles Lamb	**Selected Prose**
Samuel Richardson	**Clarissa**
	Pamela
Adam Smith	**The Wealth of Nations**
Tobias Smollet	**Humphry Clinker**
Richard Steele and Joseph Addison	Selections from the **Tatler** and the **Spectator**
Laurence Sterne	**The Life and Opinions of Tristram Shandy, Gentleman**
	A Sentimental Journey Through France and Italy
Jonathan Swift	**Gulliver's Travels**
Dorothy and William Wordsworth	**Home at Grasmere**

FOR THE BEST IN PAPERBACKS, LOOK FOR THE 🐧

PENGUIN CLASSICS

Anton Chekhov	**The Duel and Other Stories**
	The Kiss and Other Stories
	Lady with Lapdog and Other Stories
	Plays (The Cherry Orchard/Ivanov/The Seagull/Uncle Vanya/The Bear/The Proposal/A Jubilee/Three Sisters
	The Party and Other Stories
Fyodor Dostoyevsky	**The Brothers Karamazov**
	Crime and Punishment
	The Devils
	The Gambler/Bobok/A Nasty Story
	The House of the Dead
	The Idiot
	Netochka Nezvanova
	Notes From Underground and **The Double**
Nikolai Gogol	**Dead Souls**
	Diary of a Madman and Other Stories
Maxim Gorky	**My Apprenticeship**
	My Childhood
	My Universities
Mikhail Lermontov	**A Hero of Our Time**
Alexander Pushkin	**Eugene Onegin**
	The Queen of Spades and Other Stories
Leo Tolstoy	**Anna Karenin**
	Childhood/Boyhood/Youth
	The Cossacks/The Death of Ivan Ilyich/Happy Ever After
	The Kreutzer Sonata and Other Stories
	Master and Man and Other Stories
	Resurrection
	The Sebastopol Sketches
	War and Peace
Ivan Turgenev	**Fathers and Sons**
	First Love
	Home of the Gentry
	A Month in the Country
	On the Eve
	Rudin
	Sketches from a Hunter's Album
	Spring Torrents